Tender is the Night (first printing) inscribed for Dorothy Parker. Collection of Matthew J. Bruccoli.

FITZGERALD/HEMINGWAY ANNUAL 1970

Edited by Matthew J. Bruccoli

University of South Carolina

C. E. Frazer Clark, Jr.

NCR **MICROCARD® EDITIONS**
901 TWENTY-SIXTH STREET, N.W., WASHINGTON, D. C. 20037, 202/333-6393
INDUSTRIAL PRODUCTS DIVISION, THE NATIONAL CASH REGISTER COMPANY

Library of Congress Catalog Card Number 75-83781.

SBN No. 910972-03-6

Editors: Matthew J. Bruccoli

Department of English
University of South Carolina
Columbia, S. C. 29208

C. E. Frazer Clark, Jr.

1490 Sodon Lake Drive
Bloomfield Hills, Michigan 48013

Editorial Assistants: Jennifer E. Atkinson
Barbara Pinkwas
I. S. Skelton
James L. W. West III

Address all editorial correspondence to the editors.

Address orders and inquiries to NCR/Microcard Editions,
901 26th Street, N.W., Washington, D.C. 20037.

For J. M. B. and C. E. F. C.

Somme, Defensive

Aisne

Montdidier-Noyon

Champagne-Marne

Aisne-Marne

Somme, Offensive

Oise-Aisne

Defensive Sector

Verdun

Defensive Sector-Vosges Mts.

Meuse-Argonne

Chateau-Thierry

St. Mihiel

Ypres-Lys

Flanders-Syngem

Contents

Fitzgerald's *Sun Also Rises:* Notes and Comment

By

Philip Young and Charles W. Mann

Notes

Readers of Fitzgerald's letter who can neither remember the period
in which it was written or qualify as serious students of the Twenties
may need a little help with it—particularly toward the end where the
names, not all of them famous, come thick and fast. At the start there
should be no special trouble. "Bunny" is of course the Princeton
name for Edmund Wilson (1895-   ) the critic, who   wrote a novel"
later on. Maxwell Perkins (1884-1947) was Fitzgerald's editor at
Scribners, and Hemingway's; he never wrote a novel. Neither did
Katherine Tighe, who was a childhood friend of Fitzgerald's in St.
Paul, Minnesota. O. Henry (William Sydney Porter, 1862-1910),
mentioned a few lines later, was a writer of short stories, whose
"surprise endings" Hemingway's stories did much to outmode.

As for trying to get Hemingway to "cut the first part of 50 Grand,"
it should be remembered that Fitzgerald succeeded. Its author regretted the cut a good deal later on, as he seems never to have regretted junking the first part of *The Sun Also Rises*. But he did drop
three opening pages of typescript from the draft of "Fifty Grand"
that his friend read. (A photograph of the original first page appears
in the trade edition of *The Hemingway Manuscripts: an Inventory*,
1969; all three pages are reproduced in the limited edition. Why
Hemingway struck so much more than the very brief anecdote Fitzgerald—mistakenly?—thought stale is not clear.) Nor is the anecdote
in the novel that Fitzgerald found "flat as hell without naming Ford"
really all that flat, but since it appeared toward the end of the first

1

chapter-and-a-half it disappeared when that did. Hemingway never forgot either anecdote, however, and this one was related at much greater length as "Ford Madox Ford and the Devil's Disciple" in one of the funniest parts of *A Moveable Feast.*

Now for some miscellaneous items. The mysterious reference to the "age of the French women" that comes just before the objection to the Ford business was not obscure to Hemingway, since it alludes to the epigraph he supplied for his pamphlet *in our time*, 1924, where he attributed an intentionally stupid line to his friend William B. Smith, Jr. (1895-   ), who had a bit of a reputation for wit:

> A Girl in Chicago: Tell us about the
> French women, Hank. What are they like?
> Bill Smith: How old are the French
> women, Hank?

Toward the end of the letter, "God! The bottom of p. 77 Jusque the top p. 78 are wonderful," refers to the scene in Chapter VI where Cohn's mistress, Frances Clyne, is giving him a very bad time and he is "taking it all"; "p. 87," where Fitzgerald says "The heart of my critisism beats," is the place in Chapter VII where Jake and Brett, alone in his flat, feel most acutely the hopelessness of their situation.

Annotation of the rest of the letter requires identification of seven women of fact or fiction and nine men, all writers of one sort or another. As for the writers, Fitzgerald's first objection was to the fact that Hemingway was calling in print three men by their own names (as in the first draft of the novel he had used the real names of virtually all the characters); if they are nobodies, the objection ran, then there is no point in mentioning them and if they are somebodies it is "cheap." All three were somebodies, especially Ford (1873-1939). (He is made foolish in the anecdote, but a typescript of his *No More Parades*, 1925, heavily revised in his hand, was—except for this letter— the only manuscript not by Hemingway to be found in Hemingway's literary remains.) "Allister Crowly," whom Ford described as a "diabolist," is Aleister Crowley (1875-1947), an English specialist in demonology and witchcraft. "H[arold]. Stearns" (1891-1943), long-time critic of American life, became Harvey Stone in the novel.

The other male authors were named to shame Hemingway into writing better. Michael Arlen was of course an extraordinarily popular English novelist (1895-1956) of Armenian birth and doubtful merit. Robert W. Chambers (1865-1933) was another best-selling

2

writer of the period, whose influence on *The Romantic Egoist*, Fitz-gerald's first (unpublished) novel, the younger writer acknowledged in a 1918 letter to Wilson. (We have Mr. Keen, *Tracer of Lost Persons*, 1906, from Chambers' pen.) "Dr. [Samuel Parkes] Cadman" (1864-1936) was the Norman Vincent Peale of his day. "Basil Swoon's" guidebook to Paris is only a slight invention, the sober citation being Basil Woon, *The Paris That's Not in the Guidebooks*, 1926. Stephen McKenna (1888-   ) is yet another once-popular novelist of Eng-lish society. But in calling one of his own phrases a "Harding meta-phor" Fitzgerald was, typically, hardest of all on himself; the prose style of President Warren Gamaliel Harding (1865-1923) was one national scandal among many.

Of the women whose names Fitzgerald invokes, three are charac-ters from fiction, two were characters in fact, and one—whom he sus-pected of having "dramatized herself in terms of" fiction—was both. The last is Lady Twysden, Duff—the real-life Lady Ashley, Brett—of whom Fitzgerald was not an admirer. In June, 1926, he wrote Perkins that—"perhaps because I don't like the original"—he didn't like Brett in the novel; in *A Moveable Feast* he calls her "that girl with the phoney title who was so rude. . . ." Rude or not, the title was gen-uine—acquired by marriage. And the lady who held it was such stuff as legends are made on. Bertram D. Sarason, editor of *The Connec-ticut Review*, and Edward Fisher, a novelist who knew her, have helped to straighten out her actual story.* She was born Mary Duff Stirling Smurthwaite in Yorkshire in 1892. According to her she was married for not quite two days in 1917 to an "older man" (appar-ently named Byrom), before eloping with his best man, Sir Roger Thomas Twysden, who is said always to have been either drunk or "away." (There was a son, however; born 1918, died 1946, no issue.) In 1926, shortly after the action of the novel, she and Sir Roger were divorced. She did not marry Pat Guthrie, the suitor called Mike Campbell in the Hemingway version, but a painter from Texas named Clinton King, who was promptly disinherited. A painter herself, she and her husband headed an art school in New City, New York, in 1934; the writer Jerome Bahr, for whom Hemingway once wrote a preface, remembers going out drinking with her in New York. The story Hemingway told the credulous A. E. Hotchner about her fun-eral in Taxco with her ex-lovers as pallbearers (who dropped the casket, which split in two) was pure apocrypha. Apparently tubercu-

---

*Sarason. "Lady Brett Ashley and Lady Duff Twysden," *Connecticut Review*, II (April 1969), 5-13.

lar, she died Mary Duff Stirling Smurthwaite Byron Twysden King in St. Vincent's Hospital, Sante Fé, New Mexico, on June 27, 1938, and was cremated.

In theorizing that Duff dramatized herself in terms of Arlen's dramatization, Fitzgerald has in mind Iris March, promiscuous heroine of Arlen's *The Green Hat*, 1924, a very best-selling novel about some "lost generation" British. Fitzgerald was a thoughtful student of such matters; in *A Moveable Feast* Hemingway wrote that once "He gave me a sort of oral Ph. D. thesis" on Arlen's work. And it is true that Iris and Duff/Brett had some things in common. Iris affects "bravely" a green felt hat; Brett's is a "man's felt hat," and when Duff came to see Edward Fisher in his Paris apartment ("very graceful," with a "musical laugh") the hat was green. More striking, Arlen's narrator remarks that Iris was "the first Englishwoman I ever saw with 'shingled' hair. This was in 1922." Hemingway's narrator says Brett's hair "was brushed back like a boy's. She started all that." The critic and literary historian Malcolm Cowley (1898-   ) also remembers Duff's "floppy-brimmed" felt hat as green, and he reports that she "was believed to be the heroine of . . . *The Girl in the Green Hat*." If so, then Duff did not dramatize herself in terms of Arlen's dramatization so much as play—or be—herself.

The other ladies of actuality Fitzgerald mentions are Diana Manners (later, and oddly, Lady Duff Cooper, 1892-   ), the English actress whom Colonel Cantwell in *Across the River and Into the Trees* recalls playing in Max Reinhardt's *The Miracle*, and "Station Z. W. X. square," which said goodnight at the end—if not Fitzgerald himself—might refer to Zelda. (A third lady of real life was deleted when Fitzgerald wrote "Arlen's dramatization. . .of somebody's dramatization" and struck the words "maybe Nancy Cunard's." This was probably because she was not a writer or actress, but she was mistaken more than once for Brett's original. Of the Cunard Line Cunards, she "shocked society" by living among Negroes in Harlem, eventually marrying a black chauffeur. Publisher of some of Beckett's earliest work, her name crops up several times in *Waiting for Godot*. Not too long ago a correspondent to *The Times Literary Supplement* cited "authorities" to the effect that she was the model for the heroines not only of *The Sun Also Rises* and *The Green Hat* but of Huxley's *Point Counter Point* as well.)

As for the remaining ladies, all fictional. Beatrix Esmond is the lovely, fascinating but unstable coquette of Thackeray's *Henry Esmond* (1852), and "Jane Austin's Elizabeth" (Bennett) is the bright and spirited if prejudiced young lady of *Pride and Prejudice*

4

(1813). Closest to Duff/Brett, however, is "the last girl in Well's *Tono-Bungay*" (1908): Beatrice Normandy, a titled but "wasted and wasteful" lady who (recall Brett and Romero) refuses to marry George Ponderevo because she is "a woman smirched" and "spoilt." To wrap this thing up, if a little scantily, it should be reported that when Iris of *The Green Hat* is listing the three books she "most profoundly likes" she names "the last part of *Tono-Bungay*," involving Beatrice Normandy. (*Her* hat is "courageous.")

Comment

In his *Moveable Feast* Hemingway remarks that "Scott was very articulate and told a story well. He did not have to spell the words nor attempt to punctuate and you did not have the feeling of reading an illiterate that his letters gave you . . . ." If anyone was not already in on this open-secret he is now, not that it matters. Hemingway's own spelling was idiosyncratic; this Fitzgerald letter was quite sufficiently literate; the effect of its taste and candor was permanent. Hemingway got the message. He tucked it away some forty-odd years ago, and it is a pleasure to untuck it, bestowing credit where credit is overdue.

It was not hard to swallow the story as we had it in the *Feast*: Fitzgerald did not see *The Sun Also Rises* until after Hemingway had sent it to his publisher; therefore he couldn't have had much influence on the book, Q. E. D. As Hemingway told it,

> That fall of 1925 he was upset because I would not show him the manuscript of the first draft of *The Sun Also Rises*. I explained to him that it would mean nothing until I had gone over it and rewritten it and that I did not want to discuss it or show it to anyone first. . . . Scott did not see it until after the completed rewritten and cut manuscript had been sent to Scribners at the end of April.

(A note found in his papers reads, in part, "Mailed Sun Also Rises - April 25 -.")

A letter that Fitzgerald wrote John O'Hara in 1936 (Turnbull, pp. 537-38, where most of the mechanics are fixed up) once seemed to fit this account of things. Fitzgerald is talking about

> the advice that Ernest and I used to throw back and forth at each other, none of which ever had any effect—the only effect I ever had on Ernest was to get him in a receptive mood and say let's cut out everything that goes before this. Then the pieces got mislaid and he could never find the part that I said to cut out. And so he published it without that and later

5

> we agreed that it was a very wise cut. This is not literally true and I
> don't want it established as part of the Hemingway legend. . . .

This was Fitzgerald at his self-effacing best, and so far as is known the
only person to dispute Hemingway publically on when his friend got
to read the novel was Arthur Mizener. In a footnote to the 1965 revision of his Fitzgerald biography (p. 384) he quotes the sentence
which says "Scott did not see it until after the . . . manuscript had
been sent to Scribners . . ." and remarks "This statement cannot be
absolutely true . . . ." His reason: a letter from Hemingway to Fitzgerald, which he also quotes, to the effect that the novel had been
cut to start with Cohn, that all the first part had been scrapped. In
this it is clear that Fitzgerald knew what came at the start before
Cohn; since in the book nothing does, he must have seen it when
something did. It may appear unlikely that Hemingway and Mizener
could both be right here, if unequally—and Fitzgerald too, if he is
read "not literally." But that is pretty much the case.

The great bulk of the surviving manuscript of Ernest Hemingway is
stored either in the vault of a New York bank or in the study of his
widow's New York apartment. The *Inventory* of his literary remains
was prepared in both places; single finds in each place clear up the
confusion. The first was made early in the game at the bank. Inserted
in the third of the seven French schoolboy notebooks in which most
of the first draft of *Fiesta*, as the novel was then called, was pen-and-
inked were ten pages of paper folded twice into quarters. On them
was scrawled, with many deletions and insertions, some sort of unsigned letter to "Dear Ernest." Its author was easy enough to identify, but some of the phrases he cited from the book were not:
"highly moral urges," "because I believe its a good story," "the
Quarter being a state of mind." Surely they were not in the novel.
But if they weren't, what could Fitzgerald be quoting from? The
letter in Mizener did not come to mind; it was not until later that
James B. Meriwether wrote in to say that back in 1961 he had read
a copy of what was not generally known to exist, the discarded opening pages of the book. ("Aren't they terrible, though!")

Of course the clue was in the letter itself: "Please see what you can
do about it in proofs." Well then, the book had indeed been sent off
by the time Fitzgerald read it; something happened after that. What
that was became clear in the middle of a large stack of miscellaneous
papers filed in a cabinet in Mary Hemingway's study. Here rested
three galley sheets labelled *The Sun Also Rises*, which begin with the
news that this is a novel about a lady named Lady Ashley. They print

what was once the first chapter of the book and half the second, with the beginning of the story as we know it at the very end of the third galley. Fitzgerald was right beyond a doubt (not to mention Meriwether). The things he objected to are objectionable; given the brilliance of most of the rest of the book it is impossible to explain why it was feeble, irrelevant and misleading at the start.

First comes Brett, with her marital history, her present legal separation, and the fact of her son. Then we learn how she fell in with Mike Campbell one day at lunch in London, and went to Paris with him, where a hotel had only one free room and it with a double bed, which was the start of that. Mike's background follows, and Chapter I closes with a short account of their life together, mostly sleeping and drinking. Chapter II deals first with Jake—his undertaking this novel, his life in Paris, his newspaper job, his dislike of the Quarter and its inhabitants (which he has to go into, he explains, because Cohn had lived there for two years). Next we are told about Cohn himself, and his novel, and how Braddocks got Jake to read it so he wouldn't have to. This leads to the episode at the Closerie des Lilas which is told at more length about Ford Madox Ford (Madox= Braddocks) in *A Moveable Feast*, with one change. (Hemingway was alone in the nonfictional account; Jake in the novel is with "Alex Muhr"; in the first draft, before most people's names were changed, it was John Dos Passos.) Jake explains that he only tells us about Braddocks because he is a friend of Cohn's, and Cohn is the hero of the book. Then it is a little like coming into daylight to read the good old words, "Robert Cohn was once middleweight boxing champion of Princeton," which lead into the novel as we know it. (Of which Cohn is in no sense the hero, and Brett something less than the subject.)

The compilers of the *Inventory* had already told Mrs. Hemingway about the Fitzgerald letter, and with the second unearthing they showed her the uncorrected, unreturned galleys, reminding her of the way it was in the *Feast*. "Ernest lied?" she said quietly, with a bemused smile. "No, not exactly," was the response, then and now. What he did was tell the truth and nothing but the truth but not the whole truth.

Interest in this critique of Fitzgerald's has been such that the simple announcement of its existence made the pages of *Newsweek, The New York Times, The London Times,* and an uncounted number of other papers here and abroad. None of this did any harm, but a newsman from *The Washington Post,* jumping the gun without having been entered in the event, described the letter in detail on November 30, 1969 (pp. Fl, F3). He further reported that Hemingway responded to Fitzgerald by getting drunk and composing an angry letter which compared his well-intended advice, unfavorably, to horse-manure. This letter, to go on with an unlikely tale, Fitzgerald unaccountably found "snooty," and when he wrote Hemingway to that effect the latter wrote back to say he was sorry; he certainly hadn't intended to sound that way.

To misread this exchange so spectacularly requires special talents. To begin with, the first Hemingway letter referred to was neither angry nor drunken. And in the second place, none of the letters in question, subsequent to Fitzgerald's critique, had anything whatever to do with *The Sun Also Rises*. (They do have to do with an essay Fitzgerald wrote for *The Bookman,* in which he praised Hemingway, who sent his thanks, which the erratic Fitzgerald found "snooty," a reaction that a friendly clarification presumably rectified.)

Then what *was* Hemingway's response to the letter about his novel? Almost certainly it was never put on paper, save for the remarks quoted by Mizener, since no reply in writing was called for. Fitzgerald pencilled his objections, with quotations and page numbers, so Hemingway could look them up and reconsider. Except for the salutation and the "good night," his was not in the ordinary sense a "letter" at all. There was no envelope; the sheets do not look as though they had ever been folded for posting; you don't normally mail things to someone who is living practically next door. ("As I said yestiday," Fitzgerald wrote.)

The two writers had come together this time on the French Riviera, as Baker's *Hemingway* relates. The date was early June, 1926, some five weeks after the book was mailed to New York. Hemingway had gone that May to Madrid while his wife Hadley took their son John to Cap d'Antibes, where the Scott Fitzgeralds—also the Archibald MacLeishes and the Gerald Murphys—were in residence. There he joined his family (so did Pauline Pfeiffer, his wife-to-be) and his friends. He had written that he would have a carbon of the novel with him, which Fitzgerald could read if the proofs hadn't come. On his arrival, a small party of welcome was spoiled by Fitzgerald, who had started to drink before he showed up, and eventually became rude and obstreperous. But not long after this Hemingway handed over the typescript and Fitzgerald submitted his opinions. The background to this is supplied, again, in *A Moveable Feast*:

Scott was not drinking, and starting to work and he wanted us to come to

Juan-les-Pins in June. They would find an inexpensive villa for us and this time he would not drink and it would be like the old days and we would swim and be healthy and brown and have one aperitif before lunch and one before dinner. . . .

It was a nice villa and Scott had a very fine house not far away and I was very happy. . .and the single aperitif before lunch was very good and we had several more. . . . It was very gay and obviously a splendid place to write. There was going to be everything that a man needed to write except to be alone.

It is fortunate for Hemingway and his book that he was not alone, but in rather good company that was not drinking too much on one particular night to remember.

Pennsylvania State University

Letter to Ernest Hemingway

From

F. Scott Fitzgerald

Dear Ernest: Nowdays when almost everyone is a genius, at least for awhile, the temptation for the bogus to profit is no greater than the temptation for the good man to relax (in one mysterious way or another)—not realizing the transitory quality of his glory because he forgets that it rests on the frail shoulders of professional enthusiasts. This should frighten all of us into a lust for anything honest that people have to say about our work. I've taken what proved to be excellent advice (On The B. + Damned) from Bunny Wilson who never wrote a novel (on Gatsby—change of many thousand wds) from Max Perkins who never ⟨2⟩ considered writing one, and on T. S. of Paradise from Katherine Tighe (you don't know her) who had probably never read a novel before.

[This is beginning to sound like my own current work which resolves itself into laborious + sententious preliminaries].

Anyhow I think parts of <u>Sun Also</u> are careless + ineffectual. As I said yestiday (and, as I recollect, in trying to get you to cut the 1st part of 50 Grand) I find in you the same tendency to envelope or (and as it usually turns out) to <u>embalm</u> in mere wordiness an anecdote or joke thats casually appealed to you, that I find in myself in trying to preserve a piece of "fine writing." Your first chapter contains about 10 such things and it gives a feeling of condescending <u>casuallness</u>

    P. 1. "highly moral story"
        "Brett said" (O. Henry stuff)
        "much too expensive
        "something or other" (if you don't want to tell, why waste 3

wds. saying it. See P. 23—"9 or 14" and "or how many years it was since 19xx" when it would take two words to say That's what youd kid in anyone else as mere "style"—mere horseshit I can't find this latter but anyhow you've not only got to write well yourself but you've also got to not-do to do what anyone ⟨3⟩ can do and I think that there are about 24 sneers, superiorities and nose-thumbings-at-nothing that mar the whole narrative up to p. 29 where (after a false start on the introduction of Cohn) it really gets going. And to pre-serve these perverse and willfull non-essentials you've done a lot of writing that honestly reminded me of Michael Arlen

[You know the very fact that people have committed themselves to you will make them watch you like a cat. + if they don't like it creap away like one]

For example.

Pps. 1 + 2. Snobbish (not in itself but because the history of En-glish Aristocrats in the war, set down so verbosely so uncritically, so exteriorly and yet so obviously inspired from within, is shopworn.) You had the same problem that I had with my Rich Boy, previously debauched by Chambers ect. Either bring more thot to it with the re-alization that that ground has already raised its wheat + weeds or cut it down to ⟨4⟩ seven sentences. It hasn't even your rhythym and the fact that may be "true" is utterly immaterial.

That biography from you, who allways believed in the superiority (the preferability) of the imagined to the seen not to say to the merely recounted.

    P. 3 "Beautifully engraved shares"
          (Beautifully engraved 1886 irony) All this is O.K. but so glib when its glib + so profuse.

P. 5 Painters are no longer real in prose. They must be minimized. [This is not done by making them schlptors, backhouse wall-experts or miniature painters]

P. 8. "highly moral urges" "because I believe its a good story" If this paragraph isn't maladroit then I'm a rewrite man for Dr. Cad-man. ⟨5⟩

P. 9. Somehow its not good. I can't quite put my hand on it—it has a ring of "This is a true story ect."

P. 10. "Quarter being a state of mine ect." This is in all guide books. I haven't read Basil Swoon's but I have fifty francs to lose. [About this time I can hear you say "Jesus this guy thinks Im lousy, + he can stick it up his ass for all I give a Gd Dm for his 'critisism'." But re-member this is a new departure for you, and that I think your stuff is ⟨6⟩ great. You were the first American I wanted to meet in

Europe—and the last. (This latter clause is simply to balance the sentence. It doesn't seem to make sense tho I have pawed at it for several minutes. Its like the age of the French women.

P. 14 (+ therabout) as I said yesterday I think this anecdote is flat as hell without naming Ford which would be cheap.

It's flat because you end with mention of Allister Crowly. If he's nobody it's nothing. If he's somebody, it's cheap. This is a novel. Also I'd cut out mention of H. Stearns earlier.

Why not cut the inessentials in Cohens biography? His first marriage is of no importance. When so many people can write well + the competition is so heavy I can't imagine how you could have done these first 20 pps. so casually. You can't play with peoples attention—a good man who has the power of arresting attention at will must be especially careful.

From here. Or rather from p. 30 I began to like the novel but Ernest ⟨7⟩ I can't tell you the sense of disappointment that beginning with its elephantine facetiousness gave me. Please do what you can about it in proof. Its 7500 words—you could reduce it to 5000. And my advice is not to do it by mere pareing but to take out the worst of the scenes.

I've decided not to pick at anything else because I wasn't at all inspired to pick when reading it. I was much too excited. Besides This is probably a heavy dose. The novel's damn good. The central theme is marred somewhere but hell! unless you're writing your life history where you have an inevitable pendulum to swing you true (Harding metaphor), who can bring it entirely off? And what critic can trace whether the fault lies in a ⟨8⟩ possible insufficient thinking out, in the biteing off of more than you eventually cared to chew in the impotent theme or in the elusiveness of the lady character herself. My theory always was that she dramatized herself in terms of Arlen's dramatatization of somebody's dramatizating of Stephen McKenna's dramatization of Diana Manner's dramatization of the last girl in Well's Tono Bungay—who's original probably liked more things about Beatrix Esmond than about Jane Austin's Elizabeth (to whom we owe the manners of so many of our wives.)

Appropos of your foreward about the Latin quarter—suppose you had begun your stories with phrases like: "Spain is a peculiar place—ect" or "Michigan is interesting to two classes—the fisherman + the drummer."

Pps 64 + 65 with a bit of work ⟨9⟩ should tell all that need be known about <u>Brett's</u> past.

(Small point) "Dysemtry" instead of "killed" is a clichês to avoid a clichê. It stands out. I suppose it can't be helped. I suppose all the 75,000000 Europeans who died between 1914-1918 will always be among the 10,000,000 who were killed in the war.

God! The bottom of p. 77 Jusque the top p. 78 are wonderful, I go crazy when people aren't always at their best. This isn't picked out— I just happened on it.

The heart of my critisism beats somewhere apon p. 87. I think you can't change it, though. I felt the lack of some crazy torturing tentativeness or security—horror, all at once, that she'd feel—and he'd feel—maybe I'm crazy. He isn't <u>like</u> ⟨10⟩ <u>an impotent man. He's like a man in a sort of moral chastity belt.</u>

Oh, well. It's fine, from Chap V on, anyhow, in spite of that— which fact is merely a proof of its brillance.

Station Z. W. X square says good night. Good night all.*

———————

*Published with permission of Frances Fitzgerald Smith and with the approval of Mrs. Ernest Hemingway. All rights to this letter are the property of Mrs. Smith.

"Sleep of a University"—
An Unrecorded Fitzgerald Poem

The following material appeared in the November 1920 issue of
The Nassau Literary Magazine (LXXVI, p. 161)–M. J. B.

On another page of this issue appears a poem entitled "Princeton
Asleep," by Aiken Reichner. It happens that the author of the poem
is personally acquainted with F. Scott Fitzgerald, '17, the author of
"This Side of Paradise." He sent the poem to Fitzgerald for criticism
before submitting it, and in reply Fitzgerald sent him the interesting
"paraphrase" printed below. The poem as altered by Fitzgerald is a
good example of this much-discussed writer's facility in felicitous
phrasing, as well as his ability to be, on any occasion, the much-discussed writer, F. Scott Fitzgerald.

SLEEP OF A UNIVERSITY

Watching through the long, dim hours
Like statued Mithras, stand ironic towers;
Their haughty lines severe by light
Are softened and gain tragedy at night.
Self-conscious, cynics of their charge,
Proudly they challenge the dreamless world at large.

From pseudo-ancient Nassau Hall, the bell
Crashes the hour, as if to pretend "All's well!"
Over the campus then the listless breeze
Floats along drowsily, filtering through the trees,
Whose twisted branches seem to lie

Like *point d'Alencon* lace against a sky
Of soft gray-black—a gorgeous robe
Buttoned with stars, hung over a tiny globe.

With life far off, peace sits supreme:
The college slumbers in a fatuous dream,
While, watching through the moonless hours
Like statued Mithras, stand the ironic towers.

PRINCETON ASLEEP

By Aiken Reichner

Watching through the long, dim hours
Like guardian angels, stand the Gothic towers;
    Their haughty lines, severe by light,
Are softened and gain dignity in night—
    Majestic sentinels rough-hewn,
Light-shadowed by an opalescent moon.

From sombrous Nassau Hall, the bell
Tolls out the hour, as if to say "All's well!"
    And, murmuring, a drowsy breeze
Meanders on and filters through the trees,
    Whose twisted branches seem to lie
Like *point d'Alencon* lace against a sky
    Of soft gray-black—a fleecy robe
Star-studded, covering a tiny globe.

With strife far off, peace reigns supreme:
The college slumbers in a happy dream,
    While, watching through the moon-lit hours
Like guardian angels, stand the Gothic towers.

(p. 158)

15

My Friend Scott Fitzgerald

By

Elizabeth Beckwith MacKie*

This is to reverse the usual pattern. I am unable to report (or boast) that during a long friendship with Scott Fitzgerald I ever slept with him. Hardly a month passes but some new, revealing love affair, or indiscretion among the famous, comes out of hiding and into print. And so it is with a proper sense of failure that I cannot add a single flaming episode to tingle the thoughts of that vast hoard who make up Scott's admirers.

It would not have been easy to sleep with Scott, knowing as I did his ideals about the married state, which, when it could have happened, was the case with both of us. It would have destroyed too much. And yet I am not blind to the idea that it might also have brought added beauty to our relationship. There were times when I knew that he needed me, or the physical love and understanding of a woman, and I have let slip the chance to claim even one page for myself from the love life of one of the greats. The truth is that Scott never came right out—wham—and asked me!

It would be unfair to consider Scott Fitzgerald in any light other than a serious one. It would be a misconception of a man whose approach to life was anything but casual. He was dead serious about life, love, art, and friendship, and especially his dedication to his own talent.

We know he often played the clown. His biographers have recorded

---

*I am indebted to Henry Dan Piper for much help and advice in the preparation of this reminiscence.

many such instances, and I saw it happen more times than it is well to remember. But I never saw Scott laugh. I don't remember the sound of his laughter. Even when he was clowning—it was to make others laugh. He was too intent on what he was doing.

The contrast in his pattern of behavior was most noticeable, of course, when he was drinking. He was a man unfitted for the role that fate dealt him (or that he dealt himself). His public image was not the real Scott. When he was drunk he wanted to shock people, and his mind turned inevitably to sex. He would become provocative and suggestive in a way that was a complete reversal of that rather prudish and extremely sensitive, sober Scott. I believe that it was an unconscious effort on his part to equal or excell his wife, the more glittering Zelda. But he was also the victim of a tragic historic accident—the accident of Prohibition, when Americans believed that the only honorable protest against a stupid law was to break it.

I wouldn't have met Scott if it hadn't been for John Peale Bishop. John's family lived six houses and some acres away from our house, on the same street in Charles Town, West Virginia. John, who was twenty-five, was older than most of our group. A childhood illness (some said tuberculosis, but I never really knew) had slowed his progress through school, and so he had only been graduated from Princeton in June 1917. Now he was marking time waiting for the commission in the army that would take him off to officers' training camp.

We knew that John's Princeton friend, Scott Fitzgerald, was arriving for a visit, and my most cherished memento of that visit is a yellowed sheet of paper on which he wrote out for me the sonnet, "When Vanity Kissed Vanity," which he later included in *This Side of Paradise.* On it he wrote "For Fluff Beckwith, the only begetter of this sonnet."

And so the summer, which at the start seemed as routine as all other summers, was soon, in retrospect, to take on added significance by the arrival of a boy, whose name at the time was unimportant, and which I promptly forgot. Scott's visit lasted four weeks, and we were together every day.

Scott and John had entered Princeton together as freshmen in the autumn of 1913. Despite John's being considerably older than most freshmen, and Scott's having been one of the youngest (he was not quite seventeen), they soon became close friends. John, as everyone knows, was the original "Thomas Parke D'Invilliers" in *This Side of Paradise*, and Scott recorded in that novel an amusing account of their first meeting and subsequent friendship.

17

The contrast between these two personalities makes their friendship all the more interesting and unusual. John lacked Scott's good looks and exuberance. He was perhaps a head taller than Scott, with natural dignity and reserve. His friends were largely selected from the intellectual. My older sister, Eloise, was one of his special friends, and he was often at our house. John was a brilliant scholar and prolific poet. In his book of poems *Now With His Love*, he describes a Lely portrait that hung in our home.

He was instinctively attracted to the handsome, impulsive younger boy, who so flatteringly admired his talent. What they shared most of all was a common passion for the life of Art. At Princeton they worked together on the editorial staff of *The Nassau Literary Magazine*, in which they published their undergraduate writings. That eventful summer of 1917 marked the publication of John's first volume of verse, *Green Fruit*, most of which had been previously published in the *Nassau Lit.*

John, like Scott, died too soon. He was fifty-one years old, and as with Scott, his greatest recognition came after death. And so while his literary gift to posterity is limited in quantity, that which he left us is pure beauty. His work becomes more popular each year, and his first full-length novel, *Act of Darkness*, is now being published in paperback.

Scott slipped quietly into Charles Town one afternoon via the dusty old Valley branch of the Baltimore and Ohio railroad, which, except for a limited number of automobiles, was our only escape to the outside world. I had just returned from boarding school in Washington. Our group consisted of boys and girls in their late teens who were home on vacation from school and college. We had all grown up together, and it was our custom to meet almost every day, sometimes in the afternoon for a swim in the nearby Shenandoah River, or for a cross-country ride.

It was July and moonlight—at a party at our house—that I first met Scott. The clematis vine was in full bloom and the porch railing sagged deeper each year with the weight of the blossoms. The summer air was sweet. I saw him standing in the half shadow watching the dancers. Night had drained the color from his face and hair, and left him pale, but beautiful. He was twenty years old. It was the face of a poet, without sensuality.

We had been dancing to records of "Oh! Johnny" and "Sweethearts," when John came over to me and said, "Fluff, I want you to meet Scott Fitzgerald." It was an appropriate setting and his first words were a parallel of any boy and girl affair that later brought him fame. "I've been watching you," he said, "trying to guess your real name. Is it Eleanor?" "No, Elizabeth," I told him. "Then I was close," he said. "Eleanor–Elizabeth–you see, both names mean pretty much the same kind of girl."

It wasn't until I had known him for several days, and watched him with other people, that I realized that other girls all got the same carefully rehearsed treatment. But this discovery, instead of disillusioning me, merely increased my interest in him. Scott was that rare individual that went out of his way to make each girl feel very special. In a way it was nothing but a "line"–except that most boys' lines are quickly recognizable for what they are. What made Scott's different was the mixture of art and sincerity that went into every performance. He really wanted each girl to be pleased and flattered, and to respond to him, and she usually did.

The next thing I knew we were dancing together. The best description of his dancing I can think of is "lively." He had a sense of rhythm and was easy to follow, but he never attempted any trick steps. He liked to talk while he danced, and he enjoyed having a captive audience. But I liked only to feel the lovely close union of body and music, and I found it difficult to concentrate on what he was saying. But suddenly I was listening. I heard him say, "Townsend said he hoped I would meet you."

Townsend Martin was a classmate of John's who had visited him in June. He was a cosmopolite of great charm and elegance, and I was dazzled from the beginning. It was an affair that started and ended within safe range of the bridge table, but he soon cast cold water on my hopes by announcing that he was descended from "a long line of bachelors." This was a deflating experience for a girl who traditionally thought of belledom as the only way of life. A new boy, a new interest was needed to help restore a drooping ego. Afterwards, in my diary for that night of July 2, I wrote: "I met John's guest. He is good looking. He asked me for a date. We are going on a picnic tomorrow."

I remember patting my cheeks with a piece of wet pink crepe paper that next afternoon. My parents disapproved of cheek rouge as "too fast," and instead of black cotton swimming stockings, I wore my best black silk ones. Chaperones were still *de rigeur,* and our social life was organized around the rule that there was safety in numbers. We were still passionately innocent. If the picnic lasted into the tempting hours of darkness, a chaperone appeared at dusk, and joined the group until we were safely back at home.

19

Scott showed up in his bathing suit, and I surveyed him discreetly but approvingly. He wasn't terribly tall, but was strong and well-knit. And he was carrying a book. But what struck me most was his hat. I had never seen a boy go swimming with a hat. He explained that he burned so badly that he had to keep his skin covered up from the sun. And it was true. If he wasn't careful he turned a painful scarlet. He was a good swimmer, but out of the water we sat in the shade most of the time because of his tender skin.

For those of us who lived near the Shenandoah River and loved it, it wound through our lives as between its own banks. Scott soon learned to share our affection for the river, and its many moods. We knew it by heart; one minute flowing blue and lazy, the next a muddy torrent churned by a sudden mountain thunderstorm. We knew the danger spots, and the holes for diving, and the islands where the snakes were thickest. The hidden inlets—just wide enough for a canoe. The gentle rapids where it was so shallow we could lie on our stomachs, and be tossed from rock to rock. And the soft night sounds, broken by song, and echoes on the water.

When the sun dropped behind the Blue Ridge Mountains, Scott and I would drift downstream in a canoe. But the canoes were small, and too crowded for a chaperone—she sat on the bank. Most of the time I listened while he talked and talked. He loved to say things to you that would shock you, just to get your reaction and explain it so accurately that you felt completely exposed. His conversation was mainly about girls. He was always trying to see how far he could go in arousing your feelings, but it was always with words.

"Fluff, have you ever had any 'purple passages' in your life?" he asked me. I wasn't sure what it meant, but it sounded exciting. I always expected the questions to develop a more physical tone. The tingling excitement of a mood, slowly developed, yet surely building toward an exquisite moment. But this was his first exposure to southern girls, who in turn had been exposed to less timid southern boys. The southern boys I knew, despite their verbal lethargy, at least understood what it was all about, and were more aggressive and emotionally satisfying. In 1917, I'm afraid, Scott just wasn't a very lively male animal.

No photograph I have ever seen of him has captured successfully the remarkable sensitivity of his expression. It was like quicksilver. His eyes, contrary to what others have said, were neither green nor blue, but grey-blue. His hair in the sunlight was shining gold. His mouth was his most revealing feature—stern, with thin lips. The upper lip had a slight curve to it, but the lower lip was a stern,

20

straight line. All his Midwestern puritanism was there. He had never lived in that magnetic world of the senses, whose inhabitants communicate by a wordless language of intuitive feelings.

In general, however, Scott's visit to Charles Town was a small social triumph. He was in demand for all the parties, and seemed to enjoy our unsophisticated small-town amusements—and during that month I never saw him take a drink.

Much activity centered around horses. I had been proudly raised with the knowledge that one of my forebears, Sir Marmaduke Beckwith, had been responsible for introducing the first English race horses into Virginia. Scott had no such feelings about horses or horseback riding—a fact that the horse under him immediately grasped. Scott was a terrible horseman, but determined to ride at all costs. Once he was given an old nag who habitually bolted for home whenever he passed a certain familiar corner. Scott took a bad spill, but got up dusty and determined, and insisted on climbing back on. We all cheered and admired his courage, but it was clear he would never make a good horseman.

One evening just before he left Charles Town, he told me, "Fluff, I've written a poem for you," and he recited "When Vanity Kissed Vanity."

I felt chilly when he came to the line "and with her lovers she was dead." "Do you mean you think I'm going to die?" "No," he replied, "I mean you're dead to me because your other lovers have taken you from me." Later, when Edmund Wilson edited the posthumous volume of pieces called *The Crack-Up*, he published a letter Fitzgerald had written to him. It included the same sonnet, only this time with the title "To Cecilia." It was a great disappointment at first. Still, the girl was his cousin, and fourteen years older, and besides Scott had given it two months earlier to me.

August came too soon, and Scott returned to his home in St. Paul, Minnesota. And several weeks later, while I was on a trip to New York, friends introduced me to the young man who would soon afterwards marry me and share my life for the next forty-two years. Paul and I first met in Peacock Alley of the old Waldorf-Astoria, on 34th Street, a romantic encounter that Scott would surely have appreciated.

Looking back over the vista of fifty years to that eventful summer when I first met Scott, I know that he could never have been happy with small-town life. He was in search of wider horizons. He failed to discover the real core of small-town life—or its rewards. Small towns are people—there is little else. A place where one comes close to the

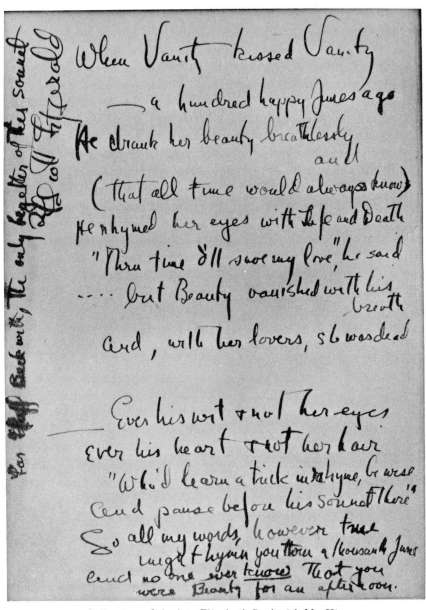

Collection of the late Elizabeth Beckwith MacKie.

pulse of human emotion. We learned early about life and living from some of the most beloved members of the colored race—exciting, intimate things, because we were not ashamed to ask. Their wisdom was earthy and uncluttered, and with the sharp intuition of their race. "That ain't no way to ketch yessef a man, you got to pleasure

22

him, honey, you got to pleasure a man." "The apple falls close to the tree." "The sweetest smell of all ain't no smell at all." I could go on and on. In the end we were gentler and wiser.

We were all excited when *This Side of Paradise* was published in the spring of 1920. John Bishop told me that Scott had said I was his model for Eleanor in the section called "Young Irony." When I read it I remembered our first meeting and Scott's having told me that Eleanor and Elizabeth were names that suggested to him the same kind of girl. I saw a vague resemblance to myself in his description of Eleanor's "green eyes and nondescript hair," and there were Amory's and Eleanor's horseback rides through mountain paths together, and the rural setting which was so obviously inspired by the country around Charles Town. And there was, of course, my poem. But the Eleanor he described only reminded me of how little he really knew me. His Eleanor loved to sit on a haystack in the rain reciting poetry. Forgive me, Scott: if that is the way you wanted it, then you missed the whole idea of what can happen atop a haystack.

It wasn't until fourteen years later, in the early spring of 1932, that I saw him again. By 1932 it seemed as though Zelda had almost recovered from her 1930 collapse. Then, that winter after her father died, she had a second mental breakdown and Scott brought her from Alabama to Johns Hopkins Hospital in Baltimore for treatment. By spring she was well enough to be released from the hospital, but her physician wanted her to remain nearby for observation and therapy.

Scott was staying temporarily in a Baltimore hotel, looking for a house to rent for Zelda and himself and eleven-year-old Scottie. Scott liked the idea of settling in Baltimore, after having spent the last ten years on and off in Europe. He no longer wanted to go back to St. Paul. On his father's side, the Fitzgeralds had lived in eastern Maryland for generations, and his father, who had recently died, was buried in the family plot at nearby Rockville. Besides, a number of his old Princeton friends were Baltimoreans.

One of his classmates, Bryan Dancy, lived next door to us. Bryan and his wife Ida Lee knew that I had once known Scott. So when they heard he was in Baltimore, they invited my husband and me to have dinner with him. A lot had happened since I had last seen Scott. He was now a celebrity, and he was at the height of his popular career. *The Great Gatsby* had not only been a highly praised novel, but also a Broadway play and a Hollywood motion picture. Besides, Scott was one of the highest-paid magazine writers of the day; *The Saturday Evening Post* featured his stories regularly. We had learned vaguely of Zelda and her illness. But most of the details were veiled in mystery, and hardly anyone in Baltimore knew her.

When Paul and I arrived at the Dancys' for dinner, Scott was standing in the living room. I paused for a moment, puzzled by what I saw. There were two Scotts: the old Scott of memory—the other, very drunk. He had run into a second-string Hollywood movie actress staying at his hotel (she was well-known then, but has since died and long been forgotten), and impetuously decided to bring her. They had tarried in the bar too long. She had said she was lonely and knew no one in Baltimore, and Scott felt sorry for her, and told her to come along. It was a chaotic evening. Scott had obviously decided to make it so, and to confirm his reputation as an unconventional guest. The more vulnerable we appeared, the sharper the attack, with realistic allusions to feminine curves and their function. It was a rejection of the Scott I had known.

As we got up from dinner he started for the front door. He struck a dramatic pose and said: "I am going home—to satisfy a need—the need for sex." He disappeared through the door, followed by the actress.

I was not entirely unprepared for this behavior. I had heard occasionally over the years from John Bishop, who had briefed me on many of the Fitzgeralds' more spectacular exploits in Europe. Compared to the fireworks that flared much of the time around Scott and Zelda, John's life was stable. In 1930 he had won Scribners' prize for his story, "Many Thousands Gone." He and his wife Margaret lived quietly as expatriates in a chateau in France, and were the parents of three sons.

All over America drinking was becoming more and more a social habit. But the rest of us had routine responsibilities, our daily jobs to attend to, and our lives were well-organized. Scott was much more of a free agent. There had been nothing of this routine to restrain him, and by the time he came to Baltimore, he had become incapable of controlling his drinking. It magnified the minor flaws in his personality, and erased the charm and good manners.

When Arthur Mizener came to Baltimore in search of Fitzgerald material for his biography of Scott, I hid. I could not at that time discuss my friendship with Scott without, I feared, hurting him. I preferred the privacy of non-recognition. How times have changed. But in spite of that unfortunate meeting, Scott and I eventually got back to a firmer relationship. No matter how badly he behaved, Scott was always sincerely sorry afterwards and would atone by a charming apology. His manners were still beautiful. Physically, he had changed very little during the last fourteen years. He was such a delightful, sensitive person, that my husband Paul, who was rather correct and strait-laced, recovered from his first impression and took a liking to him.

Apart from the drinking, I recognized the same old Scott, but a more retiring Scott than I had known before. He discouraged social invitations, much to the disappointment of the many Baltimore hostesses who had hoped to enliven their parties with such a well-known personage. Zelda, of course, was too ill most of the time to go out in public, but Scott used her illness as an excuse to dodge social entanglements. And deep, deep down he never forgot to love her.

I had not met Zelda before, and saw her only a few times during her stay in Baltimore. I knew that she had once been very beautiful. John Bishop had written me after her wedding that "she looked like an angel." Now her shoulders drooped and her skin was pallid, but there was about her still a wistful, feminine charm. One afternoon she dropped by to call, and told me she had been shopping all day for a dress with a hood in back. I remember wondering at the time if this was her way of disguising her slouching posture. Another time she invited Ida Lee Dancy and me to lunch at their home, "La Paix." She kept us waiting for an hour. And when she finally showed up, rather damp-looking, she told us that she had been in the bathtub— that part of her therapy consisted of taking a long sitz-bath to relax her nerves, with a big thermometer to make sure the water stayed the right temperature. She talked freely about her illness.

Scott often dropped by our house for a casual visit. The visits I remember with the most pleasure were those when, as he expressed it, he was "on the wagon." The length of these dry spells varied, but they sometimes lasted a month or more. It was during these visits that he often discussed the literary talents of the writers he had known, and he had interesting comments on many of the movie greats of that day. With his usual generosity toward other authors, he told me that Thomas Wolfe was the most gifted writer of his genera-tion. If we were out, he would leave an amusing note—invariably addressed jointly to my husband and me. He liked to drop in unan-nounced. But he almost always refused invitations to formal parties— especially when there might be lots of people whom he didn't know. He lacked the interest to make new acquaintances, and preferred old friends. At one of our cocktail parties to which he came, he was im-mediately surrounded by a circle of admiring, gushing women. When he finally escaped, he told me, "God, I'm sick of all those teeth grinning at me."

So although we continued to invite him, we soon grew accustomed to his polite letters of apology. After he failed to show up, we would sometimes find a note tucked in the front screen door, like the following, dated July 1933:

> Don't expect me
>   I've gone fancy
> I'm all set
>   With Bryan Dancy
> Scotty's Windbag
>   Mitchell's Berries
> Back at midnight
> Out with Fairies

My last recollection of Scott is in June, 1936. His current plans were to visit Zelda, who was now convalescing in a private sanitorium in North Carolina, and then go out to Hollywood to write for the motion pictures. As things turned out, he was injured while diving in a pool at a hotel in Asheville, and as a result of his having to be hospitalized, his departure for Hollywood was delayed until the following summer of 1937. At the time of our next-to-last meeting, however, he was planning to leave not only Baltimore but the east coast for good. Scott had come to our house to tell us his plans, and to say that he was leaving as soon as he could get rid of some furniture stored in the Monumental Warehouse in Baltimore.

Paul and I were then spending our summers in the country, and needed furniture, and so Paul bought from Scott a pair of twin beds and a painted chest of drawers. The next day I went to the warehouse. I remember how depressed I was by most of the things—they all looked as though no one had cared very much for them for a long time. I bought one more piece, a bureau, and so I went to the apartment in the Cambridge Arms, to which he and Scottie had moved temporarily, to give him a check.

It was lunch time, but Scott was still in pajamas and bathrobe. He was entertaining Louis Azrael, a well-known local newspaper columnist. He also had a severe pain in his shoulder, which he had relieved by the home remedy of strapping an electric heating pad to his back, and he was sitting on the floor plugged into the electric current. Always restless, and always the perfect host, he would get up from the floor and wander about with plug and cord clattering behind him. But there was also a wonderful dignity flowing from him that repulsed any sympathy of mine and that gave him a kind of tragic grandeur.

This was my farewell to Scott. I would never again see his handsome face, or hear him say, as he once did, when he was leaving our house and the screen door was safely between us, "Fluff, I've never had you, but I believe we always get the things we most want."

His popularity was beginning to go into temporary decline. Shortly after his death I read an obituary by Margaret Marshall in *The Nation,* February 1941. She wrote of Scott: "A man of talent who did not fulfill his early promise—his was a fair-weather talent which was not adequate to the stormy age into which it happened, ironically, to emerge."

Today Scott Fitzgerald is required reading in many schools and colleges, and my grandchildren come with school assignments, wanting to learn more about him. I show them my original copy of the sonnet, "When Vanity Kissed Vanity"—once so lightly received, and now so dearly treasured—when there is no longer cause for vanity. And one of them asked, "Grandmother, did you really kiss Scott Fitzgerald? "

Heavens! No one ever *thought* of such things in those days. Well—hardly ever.

Fitzgerald's Marked Copy of
The Great Gatsby

By

Jennifer E. Atkinson

In the Fitzgerald archive at Princeton University is a copy of the first printing of *The Great Gatsby* (1925) in which F. Scott Fitzgerald pencilled corrections, revisions, and possible alternatives to phrases. Since an author's revisions are important for what he may wish to do to the tone of a passage, a characterization, or the style of a phrase or sentence, a scholar's awareness of these changes is imperative and can affect his entire approach to a work as well as improve his understanding of how an author works.

Editors of Fitzgerald's work since his death in 1940 have either not been aware of this author's corrected copy, or they have used only parts of it. Often they have made their own emendations to *The Great Gatsby*.[1]

There are a total of 42 revisions made by Fitzgerald, of which 38 are substantives. (There is some confusion about the word "orgiastic" [218.12] and it will be treated as a special case.) These variants fall into four categories:

(I) Simple changes in which a single word or a phrase may be replaced with a different word or phrase—for example: *wonder* [*confusion*; *cafes* [*restaurants*; *Twenty-eighth Infantry* [*9th Machine Gun Battalion*; *property of* [*knowledge to* These changes appear generally to be Fitzgerald's decision in favor of a better descriptive term or phrase, or else a more accurate one.

(II) Additions of a word, phrase, or a complete sentence—for example: *her flesh* [*her surplus flesh*; *out: 'Oh* [*out: She looked around to see who was listening. 'Oh*; *work in* [*work or rigid sitting in*; *he's regular* [*he's a regular*; *added. "There* [*added as if she might*

28

have sounded irreverent "There. Such additions were sometimes made because it appears a word may have been omitted in publication, but at other times Fitzgerald seems to have been rethinking a passage and trying to make it more dramatically effective or trying to clarify a character's motivations.

(III) Omission of a word, or phrase—for example: *of ash-gray men* [*of men; had both disappeared* [*had disappeared; looked down at* [*looked at; ripped a little at* [*ripped at* In almost all instances, these omissions were made because a word was redundant in the context of the entire passage, either in meaning or because a word was actually repetitious.

(IV) In four instances, Fitzgerald completely rewrote a phrase or passage, either changing sentence structure or the meaning of a passage—for example: Through the means of subordination, Fitzgerald changed two sentences not clearly related—"We drove over to Fifth Avenue, warm and soft, almost pastoral, on the summer Sunday afternoon. I wouldn't have been surprised to see a great flock of white sheep turn the corner."—to one smooth sentence—"We drove over to Fifth Avenue, so warm and soft, almost pastoral, on the summer afternoon that I wouldn't have been surprised to see a great flock of white sheep turn the corner." In another place Fitzgerald clarifies and strengthens a passage with a rewritten phrase. In Chapter II, when Tom, Myrtle, Catherine, Nick, and others are at Tom and Myrtle's New York apartment, Catherine teases Myrtle about an old beau and declares that Myrtle had been "crazy about him." Myrtle angrily responds that she was no more "crazy about him" than she is about Nick, and she points at Nick, causing everyone to look at him "accusingly." Nick tells the reader that: "I tried to show by my expression that I expected no affection." Fitzgerald, upon rereading, probably found this statement unclear, and he rephrased it so that it makes more sense in its context. "I tried to show by my expression that I had played no part in her past." The restatement makes Nick's reaction more understandable, natural, and credible. In Chapter IV, Gatsby tells Nick of his charmed life during the war. He briefly describes one incident in the Argonne Forest when he "took the remains of my machine-gun battalion so far forward that there was a half mile gap on either side of us where the infantry couldn't advance." Fitzgerald changed this description of the vague and possibly large number of troops Gatsby led to the smaller, more impressive size of "two machine-gun detachments," thus placing Gatsby in a strategically more difficult situation and making him seem even more heroic. In Chapter V, Nick tells briefly the history of Gatsby's house and comments on the fact that the original builder had tried to get his neighbors to roof their houses with straw but they had refused. Nick concludes: "Americans, while willing, even eager, to be serfs, have always been obstinate about being peasantry." Perhaps, upon rereading, Fitzgerald found this statement too damning of his countrymen, for he softened it to: "Americans, while occasionally willing, to be serfs, have always been obstinate about being peasantry."

Concerning the problem of "orgastic"/"orgiastic" in the sentence "Gatsby believed in the green light, the orgastic future that year by year recedes before us," there is confusion as to what Fitzgerald actually intended. Apparently while the novel was still in the proof stages, some question arose about the word. In a letter on January 24, 1925, to Maxwell Perkins, Fitzgerald states clearly his choice: "'Orgastic is the adjective for 'orgasm' and it expresses exactly the intended ecstasy. It's not a bit dirty."[2] Yet in Fitzgerald's personal copy of the book, a mark has been made in the word "orgastic" and there is a very faint "i" in the margin (see illustration).[3] However, it is not certain that this "i" is in Fitzgerald's handwriting. The word remains "orgastic" in the second printing of August 1925, in which

218   THE GREAT GATSBY

in history with something commensurate to his capacity for wonder.

And as I sat there brooding on the old, unknown world, I thought of Gatsby's wonder when he first picked out the green light at the end of Daisy's dock. He had come a long way to this blue lawn, and his dream must have seemed so close that he could hardly fail to grasp it. He did not know that it was already behind him, somewhere back in that vast obscurity beyond the city, where the dark fields of the republic rolled on under the night.

Gatsby believed in the green light, the orgastic future that year by year recedes before us. It eluded us then, but that's no matter—to-morrow we will run faster, stretch out our arms farther. . . . And one fine morning——

So we beat on, boats against the current, borne back ceaselessly into the past.

five plate changes were made; it is first changed in Wilson's edition in 1941. One would like to conclude that Fitzgerald intended the word to remain "orgastic."

We can draw only one conclusion about Fitzgerald after studying these emendations. Fitzgerald, the writer, was *always* at work. Even though the novel had been published, Fitzgerald felt compelled not only to make corrections but actually to rethink, clarify, elaborate, and rephrase passages that did not satisfy him artistically. These emendations help to show us the writer at work and support the contention that Fitzgerald was a careful craftsman, always serious about his writing. This list can serve in the classroom as a device not only for the teaching of Fitzgerald's work, but also for the teaching of writing as an art.

These emendations do not reveal any wholesale revision of the novel—certainly nothing on the scale of the 750 changes Fitzgerald made in "May Day" between its publication in *Smart Set* and its inclusion in *Tales of the Jazz Age*. He does not alter the story line, character motivation, or the tone of the novel. Rather he seems to have been correcting, clarifying, and generally polishing a novel he felt did not need significant reworking. It is revealing of Fitzgerald the artist, however, that even though the novel had already been published, he still could not resist tinkering with it and polishing it a little more.

F. Scott Fitzgerald's personal emendations in the 1925 first printing of *The Great Gatsby*. The column at the right gives the corresponding page and line numbers in the "Scribner Library" edition, since that edition is most readily available for classroom use.

6.6	wonder [confusion	5.7
6.7	interesting [arresting	5.8
18.21	I began. [I said.	15.23-24
27.10	of ash-gray men [of men	23.8
28.4	days, [days	23.26
28.15	cafes [restaurant	24.9
30.10	her flesh [her surplus flesh	25.27
33.14-15	Avenue, warm ... afternoon. I [Avenue, so warm ... afternoon that I	28.12-13
35.8	had both disappeared [had disappeared	29.28
42.12	I expected no affection. [I had played no part in her past.	35.21
42.17	out: 'Oh [out: She looked around to see who was listening. 'Oh	35.26

31

43.8	saw [was	36.12
44.17	the spot [the remains of spot ⟨?⟩[4]	37.16
48.21	bobbed [shorn	40.14
50.1-2	an amusement park. [amusement parks.	41.16
57.19	First [3d	47.24
57.20	Twenty-eighth Infantry [9th Machine Gun Battalion	47.25
57.22	Sixteenth [7th Infantry	47.26
58.23	eternal [external	48.21
58.29	Precisely ⟨circled⟩	48.27
62.17	lyric again in [lyric in ⟨? in margin⟩	51.27
70.2	were lined five [were five	57.34
70.6-7	made ... circles [outlined ... gestures	58.4
76.24	work in [work or rigid sitting in	64.10
79.17	took the remains of my machine-gun battalion [took two machine-gun detachments	66.17-18
84.16	Metropole." [Metropole.	70.26
94.23	children [little girls ⟨?⟩	79.16
95.21	he's regular [he's a regular	80.11
98.15	taxi ⟨F. note: His own car⟩	82.14
99.17	looked down at [looked at	83.9
107.9	while willing, even eager, [while occasionally willing	89.23
107.17	the large [a large	89.31
116.13	man can [man will	97.14
120.11	property of [knowledge to	100.27
120.11	turgid journalism [turgid sub or suppressed journalism	100.28
121.8	Boston and [Boston to do her stuff (?) and	101.19
153.14	added. "There [added as if she might have sounded irreverent. "There	128.18-19
165.12	Mavromichaelis [Michaelis	138.11
165.25	ripped a little at [ripped at	138.22-23
166.18	metal [wire	139.12
198.17	though [as	166.5
198.19	shocked [unmoved?	166.6
218.12	orgastic [org/astic ⟨faint i in margin⟩	182.25

University of South Carolina

[1] Post-1940 editions of *The Great Gatsby* include: Edmund Wilson, ed., *The Last Tycoon* (Scribners, 1941); Malcolm Cowley, ed., *Three Novels* (Scribners, 1953); "Student's Edition" (Scribners, 1957), and Arthur Mizener, ed., *The Fitzgerald Reader* (Scribners, 1963). Malcolm Cowley seems to have been the first of these editors to consult Fitzgerald's marked copy of the book. For a discussion of the relationship between these editions and the first edition texts, see two articles: Bruce Harkness, "Bibliography and the Novelistic Fallacy," *Studies in Bibliography*, XII, 1959, pp. 59-73, and Matthew J. Bruccoli, "Animadversions on the Text of F. Scott Fitzgerald," Proceedings of the 1969 University of Toronto Editorial Conference (University of Toronto Press, forthcoming 1970).

[2] Andrew Turnbull, ed., *The Letters of F. Scott Fitzgerald* (New York: Scribners, 1963), p. 175.

[3] In addition to making corrections and revisions, Fitzgerald noted forty-four passages which had been either quoted in reviews or commented on by friends. On page 218 he marked the passage "It eluded . . . into the past." and noted in the margin the *Richmond News-Leader* and William Rose Benét.

[4] With the exception of 98.15, punctuation or words in angle brackets are notations which cannot be positively attributed to Fitzgerald.

Won't You Come Home, Dick Diver?

By

R. L. Samsell

I used to think Dick Diver was a good, kind, wise and brave sort of fellow, pretty much the way he aspired to be, that he was fully capable of sacrificing himself, heroically, for the likes of that wooden, empty-headed little doll, Nicole, and, further, that Dick's charm was an imaginative effort to make others feel at ease and important, to give them the halcyon feeling that something memorable was about to take place. I considered Dick too good for his own good, and, as it often goes with good guys, his goodness proved his undoing. I even bought the spoiled priest concept of his characterization. Perhaps my uncritical eye was due to youth, or an egocentric identification with Dick, but, now, for whatever reasons, my previous regard for Dr. Diver has given way to feelings of pity, annoyance, and frustration.

My change in attitude first came about, when, no longer able to see well enough to read, I listened to Talking Books' rendition of *Tender is the Night*.[1] Talking Books are simply records, and *Tender's* eight records, played at 16-2/3 RPM, consuming twelve hours, have been transcribed by Alexander Scourby, generally regarded as Talking Books' finest narrator. Scourby's pace is conversational, allowing time for one to become involved in *Tender's* action and dialogue. Often, when I'm wide awake, alert, I prefer to "read" with all lights out, "watching," as it were, the explosion of color ignited by Fitzgerald's magic. In darkness, *Tender* becomes a highly sensuous experience, alive with nerve-cutting colors, garlands of flowers, conveying, often, the impression that one is viewing the highly charged pigmentations of a Technicolor movie. However,

34

should anyone interrupt my movie, the picture disappears, and, although Scourby's words continue to flow, they become merely words of telling, not of showing, and, thus, each interruption requires the needle's re-setting.

Talking Books, then, do require a definite, sometimes difficult adjustment. The proper "reading" requires one's full attention. Anything less than full attention sees the graphic dimension disappear. For me, at least, there can be no skimming, daydreaming, no mental slack whatsoever. My first experiences with Talking Books found me constantly re-setting the needle, and, although the Talking Books' pace was deliberate enough, my mind wandered, or lapsed, giving me pause to wonder if perhaps my sighted reading hadn't been sullied by just such indulgences. With Talking Books, a firm listening-discipline must be achieved by the reader, but, once achieved, the Talking Books listener is thrust into the action, immersed in the scenes, and thereby comes close to living the drama. With just a little effort, one might almost feel like an eavesdropper. Thanks to Scourby's skill with *Tender*, the characters have their distinguishable cadences, intonations, and, too, with the subtlest shift of Scourby's tone, he moves out of scenes and into narrative, in and out of interior monologues; and, perhaps most important, Fitzgerald's omniscient point-of-view is readily discerned by Scourby's slightest inflections. In *Tender*, Scourby handles a half-dozen or more dialects, drunks of varying degrees, delivers his French fluently, sings a French song, and is as convincing as Jonathan Winters when he accents gay boys. In short, I feel Scourby's reading is an improvement over my own sighted readings, and, thanks to Talking Books, I feel I can now make more accurate judgments about *Tender* as a novel, Diver as a man.

Dick Diver's opening broadside suggests a complex and distinctively melodramatic chap: "It's not one of the worst times of the day,"—this he utters to Rosemary as he, clad in a jockey cap and red-striped tights, looks out at the Mediterranean. For a thirty-four-year-old psychiatrist, this disenchantment hardly seems appropriate to voice to a pretty teenager. Rosemary, sensitive and intelligent in a standard sort of way, is charmed. Dr. Diver's business, or career, is charm. Read out loud, Diver's words seem calculated to catch the fancy of the darling ingenue. Through several chapters, and through some of the finest prose, we only see Dick through Rosemary's charmed eyes, and, if we are sympathetically disposed to Rosemary, we, too, are charmed by Dick. Early in the novel, however, Fitzgerald tells us straight out that Dick's powers fall shy of the tough-minded and the perenially suspicious; and, whereas others, like Rosemary and the wastrel group surrounding Dick, are charmed by him, Fitzgerald lets us know that he is never deceived by Dick's limitations—that he, Fitzgerald, has placed himself among the tough-minded and perenially suspicious. Whenever Fitzgerald shifts the point-of-view from Rosemary to himself, the artist's critical eye cuts Dick down to lifesize, as, for example, in Book One, Chapter IV, where Dick is shown using a megaphone while Nicole responds to his words without raising her voice, and, crucially, in the same book's Chapter XX, Fitzgerald whets our curiosity about the psychiatrist by revealing him to be as fatuous as any young swain chasing a Hollywood starlet. There are other instances of Dick's frailties, each instance provided by either Fitzgerald's voice or through Nicole's point-of-view, but, for the most part, Book One is the novel's charm section, a panning of the camera across the surface of various events and personalities. Whenever Fitzgerald cuts below the surface, he does so briefly, with painstaking care—strategically—and the sound of his intrusive voice is such that we sense he will soon return to the surface of charm and events.

In Book Two's opening, the sound of Fitzgerald's prose is less lyrical, and we sense that Fitzgerald will clinically cut through the dimensions of Diver's character. Book One has precisely prepared us for Fitzgerald's deeper look. We have had quite enough of Diver's surface. Thus, the sound of Book Two's opening is a tonic. Fitzgerald, of course, knew precisely what he was about. Book Two has the sound of letting the reader in on something, and, true to this promise, Fitzgerald's scalpel moves directly to the source of Diver's charm: egotism. For ten chapters, all of which antedate Book One, Fitzgerald probes Diver's core, using his, Fitzgerald's, "inside voice," or, ruthlessly, by listening to Diver's interior monologues. Diver's monologues, heard aloud, in the privacy of one's room, reveal a conceit of such magnitude as to compel awe and abhorrence: he rejoices in his mind, in his body, informing himself that he could brief a book five years later—"if it deserved to be briefed." Further, during the Vienna cold "He thanked his body that had done the flying rings at New Haven, and now swam in the winter Danube." Still more, he whispers ebulliently, "Lucky Dick, you big stiff. . .You hit it, my boy. Nobody knew it was there before you came along." To a colleague, Franz Gregorovious, he declares he wishes to become a good psychologist—"maybe the greatest one that ever lived"—and, of his prospective book, he suggests the title *A Psychology for Psychiatrists.* Soon enough, we may infer that humility, even modesty, are not among the good-guy doctor's behavioral tenents. Is he riding for a fall? Even before Diver's wilful, egocentric marriage to Nicole, we know the kid from Buffalo is in for a tough, losing scrap. Fitzgerald foreshadows things to come by aluding to Thackeray's *The Rose and the Ring,* wherein the Fairy Blackstick speaks so shrewdly: "The best I can wish you, my child, is a little misfortune"; and the words of a fellow student, a Rumanian, vibrate through the Talking Book, warning Dick, as it were, that his problem will be—"judgment about yourself."

Having seen Dick from the outside in Book One, then from the inside in Chapters I through X in Book Two, the novel returns in time and place to Book One's opening on the Riviera. Now, with our closer understanding of Dr. Diver, and with a little misfortune having transpired—matrimony—Chapter XI begins the novel's inquiry into Dick's capacity to make judgments about himself. Immediately subsequent in time to Dick's affair with Rosemary in Paris, the sound of Fitzgerald's prose informs us that he will no longer be content with Book One's camera, but will employ, now, an x-ray as well. It is in Chapter XI of Book Two that Dick explains away his politeness as a trick of the heart, and, leaving Elsie Speers with this unexpected candor, he returns to the Villa at Tarmes where he downs an ounce of gin with two ounces of water, and, for lunch the next day he drinks an entire bottle of wine save for Nicole's solo glass. While we are wondering what Dick means by his trick of the heart, we are left to go right on wondering while Dr. Diver's self-analysis is diffused in the haze of boozey apathia. He never turns the crucial questions on himself. Fitzgerald seems to portray Diver as a kind of typically glorious post-graduate B.M.O.C., who, when his simplistic good-guy code has cracked, finds nothing left with which to fend—for, after all, shouldn't goodness be sufficient unto itself? When Dick does learn he's not all goodness and light, he becomes sulky, disturbed with his lot; but his American heritage and his ego leave him ill-equipped to do other than escape through play and popularity, which, in turn, cause a loss of control and self-respect, overcompensations in the form of showing-off, further self-effacement, deeper loss of pride, recurring self-delusions, and all the while without the searching questions which might have revealed himself to himself. It is Dick's inability to ask these questions which affords us one of *Tender's* deeper meanings: isn't Dick like so many of our contemporaries—friends, neighbors, relatives—who, too shallow to know how shallow they are, lack that essential and redemptive quality of self-inquiry, the need to be honest with one's self?

Fitzgerald cleverly lets us glimpse the stuff of which Diver is made by thrusting the Doctor into situations where spontaniety signals that which is true to his nature. In Book One, when Dick's infatuation for Rosemary rendered him heedless of his effect on her, Fitzgerald tells us Dick "went briskly around the block with the fatuousness of one of Tarkington's adolescents." We are also told that Dick's loss of control in this situation is a turning point in his life. Here, we can see him honestly involved, no longer caring what effects he produces on another, but, for perhaps the first time, experiencing emotions which transcend ego and personal consequences. In short, what he feels for Rosemary is real and its reality shows us how ingenuous he is, and shows him, for all time, the sweet freedom of being released from the grasp of one's ego. Weak, he buckles under the strain of this freedom, returning guiltily but altered to Nicole. But he never quite leaves Rosemary and he never quite returns to Nicole. With Rosemary's departure, he is left a man divided, in flux. In briefer episodes, those in which Dick's guard is down, Fitzgerald shows us the man below the surface. As Dick explains the corpse in the hotel corridor, he is heard to say to Nicole: "only some nigger scrap." Still later, under stress during the Rome fiasco, Dick is heard to yell, "Wops." As Rosemary's lover, his Puritan's inquisitiveness hardly sounds like the cosmopolitan psychiatrist: "Are you actually a virgin?" In regard to this love making, we note that it was directly after the sexual act that Dick's most pronounced avowals of love for Nicole haunt him. Dick, too, makes a fair effort to convince the Warrens and himself that he is above the mere lure of money—something of an intellectual, he decries rank materialism, and, yet, when Gregorovious mentions a prospective case, Dick inquires: "Is there any money in it?" Throughout, there are numerous examples of Dick's sub-surface which reveal him to be just another assembly line American. Perhaps Dick is unable to fathom his depths, but Fitzgerald knows him with devastating clarity.

Throughout Fitzgerald's deft handling of various points-of-view, it seems singular that Dick Diver makes so little inquiry into his heritage. Fitzgerald presses this point, informing us that Dick seldom inquired of his distant past; there being, through Dick's point-of-view, only the recollection of finer moments at Yale, until, upon his receiving word of his father's death, he finally expresses brief sentiments of his bygone Buffalo days. At one point, in Chapter I of Book Two, we hear Dick chide himself for sounding like an American: "He mocked at his reasoning, calling it specious and 'American'—his criteria of uncerebral phrase-making was that it was American." Thus, we see that Dick's self-inquiry is blocked by a typically American affectation, that of the intellectual who thinks he has outgrown his roots. Upon Dick's return to America after his father's death, Fitzgerald is careful to inform us that Dick did not identify with his native land until after his travels from Buffalo to Westmoreland County—when he saw the cold moon over Chesapeake Bay. At the gravesite, Dick expresses the thought that he has no more ties in America. Throughout the novel, he expresses not one hint that his character and conduct can be attributed to his origins; yet, Fitzgerald details Diver's American biography with compellingly selective facts. But Diver says goodbye to his father—goodbye to all his fathers, never dreaming he is indigenous to his native soil, not to Gausse's beach. For a psychiatrist, this is at least curious. But his pride has hermetically sealed his past.

In the novel's final book, we hear his futile efforts to solve his nature. His analysis, sound enough, simply lacks depth. He blames Nicole and the Warren money, thereby achieving convenient martyrdom: "I was swallowed up like a gigolo." But Nicole, the indolence and frivolity of the very rich, his idleness—"Listening to time"—these are but the exterior pressures, or atmosphere, by which his native weakness is nurtured. An ego such as Dick Diver's must prevail, or, failing this, the resentments set in, rationalizations begin, and, succored by alcohol, the grandiose become grander, ever more delusive, until Christ-like, the ego enjoys the crucifixion wrought by those very souls the martyr hath saved: "I wasted eight years teaching the rich the A B C's of human decency . . ."—when, in truth, his performances were only ego gratifications, by no means instructive, and to an audience hardly receptive to instruction of any kind, much less that of human decency. The strongest illustrations of Diver's baseness are dramatized for us in the book's closing chapters. In saving Mary North Minghetti and Lady Sibley-Biers, there is nothing instructive nor priest-like in the string of lies rendered in his voice of sincerity. We cannot be certain, but there is the suggestion that Dr. Diver shares Nicole's suspicion that he affected her cure by having willed events which bring her strength and independence. But we should recall that as early as the Renault wreck in Book Two, Chapter XV, Dick had discharged himself as Nicole's savior. Her cure, ironically, was simply affected by his failure to affect a cure. Of course, the grossest, culminating delusion takes place as Dick gives the benediction from above Gausse's beach. To the end, he assumes a divine role, blessing the lost, leisurely souls who bask in the laziest of secular sunshines. In the novel's opening, Dick was giving a performance, and, consistent to the end, he is still performing, but on a grander and now delusive scale. Recall that earlier that day Dick had taken a long draught from a three foot high bottle of brandy. Thus, Dr. Diver, after too many compromises for too many others, having lost his identity from the abrasions of too many adjustments in the name of human decency, must find his identity from deep inside the bottle, and, thus fortified, he makes the traditional transmogrification of the inveterate boozer—he rises from the depths to the heights, taking pity on those he has transcended; when, as Fitzgerald clearly knows, and we are soon told, it is Dick who is damned—damned from the beginning. His cross is only the denouement of the sick extremes to which his fancy has flown.

Perhaps you see it differently? But I hear the Diver drama as an American epic, rendered more American by its contrasting, European locale. I hear the novel, too, as virtually flawless in form and substance. The chronology is slipshod, but this is simply arithmetic. Fitzgerald's task was an onerous one. Imagine his difficulties in portraying a downbeat character who is from the outset on a downhill slide. Consider, too, that he's an egocentric phony, surrounded by dolts even duller than himself, that, in this environment, he never has a worth while discussion with himself or others, that the extent of his self-knowledge is that his charm is a trick, that he needs to be loved—that, in whatever event, he interprets the consequences as those somehow fashioned or ordained by his wizardry. Is it any wonder the novel begins with the upbeat Rosemary, not merely to achieve the impact of Dick's charms through the impressionable young girl, but to give the novel a lift and momentum, which, even when closely scrutinized, virtually disguises the tragedy taking place? Further, Rosemary's point-of-view, showing Dick at his strongest, is sharply contrasted to that of Nicole's during the final chapters of the novel, where, through Nicole's emergent independence, Dick is viewed mostly with contempt, and, thus, his deterioration is more sweeping in its effect. Legend to the contrary, *Tender* sounds like it was written cold sober. The novel's symmetry and balance are exact. Throughout, the prose is finely honed. One critic, Henry Dan Piper, has taken exception to the clumsy writing in Chapters XI to XXII of Book Two, but here is where Dick's disintegration requires an appropriate loss of smoothness, although, within these same chapters, when the situations require grace, or beauty, anything compelling, Fitzgerald braces the style, becoming florid only when the melodramatics call for it. Fitzgerald's relentless flattening of Dick's spirit had to be achieved by detachment. Moreover, the precise pacing of numerous episodes through the novel's broad conception could only have been achieved by a first-rate novelist in full control of his talents.

In the foregoing, I have linked phrases and events to illustrate why, in studying *Tender is the Night* through Talking Books' rendition, I no longer hold Dick Diver in esteem. In fairness, however, there are many episodes which reveal Dick as the good, kind, wise, and brave man he intended to be. He helped others, yes, and he gave freely of his time and energies. Fitzgerald, after all, gave us a character in the round. Perhaps the Talking Book reading-approach can be a little harsh, even merciless, for Dick's vanities, weaknesses and indulgences are amplified when effectively dramatized for an alerted ear. For example, Scourby as Dick Diver, the drunk, may well leave no room for sympathy, whereas the non-thesbian sighted reader might not do Dick's character the damage that Scourby's drunkenese does. That leaves us with this question: What does an actor-reader like Scourby add to or take from Fitzgerald's intended prose effects? In my opinion, Scourby neither intends nor accomplishes any improvement on Fitzgerald. His reading is merely an appropriate response to the demands of Fitzgerald's material. More than this, strong prose is an intimidating force on any reader, especially one, like Scourby, who is seasoned to do a professional job. I have heard three different readers dramatize major sections of *Tender is the Night*, and, with each reader, the effects were the same. Fitzgerald, at least, leaves no room for any variations on the theme. Try it out yourself. I think you'll find you are forced along by the unremitting pressure of Fitzgerald's style, precision, and eloquence.

Finally, I should like to rebut those who have criticized Fitzgerald's apparent scanty portrayal of Diver as a psychiatrist. Such criticism is convenient, but hardly intelligent. Diver's goal was success, his means mere ambition; his pride is in himself, not in his calling. *Tender* is the story of a man who forsook his work for play and posturing, not the story of a serious psychiatrist. It is the chronicle of a frivolous American charmer, who, ironically, as a psychiatrist, lacked the capacity for self-analysis. As Diver informed Gregorovious, he became a psychiatrist for no better reason than that a pretty girl happened to attend the same lectures at Oxford. Nowhere in the novel does Fitzgerald show Diver expressing any deep interest in psychiatric cases and/or problems. But Fitzgerald shows Diver with just sufficient interest to qualify him for a limited time as a practitioner at Gregorovious' country club of a clinic. Dick does well with his bedside manner, but he finds no real intrigue in his work. Yet, subtly, and brilliantly, while Diver reveals his limitations as a doctor of the psyche, Fitzgerald dramatizes virtually every aspect and phase of the doctor's development and decline, detailing behavioral patterns, motivations, prognosticating Diver's spiritual demise. Fitzgerald, himself, is the psychiatrist, analyzing an American prototype, and forcing upon us, as is the psychiatrist's job, a glowing question mark as to Diver's being, his heritage, the interplay of those ingredients. The patient, Dick Diver, is unable to face up to that question mark; but readers, by Diver's example and tragedy, should ask themselves why he cannot, and, hopefully, they should then face up to the questions interrelating their identities with their backgrounds. As a psychiatrist, then, Fitzgerald would have us inquire of ourselves. This is the novel's intent. This is the novel's success.

---

[1] Talking Books are recorded in the Talking Book Studios of the American Foundation for the Blind, New York, New York, pursuant to federal legislation, 1931, whereby Congress appropriated $1,000,000.00 per year, for the purpose of recording and making available books for the legally blind. In recent years, the appropriation was increased to $2,000,000.00 per year. Talking Books are recorded at 16-2/3 RPM and circulate through the mails in plastic containers, postage free, and are generally distributed by various blind agencies, i.e., Braille Institute of America, Los Angeles, California, where thousands of Talking Books comprise a circulating library.

The Passion of F. Scott Fitzgerald

By

R. W. Lid

Critics of *The Great Gatsby* frequently, and quite understandably, focus their attention on the magnificent overt symbolism of the novel, particularly Dr. Eckleburg and the ashheaps his brooding presence dominates. So powerful are these symbols, and certain others in *Gatsby*, that it is sometimes assumed that the meaning of the novel resides in them. Readings of the novel through the eyes of Dr. Eckleburg overlook a simple truth about fiction, which is that narrative pattern is the total mode of symbol. The major meaning of a work of fiction is by and large carried by the narrative—and this narrative is in turn symbolic of the novel's larger meaning. In terms of the structure of *Gatsby* it is questionable whether symbolically Eckleburg is as important to the novel's meaning as the less eye-catching dog-leash which Myrtle Wilson buys for her mongrel pup and which, in a complex way, mirrors her relationship with Tom Buchanan. What our fascination and preoccupation with the occulist's sign, with "owl eyes," the ashheaps, and other such symbols, reflect, I think, is the depth of our immediate response to the powerful moral quality which pervades the book. At the root of Fitzgerald's success in *Gatsby* lies something we can only attribute to the author's personal passion. Ultimately, as I hope to show, Fitzgerald used his narrative art to curb and express this passion. In effect he manipulated the processes of his own heart, and in so doing enlarged the dimensions of narrative in twentieth century fiction.

The sources of contention surrounding a major work of fiction are almost always various and complex. In part contention derives from the work itself—from its characters, themes, symbols, structures, modes of development and the ways critics have viewed these and similar elements in the work. In part contention derives from the discoveries of biographers and historical critics about the relationship between the author's life and his work and the meaning these discoveries hold for the author's art. In the case of *Gatsby* the areas of contention as I have described them have always tended to blur, merging as critics have pursued Fitzgerald's elusive genius and attempted to account for the originality of the novel. Fitzgerald's reading habits, for example, have been used to support interpretations of the structure and meaning of the novel which see small and large parallels with the works of Conrad, while Fitzgerald's own character and behavior have assumed a fictional formulation which sees an essential dichotomy in the man and hence finds segments of his person in the novel's narrator and also in its putative hero.

Most of us are familiar with this body of criticism. It has grown by accretion, one is almost tempted to say by agglutination. Some of it is of long standing, a first sounding of the man and his work. Some of it has been repetitive, a recasting and elaboration of earlier work by critics. A good deal of it has been original in focus and discovery, and much of it has contributed to an illumination of the man, the career, the novel. Yet all of it falls short in my eyes of explaining the roots of Fitzgerald's genius or of accounting for the technical skill which underlies the making of *Gatsby*. We have not, as I see it, really examined the grand strategy of the novel closely, and we have not used the available material surrounding the man's life to suggest the highly personal context which made his art possible. In effect, we have been blinded, like Gatsby, by the cynosure of light shining at the end of the dock on Daisy's Long Island estate.

The situation is not, I would suggest, one of having to disavow parallels with Conrad or to disallow Fitzgerald his place in the Conradian or, more accurately, the Flaubertian tradition. Nor is it a case of denying the influence of American writers on his work or of failing to see him in some general American tradition, for Fitzgerald had to work, if only subconsciously, within the radical boundaries set on the one hand by Melville in his use of a personal narrator and on the other by James in his development of point of view. Rather, it is a case of seeing the individuality of the writer in the perspective of his own works and life. The issue, it seems to me, is crucial for Fitzgerald—as it is for Hemingway, where again so many of the questions concerning the works go directly back to questions concerning the division between man and writer, the author's involvement with his subject, and its relation to his art. In each instance, I would argue, the understanding needed depends in part on seeing in different perspective the alignment between authorial intent and personality and narrative technique.

I am going to try to show with specific reference to *Gatsby* that Fitzgerald's narrative sense was in an extraordinarily personal way the direct expression of his moral experience as a man. I use the phrase "narrative sense" for lack of a more precise term. Yet what I mean is not very difficult to see. It resides in the fragmented narrative line of *Gatsby* and the skill which Fitzgerald, through the agency of his first person narrator, Nick Carraway, exercised in putting it together. I would like to stop over one isolated instance of Fitzgerald's use of Nick Carraway at the beginning of Chapter VI to illustrate the point I wish to make. This is that Fitzgerald's swift, breathless, and apparently rather random ordering of his material is actually so tightly controlled that the reader's mind is led through each involution of narrative. If this particular instance is somewhat flashier, and less complex, than others I might have chosen right off, it has the virtue of being short and uncomplicated, in the sense that it does not directly involve the personality of the narrator or larger questions about the structure or meaning of the novel. It is also a small but significant instance of Fitzgerald's remarkable narrative boldness, a quality of *Gatsby* which has never been sufficiently remarked upon.

Chapter VI lies roughly at the halfway point of Fitzgerald's novel. We have already met Nick Carraway, and he, in turn, has introduced us to Daisy and Tom Buchanan, to Jordan Baker, to Myrtle Wilson and her husband, and, finally, to Gatsby. Nick has gone along with Tom to New York City and a party at Tom's and Myrtle Wilson's apartment. Nick has also attended a party at Gatsby's and there met his next door neighbor, the "elegant young roughneck" whose mysterious activities have bred extravagant rumors and whose unknown origins have caused endless speculation.

For all of this, however, it is not until the fourth chapter of the novel that the seemingly random pieces of Nick's account of the lives of these various people begin to fit together. We learn for the first time, through Jordan Baker's reminiscence, of Gatsby's earlier relationship with Daisy (this is more than a third of the way through the novel, to speak of narrative boldness); a few pages later we learn the reason for Gastby's West Egg mansion and its splendors: "Gatsby bought that house so that Daisy would be just across the bay." He had romantically hoped to attract Daisy by the brightness of his parties, as a moth is attracted by light. But Daisy has never come. Gatsby's notoriety has escaped her; West Egg is not the stamping ground of the socially elite. Now, Gatsby wants Nick, who is Daisy's cousin, to have them both to tea and hence bring them together. Chapter V is given over to that afternoon tea, including a poignant tour of Gatsby's mansion. It concludes with the three of them listening to Klipspringer, "the boarder," play show tunes on the piano in the gathering dark of Gatsby's music room. This is the day Gatsby has waited almost five years for. "There must have been moments even that afternoon," Nick remarks, "when Daisy tumbled short of his dreams—not through her own fault, but because of the colossal vitality of his illusion. It had gone beyond her, beyond everything."

Chapter V, then, completes one narrative rhythm, or movement, as it were, in the developing plot of the novel. The romance which Gatsby has stored up in his "ghostly heart" for five years has made contact with reality. Chapter VI begins a new movement, and with it a new tone appears in the narrative. The chapter begins in the following manner:

> About this time an ambitious young reporter from New York arrived one morning at Gatsby's door and asked him if he had anything to say.
>
> "Anything to say about what?" inquired Gatsby politely.
>
> "Why—any statement to give out."

The reporter, we learn, has come out to West Egg on his day off. Some rumor, some half understood remark in the office, has sent him energetically in search of a story about Gatsby. "It was a random shot," Nick remarks, "and yet the reporter's instinct was right. Gatsby's notoriety . . . had increased all summer until he fell just short of being news."

> Contemporary legends such as the "underground pipe-line to Canada" attached themselves to him, and there was one persistent story that he didn't live in a house at all, but in a boat that looked like a house and was moved secretly up and down the Long Island shore.

"Just why," Nick goes on, concluding the paragraph with a sudden, and upon first sight seemingly unexpected, revelation. "Just why these inventions were a source of satisfaction to James Gatz of North Dakota isn't easy to say." And the next paragraph abruptly begins: "James Gatz—that was really, or at least legally, his name." With as little overt preparation as this single page of the novel, the misty grandeurs of the Gatsby legend are suddenly blown away to reveal an unglamorous patronymic and an unromantic birth place. And then, before we have time to cease wondering over our new insight, the next sentence plunges us backwards in time, to Dan Cody and the incident of the *Tuolomee*, to events which Nick learns only later, on the final night he spent with Gatsby (see pp. 102 and 148 of the Scribner Library Edition).

It is true, of course, that we have been expecting some such revelation about Gatsby's background for some time. The rumors spread by the guests at his parties, "the bizarre accusations that flavored conversation in his halls," have been compounded as Fitzgerald's tale has progressed. Gatsby's own account of himself to Nick in Chapter IV ("I'll tell you God's truth") has left Nick half incredulous. The luncheon with Meyer Wolfshiem has added another dimension to the mysteries surrounding the man, and Jordan Baker's account of Gatsby's relationship with Daisy has also contributed to our growing expectation of some revelation. But we have not expected it to come as starkly or as boldly as it occurs at the beginning of Chapter VI, and certainly not at this moment, in this way. Yet a closer examination of the passage shows that the revelation has been subtly prepared for.

The success of Fitzgerald's narrative boldness derives from the particular relevance of the apparently random occurrence of the newspaper reporter at Gatsby's door and the pattern of suggestion it creates. The reporter's instinct, that a story concerning Gatsby is about to break, is, Nick tells us, the right instinct to have; the truth about Jay Gatsby, the incident suggests, is near at hand. There is an added suggestion of this in the emphasis on the season; before summer is over, the implication runs, Gatsby will be news. Time, we are made to feel, is about to run out on Gatsby's masquerade—and before the paragraph is over, he has become James Gatz.

Gatsby, of course, doesn't have "any statement to give out" to the young reporter; but he does have, we know, a detailed statement to give Nick, and it is ultimately our knowledge of this that gives the incident its relevance and the transition its effectiveness. For Nick is our reporter. We are waiting for his account of Gatsby's life, for the "news" about James Gatz. The reporter's arrival and reaction have been merely the occasion for revealing the real story behind Gatsby. What we might call Fitzgerald's calculated "rhetoric of narrative" in this instance serves a similar function at a number of crucial junctures where Fitzgerald is bridging difficult gaps in his fragmented narrative scheme. Without such imaginative rhetorical movements on the part of Nick Carraway, no rearrangement of chronology, however clever, would be effective. A good deal of the technical brilliance of

Gatsby stems from Fitzgerald's narrative sense at precisely such moments.

It was Fitzgerald's narrative sense, I think, which partly enabled him to achieve the extraordinary effect of compression *Gatsby* gives. Writing to the author some months before the novel's publication, Scribner's editor Maxwell Perkins remarked: "It seems, on reading, a much shorter book than it is, but it carries the mind through a series of experiences that one would think would require a book of three times its length." And Fitzgerald, in his Introduction to the Modern Library reprint of the novel, remarked: "What I cut out of it both physically and emotionally would make another novel." The contours of Fitzgerald's story would more than prove the truth of such a statement. For one problem Fitzgerald faced, and solved, was the burden of narrative. He had too much story on his hands. Any one of his isolated narrative fragments—Gatsby's courtship of Daisy, Tom's and Daisy's wedding, Dan Gody and Ella Kaye—could have commanded a great deal more space

In *The Fictional Technique of F. Scott Fitzgerald*, James E. Miller, Jr. demonstrates at considerable length that Fitzgerald had a "sure touch" for selection, for knowing which events to dramatize, which to present obliquely, to summarize, to omit, and so on. Some similar account also has to be given of Fitzgerald's "sure touch" in the selection of his major narrative elements. For one reason for the brevity of the novel and its extraordinary effect of compression is that basically the plot of *Gatsby* is that of a short story, not a novel. Fitzgerald fashioned the narrative framework for a major American novel from the thin story-line of two sexual affairs (Gatsby and Daisy, Myrtle Wilson and Tom Buchanan), one of which he does not even recount, and he resolved both lines of action by a single violent action on the road to West Egg. So the novel appears in outline.

The narrative scheme of *Gatsby* is built around two strands of story—the story of Gatsby and the story of Myrtle Wilson, parallel characters who share parallel dreams and parallel fates. In terms of structure, the novel is as much Myrtle Wilson's story as James Gatz's, and the novel's most tragic moment is when her body is found on the road to West Egg, the left breast "swinging loose like a flap." "There was no need to listen for the heart beneath. The mouth was wide open and ripped at the corners, as though she had choked a little in giving up the tremendous vitality she had stored so long." I am not suggesting for a moment that Myrtle Wilson is the central figure of the novel, or even that Fitzgerald was as absorbed by her story as

Gatsby's, but that she carries the burden of narrative which her more glamorous counterpart cannot sustain. She is the ballast which prevents Fitzgerald's balloon of romance from sailing off into the blue and out of sight.

Myrtle Wilson, of course, was not part of the nucleus of fact out of which Fitzgerald first conceived his novel, and it is impossible to reconstruct what led him to seize upon her story and develop it to such lengths—except to say that his extraordinary narrative sense guided him. Her story is a second, less glamorous, more soiled version of the American Dream. Its realities are crude, its plot openly one of adultery and exploitation. Its characters are distinctly unpleasant people. Myrtle is seen at her most vulgar, Tom Buchanan at his ugliest. Then there is Wilson, a tragically broken man who lives in a blighted world with his own dreams of success. And at the party in Myrtle's and Tom's apartment, the dark counterpart of all the glamorous parties on Gatsby's estate, there is Myrtle's sister Catherine and the McKees, characters which reinforce Fitzgerald's point. The Sunday afternoon party occurs before we see any of the exotic affairs at Gatsby's on Long Island. It stands at the front of the novel providing ironic commentary and judgment on events to follow. The accidental violence which is to occur on the road to West Egg is prefigured by the violent outburst of emotions with which the party breaks up near midnight.

The world of Myrtle Wilson is the world of Gatsby seen in a glass darkly, but truly. Her story is unlike the romanticized version of the dream in the Gatsby narrative strand, with its glamorous parties, Gatsby's exemplary if preposterous conduct, his idealized vision of Daisy: "High in a white palace, the king's daughter, the golden girl." Gatsby's illegal activities are never spelled out. Romance and myth hang over them, and they are largely dealt with by the author through conjecture and suggestion. We are never allowed a close view of the ways Gatsby made his money ("I was in the drug business and then I was in the oil business. But I'm not in either one now."), nor do we see the gradual transformation of a personality, or the steps by which he arrived in West Egg. In contrast, we follow Myrtle Wilson step by step from the garage in the ashheaps to the apartment in New York City. Her dissatisfactions, her dreams of wealth, betterment, and a more sophisticated life mirror the dark realities we are only allowed to glimpse in the Gatsby story.

Fitzgerald makes us acutely aware of the web of material things out of which Myrtle fashions her alter life, from the copy of *Town Tattle* and the notions she purchases in the Pennsylvania Station, to the over-priced mongrel she makes Tom Buchanan buy her. To

Myrtle, the alleged Airedale ("Undoubtedly there was an Airedale concerned in it somewhere," Nick remarks) is the symbol of her escape from the ashheaps into affluence. " 'I want to get one of those dogs,' she said earnestly, 'I want to get one for the apartment. They're nice to have—a dog.' " At the climax of the novel we learn that one of the things that made Wilson suspicious of his wife's conduct and set him off was a "small, expensive dog-leash, made of leather and braided silver" that he found in a drawer. No doubt the leash was also bought with Tom Buchanan's money and like the dog represents social position to Myrtle. But the leash is also symbolic of her relationship with Tom Buchanan. To her, he is an animal on a leash, to be exploited—just as he is exploiting her. Tom's true feelings about Myrtle, on the other hand, emerge in the scene in the cab in New York City. As Myrtle takes the dog onto her lap and fondles "the weatherproof coat with rapture," and the sidewalk salesman continues to extoll the animal's virtue, the seemingly casual dialogue suggests a second level of meaning.

"Is it a boy or girl?" she asked delicately.

"That dog? That dog's a boy."

"It's a bitch," said Tom decisively. "Here's your money. Go and buy ten more dogs with it."

Included in Tom's statement is the innuendo that Myrtle herself is a bitch and he has bought her. But while Tom begrudges Myrtle the over-priced mongrel, he nevertheless buys it for her. The terms of their relationship are clear to both of them.

As the Sunday afternoon party progresses in their apartment, Myrtle gradually transforms herself from the wife of a filling station operator to the mistress of a socialite millionaire. At one point she changes into an elaborate afternoon dress of cream-colored chiffon (" 'It's just a crazy old thing,' she said. 'I just slip it on sometimes when I don't care how I look.' "), and is metamorphosed. "The intense vitality that had been so remarkable in the garage was converted into impressive hauteur. Her laughter, her gestures, her assertions became violently affected moment by moment, and as she expanded the room grew smaller around her, until she seemed to be revolving on a noisy, creaking pivot through the smoky air." Like Gatsby, who piles mounds of shirts before Daisy—"shirts with stripes and scrolls and plaids in coral and apple-green and lavender and faint orange, with monograms of Indian blue"—Myrtle has been transformed by the power of things, only here the material shabbiness of the dream breaks through the surface and dominates the scene. With his gesture, of course, Gatsby is inarticulately searching for some equivalent to his "heightened sensitivity to the promises of life," his "romantic readiness." Myrtle is allowed no such redeeming grace, only her vitality and vulgarity. There is nothing to parallel Daisy's outburst to Gatsby: " 'They're such beautiful shirts,' she sobbed, her voice muffled in the thick folds. 'It makes me sad because I've never seen such—such beautiful shirts before.' "

About Gatsby's and Daisy's relationship after they are reunited by Nick, Fitzgerald tells us nothing. Writing to Edmund Wilson at the time of the novel's publication he remarked: "I gave no account (and had no feeling about or knowledge of) the emotional relations between Gatsby and Daisy from the time of their reunion to the catastrophe. However the lack is so astutely concealed by the retrospect of Gatsby's past and blankets of excellent prose that no one has noticed it—though everyone has felt the lack and called it by another name." Another reason the lack is so astutely concealed, it seems to me, is that the brute realities are so acutely present in the narrative strand revolving around Myrtle Wilson. It is almost as if Myrtle Wilson's world were a substitute for the real world of Gatsby which the exigencies of Fitzgerald's narrative purpose caused him to gloss over.

Assuredly it was a stroke of narrative genius on Fitzgerald's part which found the resolution of his two narrative strands in a single event on the road to West Egg—but it was Fitzgerald's narrative sense which enabled him to join together his two fragmented lines of story so that they not merely reflect each other but become a single unit of narrative. The effect he achieves is much like that of a composer orchestrating two themes which sometimes reinforce each other, sometimes clash, but which always provide continuous commentary on each other. From the pattern of consonances and dissonances emerges the larger meaning of *Gatsby*.

It is in creating the resonances between the two narrative strands that Fitzgerald's narrator plays such an important role. I do not myself believe that sufficient attention has been paid to this role. Take, for example, the famous climax of the novel in Chapter VII, the movement which comes to a close at the end of the scene in the hotel room in New York City. Gatsby and Tom at long last clash directly over Daisy. The scene reaches a climax, we recall, with a bitter exchange between the two men about Gatsby's illegal activities, particularly those which involve Tom's friend, Walter Chase. As revelation follows revelation, Daisy's spirit withers until, in the end, Tom knows that Gatsby has lost her. Assured that "whatever intentions, whatever courage" Daisy had had, is gone, Tom insists that Daisy and Gatsby start home in Gatsby's car.

Jordan, Tom, and Nick also prepare to leave. Before they go, Tom offers Jordan and Nick a drink from an unopened bottle of whiskey he is wrapping in a towel. Nick, lost in thought, fails to answer, and Tom asks again: "Want any?" Nick replies: "No . . . I just remembered that today's my birthday."

With Nick's unexpected answer, the scene in the hotel room comes to a close. Now Nick directly addresses the reader: "I was thirty. Before me stretched the portentous, menacing road of a new decade." A single paragraph follows in which, amidst a recounting of the start back to Long Island in Tom's coupe, Fitzgerald plays upon the loss of Nick's romantic dreams.

> Thirty—the promise of a decade of loneliness, a thinning list of single men to know, a thinning briefcase of enthusiasm, thinning hair. But there was Jordan beside me, who, unlike Daisy, was too wise ever to carry well-forgotten dreams from age to age. As we passed over the dark bridge her wan face fell lazily against my coat's shoulder and the formidable stroke of thirty died away with the reassuring pressure of her hand.

The next paragraph, a single sentence, abruptly states: "So we drove on toward death through the cooling twilight." And the next paragraph begins: "The young Greek, Michaelis, who ran the coffee joint beside the ashheaps was the principal witness at the inquest."

Fitzgerald's time-shift is abrupt and seemingly unexpected, yet, as in our earlier instance in Chapter VI, it has been subtly prepared for. For one thing, the figure of speech Fitzgerald selects ("the portentous, menacing road of a new decade") is in itself suggestive of the approaching accident. The submerged analogue, of course, is that of the road of life, which is the relevance behind Nick's remarks about being thirty, and the pivotal sentence—"So we drove on toward death through the cooling twilight"—carries the force of this second meaning with it. There is, moreover, "the dark bridge," which marks their re-entrance to Hades, the Valley of Ashes, and beside Nick, a perverse Beatrice leading him downward instead of upward, sits Jordan—Jordan who with her "wan face" appears as if she were a living ghost of a departed Daisy. ("They were gone," Nick remarks of Daisy and Gatsby after they have left the hotel room, "without a word, snapped out, made accidental, isolated, like ghosts, even from our pity.") Nick's birthday and the rhetoric which Fitzgerald builds around it here serve the difficult task of uniting the novel's two main narrative strands.

It is often said by critics of *Gatsby* that Fitzgerald's narrator not merely records the events of the novel but also embodies the meaning of the experiences he witnesses. Certainly Nick Carraway is one of the most engaging narrators in twentieth century fiction. He is warm, human, fallible. From the first page of the novel, when he presents his credentials in a humorous, self-depreciatory yet quietly authoritative voice, much like Melville's Ishmael, we consciously identify with him. For this reason, among others, critics have felt the need to elevate his status from mere narrator to active participant. On occasion Nick Carraway has even been viewed as the novel's hero, and at least one critic, Robert Wooster Stallman, has gone so far as to find him an "unreliable" narrator.

The most commonly held view of Fitzgerald's narrator is not so extravagant in its claims, and it bears closer examination. In the introduction to his anthology of *Gatsby* criticism, the late Frederick J. Hoffman neatly summarized this view. After discussing Fitzgerald's fragmented narrative, Mr. Hoffman went on to say:

> This interweaving of present and past is especially important, in light of Nick Carraway's role as narrator. The real triumph of *The Great Gatsby* lies in its combining two principal strands of emotional and intellectual development: Carraway moves toward an understanding of Gatsby (he must "solve the mystery" of what appears to be a "purposeless splendor"); but he also comes to accept Gatsby, as the mystery recedes and the "young roughneck" vulgarity is discounted, for the "romantic readiness for hope" that transcends it.

He concluded his summary in the next paragraph: "These are the major means of the novel. It is, therefore, a novel with both Gatsby and Carraway as heroes." Now in one sense this is obviously true. The experience is Nick's, we share it with him. Yet does such an account at all reveal the essential narrative structure of the novel, as it would seem to—or is our reading of the novel here being influenced once more by the spectre of Conrad and the form of *Heart of Darkness*? Put another way, does such a reading really account for Fitzgerald's actual narrative practice, that is, for the uses to which he puts Nick Carraway?

At both the outset and close of *Gatsby* Fitzgerald's narrator is a highly self-conscious young man, but for the rest of the novel he is overshadowed by the more glamorous and romantic Gatsby, just as

Myrtle Wilson is. In fact, Nick does not even have the status as a character in the plot that Mrs. Wilson does. The change he undergoes, moreover, is largely a superficial one. That is, Fitzgerald adopts a stock development of a fairly standard character which he expects his readers to accept immediately at the level of convention. This would seem to me to be the reason for so carefully presenting Nick's credentials as moral agent in the opening pages of the novel, as well as for presenting the outcome of his experience so early. The novel, moreover, is told in the past tense. The action is over, all of Nick's judgments have in effect been made. We do not see him in the course of his narrative making elaborate revisions in his opinions, nor do we see him involved in real moral ambiguity.

What Fitzgerald gives us instead are largely gestures of a changing moral attitude. For example, after breakfast with Gatsby, on the morning after the accident, Nick shouts across the lawn to Gatsby as he leaves: "They're a rotten crowd. You're worth the whole damn bunch put together."

> I've always been glad I said that. It was the only compliment I ever gave him, because I disapproved of him from beginning to end. First he nodded politely, and then his face broke into that radiant and understanding smile, as if we'd been in ecstatic cahoots on that fact all the time. His gorgeous pink rag of a suit made a bright spot of color against the white steps, and I thought of the night when I first came to his ancestral home, three months before. The lawn and drive had been crowded with the faces of those who guessed at his corruption—and he had stood on those steps, concealing his incorruptible dream, as he waved them good-by.
>
> I thanked him for his hospitality. We were always thanking him for that—I and the others.
>
> "Good-by," I called. "I enjoyed breakfast, Gatsby."

Here, as at a number of other places in the novel, one becomes acutely aware of the extent to which grammar and syntax and diction convey moral meaning, and involve moral choice for the author. But there is no question about Nick's (or the author's) attitude toward Gatsby. Nick's journey to understanding is assumed by author and reader alike; he is not in any real sense a growing or developing character.

What Fitzgerald gives us about Nick are largely tokens of character—"a short affair with a girl who lived in Jersey City and worked in the accounting department," a growing interest in Jordan Baker, with whom he goes to a house-party up in Warwick, the formidable problem of breaking off with a girl back home who remains nameless. In other words, he presents no more account of Nick's background or of his routine life during the summer in which the major events in the novel take place than is necessary to make him convincing to the reader. Even Nick's sensitivity is determined, it seems to me, by the requirements of Fitzgerald's narrative. "I was thirty. Before me stretched the menacing road of a new decade." This particular metaphor of aging is necessary to Fitzgerald's purposes. The road Nick is driving on, I repeat, becomes the road of life.

As has been pointed out more than once, Nick's relationship with Jordan Baker is not very adequately treated in the course of the novel. The reason for this, it seems to me, is that Fitzgerald is not really very interested in them as persons, or, for that matter, in any parallels their abortive affair presents to the other couples. Both Nick and Jordan are much more important to Fitzgerald on other levels of narrative construction. Jordan is in effect Daisy's stand-in, her double. She reflects the dark side of Daisy's personality, her moral shabbiness and self-centeredness; she is both figure and commentary, just as Myrtle Wilson is. Such reflexive figures are needed to fill out Fitzgerald's purpose, for both Daisy and Gatsby are mere ghostly presences in the book. That is, Fitzgerald's "golden girl" and his "elegant young roughneck" are figments of his vision of his own life and of the life he shared with Zelda. At precisely the points where it can be said that his critical intelligence wavered and his insights became blurred, his narrative imagination supplied both perception and sensibility.

Nick's function is another matter. If we turn to the most complex instance of Fitzgerald's weaving together of his narrative strands, his role becomes clearer. After the breakfast with Gatsby, on the morning after the accident, Nick goes up to the city. He tries "for a while to list the quotations on an interminable amount of stock," then falls asleep in his swivel chair. At noon he is awakened by the phone. It is Jordan Baker. "Usually," Nick remarks, "her voice came over the wire as something fresh and cool, as if a divot from a green golf-links had come sailing in at the office window, but this morning it seemed harsh and dry." Jordan tells Nick that she has left Daisy's house. "Probably," Nick remarks, "it had been tactful to leave Daisy's house, but the act annoyed me, and her next remark made me rigid." Jordan complains that Nick wasn't "so nice" to her the night before. ("How could it have mattered then?" he replied.) Nevertheless Jordan wants to see Nick that afternoon. But Nick, responding to the suggestion of cowardliness in her leaving Daisy's, and to her essential selfishness and lack of concern over what has happened, doesn't want to see her. "I don't know which of us hung up with a sharp click, but I know I didn't care. I couldn't have talked to her across a tea-table that day if I never talked to her again in this world."

> I called Gatsby's house a few minutes later, but the line was busy. I tried four times; finally an exasperated central told me the wire was being kept open for long distance from Detroit. Taking out my time-table, I drew a small circle around the three-fifty train. Then I leaned back in my chair and tried to think. It was just noon.

Now there occurs a space break on the page, possibly to suggest that the thoughts which follow could occur to Nick as he reclines in his chair, and then a time-shift carries us back to the morning.

> When I passed the ashheaps on the train that morning I had crossed deliberately to the other side of the car. I supposed there'd be a curious crowd around there all day with little boys searching for dark spots in the dust, and some garrulous man telling over and over what had happened, until it became less and less real even to him and he could tell it no longer, and Myrtle Wilson's tragic achievement was forgotten.

A final, abrupt sentence closes the paragraph: "Now I want to go back and tell what happened at the garage after we left there the night before." With that sentence time shifts first backward, to the night before and events at the garage, then forward to the events of the day leading to Gatsby's death.

About the detailed events crowding around Wilson and Michaelis in the hours after the accident—which Fitzgerald describes immediately after the paragraph quoted above—Nick can know only what newspaper accounts or Michaelis's testimony at the inquest revealed. Nick's "Now I want to go back and tell what happened . . ." seemingly violates point of view. A less assured and less skilled writer than Fitzgerald, one can theorize, would have handled the matter less swiftly and less boldly. Conceivably he might have had Nick interview Michaelis. More likely, he would have taken pains to show Nick piecing things out from various sources, or he would have planted an eye witness who directly tells Nick what happened. But such devices used in this fashion would have obtruded technique upon subject matter, and Fitzgerald is too good a writer to do this. Actually Fitzgerald does use these devices but much more subtly and imaginatively. In scattered references to Michaelis's testimony and to newspaper accounts in the pages which follow Nick implies that he has gathered the information which he dramatically retells, while the suggestion of an eye witness—"some garrulous man telling over and over what had happened"—is represented in the ghostly person of Nick.

Riding the train that morning, we recall, Nick had avoided viewing the scene of the accident by changing his seat to the other side of the car. Nevertheless he had imagined a curious crowd at the ashheaps, little boys searching for dry spots of blood, and his garrulous talker retelling what had happened. Had Nick looked out of the train window, hours after the accident, it is extremely unlikely that he would have seen anything but a stretch of road, passing cars, and a deserted garage and gasoline pumps. Nick's imaginative rearrangement of the landscape, with its heightened tragic overtones, artistically prepares us for the return to the night before, while the analogue of the garrulous storyteller suggests that the information was readily available to everyone.

A glance at the larger scheme of Fitzgerald's narrative reminds us that this is not the first but the second time he is covering the ground of the night before. We have already visited the scene of the accident with Tom and Nick, learned something of events from five o'clock on through Michaelis, gone on to the Buchanan's home, left Gatsby at his lonely vigil outside, and then later, together with Nick, spent the remainder of the night with him. Nick's reconstruction of the scene comes at a point where Fitzgerald is recharging his narrative. Now we return to the scene of the accident, this time with events leading swiftly in a single unbroken narrative line into the next day and Gatsby's death. We move so swiftly that it is not surprising the story out-distances Nick's knowledge of events and in the final moments of Gatsby's life Fitzgerald must rely on Conrad's technique of narrative by conjecture. Yet the effect is, to use Fitzgerald's words from his 1934 Introduction to the novel, "truth or rather the equivalent of truth, the attempt at honesty of imagination."

Fitzgerald's rearrangement of time juxtaposes the deaths of Myrtle and Gatsby. It also allows Wilson's story of his life with Myrtle, his growing suspicion of her other life, his discovery of the dog collar, and his quarrel with her to be part of the main narrative instead of mere flashback or isolated story. But such re-ordering of chronology also produces unexpected breaks in narrative, sudden stops and swift starts, awkward gaps that have to be filled. It is precisely at these moments that the presence of Fitzgerald's narrator, who is not bound by time or scene, maintains the unbroken rhythm of the plot. But Nick is not merely the author's stand-in. The relationship between authorial intent and personality and narrative technique remains complex.

In his biography of Fitzgerald, Arthur Mizener remarks: "His use of a narrator allowed Fitzgerald to keep clearly separated for the first time in his career the two sides of his nature, the middle-western Trimalchio and the spoiled priest who disapproved of but grudgingly admired him." Mr. Mizener's remark, in the sense in which I think he intended it, is obviously true. *Gatsby* exhibits a measure of control over subject matter which Fitzgerald failed to achieve in his other books, and this control resides in Fitzgerald having found, through his use of first person narration, a way not only to sort out the attitudes he shared with his characters but also to provide legitimate commentary on these attitudes.

It might even be said that in *Gatsby* Fitzgerald's selves are converted into a narrative pattern to be worked out by his characters. From our earlier examination of the structure of the novel, it is obvious that more persons than Gatsby and Nick are involved in this design. Hence the caution with which one must approach Mr. Mizener's interpretation. Interpretations substantially the same as his of the relation between the author and his hero and narrator have on occasion been used as additional support for the view that Nick is one of the dual heroes of the novel. Mr. Mizener, of course, does not take this step. He is not insisting, to put it crudely, that Fitzgerald mysteriously divided himself in half, and one part found expression in Gatsby, the other in Nick Carraway. He is merely indicating the obvious extent of the author's personal involvement in two of his characters. I would suggest that Fitzgerald is equally involved in a number of his other characters, for there is a sense in which he is also Daisy and Myrtle and "owl eyes"—and even George Wilson. In his biography, *Scott Fitzgerald*, the late Andrew Turnbull quoted a remark Fitzgerald once made to his secretary, Laura Guthrie. "I take people to me and change my conception of them and then write them out again. My characters are all Scott Fitzgerald. Even my feminine characters are feminine Scott Fitzgeralds."

It is a commonplace of Fitzgerald criticism that the characterization in *Gatsby* is not deep, is at times no more than adequate; and we ourselves have seen how minimally Nick Carraway and Jordan Baker exist as people. But what has never been posited is that perhaps Fitzgerald is using first person narration here to avoid characterization. That is, in *Gatsby* the deliberate pressure of narration frees Fitzgerald from a blinding sense of identity with any one character in the working out of his fable; in effect, he is able to curb and express his personal passion.

Ultimately, of course, Fitzgerald does create a magnificent figure in

Gatsby, one with depth and possessed of profound moral seriousness, but that figure is neither Jay Gatsby nor Myrtle Wilson. Nor is it Nick Carraway. It is, I would suggest, Scott Fitzgerald, both man and writer, or, rather, the man-as-writer. Brooding over his domain of ashheaps and the drama which unfolds upon it are not merely the eyes of Doctor T. J. Eckleburg but the intelligence and conscience of the author. "I am not a great man," he wrote his daughter in 1939, "but sometimes I think the impersonal and objective quality of my talent and the sacrifices of it, in pieces, to preserve its essential value has some sort of epic grandeur."

From the vast biographical material available about Fitzgerald, including that provided by his *Letters*, it is clear that he wrote out of himself, in effect put himself directly on paper, in a way that earlier writers cannot be said to. His goal was the modern novelist's goal of self-understanding. What separates Fitzgerald from his immediate predecessors, it seems to me, is the extent of awareness of self in his fiction. It is not that Fitzgerald was more honest than, say, Conrad, but that by the time Fitzgerald wrote, it had become possible to accept blame. For Fitzgerald's generation, self-knowledge had become a human discovery, and Fitzgerald shared in that discovery. Overshadowing both the man and his work is the deeply tragic understanding that he is the personal author of his own wreckage.

In *Gatsby*, Fitzgerald's heightened awareness that his vision was partial, incomplete, uncertain, tentative, hesitant, led him to use character and fable to test a series of passionately held hypotheses about life. The final success of Fitzgerald's narrative technique can be measured by Edmund Wilson's description of the book as an "organized impersonal" novel.

San Fernando Valley State College

"I Just Can't See Daylight...."

By

Paul Wagner

When Ted Coy, the legendary Yale back, died in September 1935, Scott Fitzgerald was stunned. He had put Coy in some of his stories, and the death of one of the pre-eminent idols of his youth weighed heavily on him. Coy had, Fitzgerald was sure, died an alcoholic, and his death assumed a premonitory complexion, pitching Fitzgerald into a deep funk during the last days of that Asheville summer.[1]

Born to moderate wealth and the gentle traditions that informed the eastern upper class of the Eighties, Edward Harris Coy, like many of Fitzgerald's heroes both real and imagined, was a child of advantage. At the time of Coy's birth on May 24, 1888, in Andover, Massachusetts, his father was a classical scholar; his mother was possessed of a better-than-decent fortune for the day; and he was, further, by heritage party to an aristocratic academic tradition. His family included several prominent Yale alumni, among them Timothy Dwight, who was president of the University in the 1880's and '90's, and when the elder Coy assumed the headmastership of Hotchkiss School, Ted was commited to preparing there for his own career at Yale, which began ordinarily enough in the fall of 1906 and ended when he was graduated with the Class of 1910 and set out into the world a national celebrity.

Ted Coy was, quite simply, a superb athlete. A member of the freshman football, baseball, and track teams, he continued by distinguishing himself on both the College and University baseball teams and the University track and football teams. But it was in football that he excelled. He was an exemplary fullback: he had speed, a high-kneed, piston-like gait; he could punt a long, high ball—on the run if necessary—and he was a first-rate drop kicker. He could pass, tackle, and block, and he never tired. Adversity brought out the best he had to offer, and his best was rarely surpassed.

In his three years of University football, Coy played in only one losing game, and in his senior year as captain, he and his teammates not only defeated each of their ten opponents, but also prevented any of them from scoring, their losses fated to hang like a string of eggs down the margin of the Yale record book for 1909. Coy left the field at Cambridge on November 20, that year, the victory over Harvard ending an uncommonly glamorous undergraduate career that had captured the imaginations of sports-minded romantics throughout the country.

At six feet and 195 pounds, Coy was powerfully built, and his physical agility and brainy playing were in no way compromised by his being wholesomely goodlooking with a puckish eye, an up-turned nose and a wave of blond hair breaking over his high forehead. In an age when almost everyone knew Frank Merriwell's fictional exploits at Yale, it was good to believe that life could in fact imitate art.

And imitate art it did. Coy was hardly less magnificent than Merriwell either as player or man. As a player his position in football history was assured by the skill alone with which he translated superior thought into superlative action. As a man, however, he entered a realm that appealed to the highest romantic instincts of both his male and female admirers.

Two weeks before the opening of the 1909 season, Coy had undergone an appendectomy, and, having been sidelined for the first four games of his captaincy, he begged to be sent in to quash an imminent Army score. Allowed to play after having promised to do no more than pass and kick, he obeyed his trainer's orders by limiting himself to punting and then to passing at a critical moment to an obliging teammate who supplied the rough-and-tumble muscle to prevent Army's impending success. It was a bravura gesture that unified the Yale effort, and the fans loved Coy for it. His was the kind of manly, imaginative decisiveness that made legends.

By the end of his final season, Coy was a god, and of that last game at Harvard one reporter wrote:

> . . . . Yesterday it was his remarkable personality as well as his drop kicking ability that won the game for his team. He held his eleven in the hollow of his hand, laying a restraining hand on the arm of the man who showed signs of losing his temper, rebuking the player who wanted to talk to his opponent in the line, and so surely dominating the Yale situation that during the whole game the Elis suffered but two penalties. . . . In the quiet

smiling manner of his leadership and in the sportsmanship that prompted every move, Coy added greatly to the fame that he has gained in all his football exploits.[2]

According to the New York *Times*, he received more than fifty proposals of marriage within a few days after that last victory at Cambridge, but romantic involvements were not yet a part of his life. He had still to graduate, and by the time he had, seven months later, he had accumulated a substantial list of honors and extracurricular credits.

In addition to his athletic achievements, he had, among other things, sung tenor with the Apollo Glee Club and had sat on the Senior Council; he was a member of Delta Kappa Epsilon, and on Tap Day had gone to his room a Skull and Bones; scholastically his accomplishment had been respectable, and at the time of his graduation he said that he expected to go into business.

Although a mere summary of his versatility and popularity— especially at a remove of some sixty years—can only vaguely suggest the appeal he held for a hero-worshipping age, Ted Coy's celebrity lasted well beyond his undergraduate days. As late as 1928, he appeared, barely concealed behind the name Ted Fay, as a secondary but nonetheless important character in Scott Fitzgerald's "The Freshest Boy," one of the Basil Duke Lee stories.

Fitzgerald's portrait of Coy-Fay aches with the nostalgia of the unregenerated hero-worshiper observing an awe-struck adolescent and a remote, clear-eyed god unapproachably immured in the amber of his golden, supremely ineffable glamour.

> [Basil] found the theatre and entered the lobby with its powdery feminine atmosphere of a matinée. As he took out his ticket, his gaze was caught and held by a sculptured profile a few feet away. It was that of a well-built blond young man of about twenty with a strong chin and direct gray eyes. Basil's brain spun wildly for a moment and then came to rest upon a name—more than a name—upon a legend, a sign in the sky. What a day! He had never seen the young man before, but from a thousand pictures he knew beyond the possibility of a doubt that it was Ted Fay, the Yale football captain, who had almost single-handed beaten Harvard and Princeton last fall. Basil felt a sort of exquisite pain. The profile turned away; the crowd revolved; the hero disappeared. But Basil would know all through the next hours that Ted Fay was here too.[3]

Earlier there had been a hint of Coy in Amory Blaine's image of himself as a St. Regis football hero,[4] and there was a bit of him too perhaps in Tom Buchanan, though Buchanan had been an end:

". . . a national figure in a way, one of those men who reach such an acute limited excellence at twenty-one that everything afterward savors of anticlimax. . . ."[5] ". . . a sturdy straw-haired man . . . . you could see a great pack of muscle shifting when his shoulder moved under his thin coat. It was a body capable of enormous leverage. . . . His speaking voice, a . . . husky tenor. . . ."[6] But if there is a touch of Ted Coy in Tom Buchanan, it is a part of the later Coy—the part Fitzgerald was to find so frightening in the late summer of 1935.

In the first months following his graduation from Yale, Ted Coy worked for a Minnesota lumber company, returning on invitation to New Haven in September as head coach of the 1910 University football team, but he proved an indifferent coach, and at the end of the season, having taken time out to write a series of articles on football for *St. Nicholas*, he moved on to Chattanooga where for the next two years he worked in relative anonymity as a minor executive for a coal and iron company. Business was in fact to be his future, and he was on his way up.

During the summer of 1913, Coy, in Savannah briefly, in part to umpire a game, met and fell in love with Sophie d'Antignac Meldrim, the daughter of Frances Casey, a celebrated Georgia beauty, and of General Peter W. Meldrim who had been, or was yet to be, mayor of Savannah, president of the American Bar Association, commander of the state's military forces, and a judge of the Chatham County Superior Court.

The romance was precipitate. Coy and Miss Meldrim eloped to Asheville where they were married on August 31. The elopement was a gossip's delight, and the marriage was considered on all counts a love match of the first order, which indeed it seemed to be for the next decade.

Coy pursued his business interests, first as the manager of a bond department in Washington and subsequently as office manager and member of the firm of Davies, Thomas & Company of the New York Stock Exchange, and he continued to write, principally for newspapers, on financial matters and, more extensively, about sports. But by 1922 there were rumors of his wife's intention to sue for divorce, and a year later she went to Paris to file charges only to change her mind and return to the States. By late 1924, however, their marriage was over, and she returned to Paris, accused Coy of having deserted her, and was granted a divorce and the custody of their two sons. The divorce, according to the New York *Times*, thrilled scandal-conscious Savannah just as much as the elopement and marriage had a dozen years earlier.

In the meantime, Coy had met and become infatuated with Jeanne Eagels, who, at the time of their first meeting, was starring in *Rain*, the immensely successful Broadway adaptation of Somerset Maugham's "Miss Thompson." A star of unchallenged popularity, Jeanne Eagels was a tempestuous genius who could curse like a drover, string along Stage-Door Johnnies and Sugar Daddies, and still appear in her publicity photographs demure, fresh-eyed and cameo-profiled—just the sort of girl any fellow could take home to mother.

She was, above all, the consummate artist. Her work was her glory and apparently her only immutable love. Born in Kansas City, she had acted first at the age of seven—or possibly eleven, since she was known to fib about her age—as Puck, progressed quickly to the tent shows of the turn-of-the-century mid-west and from there to her New York career which began in 1911 in Richard Carle's *Jumping Jupiter.* During the next decade she appeared in *The "Mind-the-Paint" Girl* and *The Crinoline Girl*; in George Arliss's revivals of *Disraeli* and *The Professor's Love Story* and in his production of *Hamilton*; in Belasco's *Daddies*; in *A Young Man's Fancy*, *The Wonderful Thing*, *In the Night Watch*, and a handful of other plays which either closed before they reached Broadway or from the casts of which she purposely withdrew. She also appeared in films, most notably in a silent version of *The Outcast*, in a role which she had also played on the stage.

At one point Florenz Ziegfeld offered Jeanne $150 a week to help him glorify the American girl; she was then earning only thirty-five, but refused his offer, explaining that she was a dramatic actress and not a chorus girl. She had a specific goal in the theatre, and becoming anything less than the American Bernhardt was inconceivable.

The Ted Coy-Jeanne Eagels romance began, so far as the public was concerned, with a denial. No, she had not married him. It was now barely three months after his divorce. Wasn't Coy staying in a downtown Cleveland hotel while *Rain* was there? reporters asked. Was there no special significance in that? Jeanne Eagels resolutely refused to say another word.

Finally on August 26, 1925, she and Ted Coy were married in Stamford, Connecticut, at the home of Fay Bainter. The *New York Times* in reporting the wedding and the reception which followed at Jeanne's Ossining, New York, estate also noted that she claimed to have no intention of giving up her career and that she in fact planned to re-open in *Rain* the following month.

Ted Coy's marriage to Jeanne Eagels began happily enough; it was, she said, a love "that will last forever."[7] But Coy, continuing his investment interests in New York and at the same time ostensibly managing the Ossining estate, found himself at a loss among his wife's friends. To many of them he was simply "Mr. Eagels," for she was a star while he—well, his exploits at Yale were so far in the past and his more recent achievements so ordinary that he was figuratively if not quite literally in eclipse.

As early as December 1926, the love destined to last forever had ended according to the *Chicago Daily Journal*. But the *Journal* was wrong—at least for the moment, for the Coys were sticking it out, while Jeanne began rehearsals early in 1927 for *Her Cardboard Lover*, which opened in New York at the Empire in March.

When she went to Hollywood later in the year to make *Man, Woman and Sin* at MGM with John Gilbert, Coy followed. Gossips surmised Jeanne's infatuation with Gilbert and speculated on Coy's irritation with her drinking, which had already earned her the sobriquet "Gin" Eagels, since, it was alleged, she drank hot gin, of which she was unduly fond, to kill the pain of persistent neuralgia with which she had long been afflicted. Coy, who objected to her drinking, drank to excess himself in order to shame her, and she in turn drank still more to punish him for presuming to correct her.

Upon completion of *Man, Woman and Sin*, a road company of *Her Cardboard Lover* was assembled for the interim till Jeanne's new play for Sam Harris, scheduled for the fall of 1928, went into rehearsal. But by mid-January of that year she was well into a series of indispositions which prevented her from fulfilling her obligations to the tour.

She had for several years been treated for various nervous disorders which had manifested themselves in bizarre behavior including her insistence on one occasion that a performance of *Rain* be stopped and the curtain lowered while a door backstage was shut, and, on another, by her halting a performance of *Her Cardboard Lover*, demanding that Leslie Howard get her a glass of water. Her excuses for failing to appear—laryngitis and food poisoning—did not wash with Actors' Equity, which she had joined with some reluctance in 1924, and in April 1928, she was fined and suspended, forbidden to appear in Equity productions for the next eighteen months.

In the weeks that followed, she made several attempts to reverse the Equity decision; she also organized a vaudeville tour which could not be intruded upon by union rules, and in the midst of it all—her behavior becoming increasingly unpredictable—she sued Ted Coy for divorce.

The divorce, granted in Chicago in mid-July 1928, added to

Jeanne's already gaudy reputation for raising hell. She claimed that Coy had at various times mistreated her, bruised her wrists on one occasion, knocked her down and dislocated her jaw on another, and quarreled with her almost continuously. Further, Jeanne's mother testified that Coy had once threatened to "ruin his wife's face for the movies."[8] Coy denied none of it, but later, after Jeanne's death, her biographer Edward Doherty elicited a less damning version of the jaw-dislocation incident from Coy, and Doherty concluded that Jeanne's humiliations and her mother's testimony notwithstanding, Coy had been too much the gentleman to defend himself against their allegations. He and Jeanne were both intensely unhappy, and it was simply easier for him to let her have her own way.

For the remainder of her suspension, Jeanne played in vaudeville, planned her return to Broadway, and also continued to work out a three-picture contract for Paramount at their Astoria studios. She had already made *The Letter* and was filming *Jealousy* with Fredric March, when her turbulent emotional life again surfaced in the public prints. The *Times* reported her weeping alone on the *Jealousy* sound stage as it was being cleared in deference to her trauma of the moment, but whatever problems she may have had during the shooting, there was no trace of them in the completed picture. Of her performance the *New Yorker* said she was "as superb as ever": "Jeanne Eagels . . . could read Mrs. Rorer's cookbook and hold an audience absorbed and entranced with her interpretation."[9]

Still her behavior became increasingly disturbed: she sold the Ossining estate where she and Coy had lived, then bought another house nearby, where, according to Doherty, she drove her staff and guests to distraction, even to the extent of accusing Fay Bainter of having dug up and transplanted some of the trees.

Her various physical and nervous ailments aggravated by misuse of drugs and an excess of alcohol, she submitted in September 1929 to an operation to mend her eyes which had become ulcerated, but less than a month after her release from the hospital she was dead from an overdose of chloral hydrate, a sedative with delirium-producing properties. Within the next year, however, the *Times* would also without qualification attribute her death to heroin addiction.

For those who savor life's minor mysteries, it may be of interest to know that when she died on October 3, 1929, only three days short of the end of her Equity suspension, Jeanne Eagels was still wearing her wedding band, the little circlet of diamonds she had received from Ted Coy.

Coy had remarried less than a month after his divorce from Jeanne, and with his new bride, Lottie Bruhn of El Paso, went to live in California, where he continued to write about sports for the San Francisco *News*, and to work as an investment adviser with a former Yale classmate. But when the Depression struck, he became a salesman for the Fuller Brush Company in Berkeley, returning to the east a year later and eventually joining the firm of another Yale alumnus as an insurance broker.

In early March 1933, at the beginning of the New Deal, Ted Coy filed in bankruptcy court, listing personal assets of $730 and liabilities in excess of $13,000. When reporters picked up the news and asked for a statement, Coy replied in the same even-handed manner that had won him respect on the playing field: "I've carried my burden so long I've got to let it down to regain a little strength. All a man can do is the best he can and then take his medicine. I'm repudiating no debts or obligations. I just can't see daylight ahead at present. All I'm looking for is a chance to work on unhampered, and I'll come through all right."[10]

The money he had inherited from his mother was long gone toward the support of his family, and gone too apparently was the aura of his celebrity, for his bankruptcy was the last that most people ever heard of him until he died two-and-a-half years later on September 8, 1935, in New York from a heart attack complicated by pneumonia. He was forty-seven.

Ted Coy's funeral was a simple one at the Broadway Tabernacle, a few blocks from the scenes of Jeanne Eagels' greatest successes. The service was brief. The Reverend Dr. Henry Sloane Coffin officiated; there was a reading from the Holy Scriptures, and someone read a poem by Whittier. There was no eulogy, nor was there need for one, for the three hundred mourners included many of Coy's old teammates and several of his former adversaries as well, all of whom had come out of loyalty to a man they loved, a man who had helped to inform the spirit and the ideals of their generation. They, by their presence, were his eulogy.

His ashes were buried in New Haven, less than a mile from the Yale Bowl, where, when it was still Yale Field, he had earned the all-time all-America accolades of Walter Camp and Parke H. Davis who had named him for perpetuity to the company of the nation's greatest athletes.

Ted Coy is not much remembered anymore, but his legend lives on in the football record books—he was elected to the National Football Foundation Hall of Fame in 1951—and in the chronicles of the

Twenties, when his unhappy star drifted into the path of the plummeting comet that was Jeanne Eagels. He lives, too, disguised as Johnny Donahue, a Princeton man, in Columbia Pictures' *Jeanne Eagels*, now a late-night television perennial, in which he was portrayed by Charles Drake, and finally, of course, he will forever be Ted Fay, the god-like football hero who teaches Basil Duke Lee—just as the real Ted may have helped to teach Scott Fitzgerald—". . . that life for everybody [is] a struggle, sometimes magnificent from a distance, but always difficult and surprisingly simple and a little sad."[11]

That's not a bad sort of immortality.

Princeton University Library

---

[1] Laura Guthrie Hearne. Diary. Typescript. Princeton University Library, p. 134.

[2] "Ted Coy's Right Foot gives Yale 8-0 Score over Harvard Eleven," an otherwise unidentified press cutting in the William Charles Wurtenberg scrapbook of news clippings about Yale football, 1902-1915. Yale Archives Collection. Yale University Library.

[3] F. Scott Fitzgerald, "The Freshest Boy," *Taps at Reveille* (New York: Scribners, 1935), p. 44—hereafter cited as *TR*.

[4] Fitzgerald, *This Side of Paradise* (New York: Scribners, 1920), p. 35.

[5] Fitzgerald, *The Great Gatsby* (New York: Scribners, 1925), p. 7.

[6] *Ibid.*, p. 8.

[7] *New York Times*, 30 June 1928, p. 11.

[8] *New York Times*, 1 July 1928, p. 22.

[9] *New Yorker*, 21 September 1929, pp. 12, 91.

[10] *New York Times*, 9 September 1935, p. 19.

[11] Fitzgerald, *TR*, p. 50.

Fitzgerald's Second Thoughts About "May Day": A Collation and Study

By

Colin S. Cass

Scott Fitzgerald was only twenty-three in July of 1920, when *The Smart Set* magazine published his novelette, "May Day."[1] Except for his contributions to Princeton's literary life, he was very much a newcomer to publishing: he had first sold a story, after many rejections, only thirteen months before,[2] and his first novel, *This Side of Paradise*, reached the public four months before "May Day" appeared.[3] His age and lack of professional exposure thus imply the artistic immaturity that is, in fact, to be found in the *Smart Set* version of the novelette.

A mere five years later, however, Fitzgerald had somehow gotten his talent so thoroughly under control as to produce the impeccable *Gatsby* for which he is best known. In those five years a published amateur developed into a finished professional.

Insight to that remarkable process of maturing is afforded by "May Day," because Fitzgerald thoroughly revised it for its second publication two years later in his second collection of short works, *Tales of the Jazz Age*.[4] The ensuing discussion is thus based on an examination of "May Day" in its original *Smart Set* text (1920), collated with its revised (and now widely reissued) text as it appears in *Tales of the Jazz Age* (1922). Because Fitzgerald's revision was very extensive, the collation affords us a long close look at his craftsmanship: we can see him, as it were, criticizing his own work and improving on it.

His revisions are distributed densely and quite evenly throughout the text. There are 395 citations in the collation, each representing at least one and sometimes a cluster of many substantive variants;

69

the average is almost 5.9 locations of substantive change per page of *TJA* (*Tales of the Jazz Age*) text. And none of the 67 pages of *TJA* is without at least one substantive change. All considered, the revision extends from a great many changes in accidentals (punctuation, spelling, indentation, etc.) on the one hand, to substantive changes (additions, deletions, substitutions of single words or whole sentences and paragraphs) on the other.

The most noticeable change is in the ending. Fitzgerald excised the last four paragraphs of the *Smart Set* version, and in their place supplied a new paragraph showing us what he originally had only implied, that is, Gordon Sterrett's suicide. But if it is the most obvious change, the new ending is nevertheless merely one instance in the much more pervasive system of changes that redefines Gordon Sterrett. He, like the other major characters, is made to seem a more respectable and substantial person than he was in the original version. Like the others, he is given a greater distance to fall. The personal and circumstantial causes of his decline can therefore be identified more readily, and are more impressive because less obvious at the outset.

It is nevertheless true that the *TJA* text is better characterized as a thorough polishing and refinement than as a drastic rewriting. None of the material in the revised text has been moved more than a paragraph away from its original location, and even minor relocations are rare. Fitzgerald's usual practice was to improve on what he had, especially by discarding unnecessary words, sharpening description, and adjusting tone.

To make the appended collation more useful, I shall survey the various kinds of revisions to be found there. I make no claim to exhaustiveness in this survey, though I shall discuss all the changes that are especially helpful in interpreting "May Day"; and of course, in the collation I have sought to record every substantive variant.

Although Fitzgerald made several changes which are important enough individually to affect our understanding of the entire novelette, most of his revising improved the work in less striking but cumulatively more important ways. The collation shows that he worked hard to improve tone. A defect that he recognized in the *Smart Set* version is its burden of emotional writing, both in narration and dialogue. Gordon Sterrett in particular suffers from this defect. For example, Fitzgerald originally described him as being "spiritless, a picture of utter misery," but in *TJA* revised this to "spiritless" (67.27). As Fitzgerald probably realized, this revision conveys roughly the same idea about Sterrett, but the reader is less likely to object that the narrative is maudlin. Similarly, Sterrett's self-pitying lines are drastically reduced. He tells Philip Dean (that is, Philip Cory in the original), that "I'd get a few drinks in me and somehow, somehow the struggle'd seem a little more dignified" (66.16). This line, like others equally self-indulgent, was deleted. We shall return to the portrayal of Sterrett, but we should notice here that Fitzgerald's effort to govern tone is not limited to passages about Sterrett. Words like "misery," "dismay," "jovially," "jubilantly," and "fairy night" are often removed regardless of where they occur; and the novelette thereby gains in seriousness and genuine emotional power.

Insofar as it tries to get something for nothing, triteness is akin to sentimentality and emotional exaggeration in writing. For this reason, presumably, Fitzgerald removed such commonplaces as "I drink— therefore I am" (118.23), and "That was what he needed after all, he thought—a good woman" (72.33-34). At one point a 59-word description of the girls at the Gamma Psi ball is reduced to ten words (73.13), probably because Fitzgerald saw that he had cataloged nothing but clichés about Western, Southern, and Eastern types. Likewise, "the struggle of life" (74.20) is deleted, as is Henry Bradin's facile remark, "There always have been a lot of fools. . ." (106.6-8).

Wordiness weakened the *Smart Set* version considerably, as is suggested by the fact that Fitzgerald shortened 135 sentences for *TJA*, but lengthened only 81. Moreover, he deleted 51 complete sentences but added only eight. The entire collation is evidence of his search for more direct and economical expression of his ideas. Even the 135-to-81 ratio is not full testimony to the severity of his revising, for his additions are seldom wordy, but are often succinct elaborations that began by clearing out verbiage. The economy can be seen in various kinds of changes. Sometimes it was just a matter of condensation: "the effect given was that" became "In effect" (120.6); "made a quick resolution" became "resolved" (65.35); "all my friends and acquaintances" became "everybody" (66.8). Elsewhere, though, the problem was in identifying nonessential information. Compare these passages:

> . . . it floated vaguely into her mind that she had heard that very hour mentioned lately in some significant connection. Where?
>
> Then she remembered, her brother . . .

as opposed to:

> . . . it floated vaguely into her mind that her brother . . . (99.32).

71

Ordinarily he sensed what the reader's imagination will respond to. In the following, the best detail, "hatless," is retained in the revision: "marvelous young ladies in opera cloaks of blue and yellow and rose, hatless and elaborately coiffured . . ."; this became "marvelous, hatless young ladies" in *TJA* (79.24). He had spied the detail that would best realize the Jazz Age scene. The original passage is also noteworthy because of its similarity to another line where, to affect an exaggerated biblical style for the prologue, he revised in favor of the unbroken series that he rejected in the "hatless" example. The revised line from the prologue reads: "bags of golden mesh and vari-colored slippers of silk and silver and rose satin and cloth of gold" (61.17-19). The opposite tendencies of these revisions indicate his growing ability to discriminate between the rhetorical effects of descriptive profusion on the one hand, and incisiveness on the other. He usually worked toward the latter.

In some of his revisions, pairs of ideas that are intellectually distinct, like "deliberation and consultations" (72.13), are simplified by making one of the words stand in place of both. He concluded, apparently, that readability can be a higher virtue than semantic accuracy. Certainly it is true that the *TJA* version is much more readable, and also that abstractions like "deliberation and consultations" and "unexpected, unexplainable" (86.14) are less numerous. Usually his changes are toward particularity: "the door" becomes "his door" (63.2); "fact that" becomes "news that" (80.25); "some undergraduate named Barton" becomes "a junior named Peter Himmel" (72.2). He deliberates, moreover, about which details we should be asked to imagine: when Edith leaves Delmonico's and walks to her brother's office, the number of the street she takes is eliminated, but the location of the building she goes to is added (103.14).

His desire for efficient prose makes him relentless in getting rid of vagueness. Such expressions as "an air of," "a sort of," "somehow," "quite," and "perhaps a little" are almost always deleted. The result is not only a less foggy prose: in eliminating vagueness, he sometimes changes his stand altogether and becomes very decisive where before he has been the reverse. Thus, the "city perhaps a little fed up with soldiers" emerges as "city thoroughly fed up with soldiers" (71.10).

There is also abundant evidence that he was testing the plausibility of his material. Some of the expressions in the *Smart Set* text make little sense, and these he generally spotted. He discarded "hearty metriculousness" (63.34), whether for the misspelling or the improbability I don't know. He recognized the difficulty that comes of saying that liquor on a man's breath made Edith feel "quite at home" (88.25). He saw that with only three persons in the news office and two of them conversing, it made no sense to write that "Someone had uttered a grunt" (107.20) when it was obviously the third person. Likewise, when Gordon and Philip leave the hotel room, Fitzgerald has to change "definitely and completely hated" to "suddenly and definitely hated" (70.17), because the entire scene would have been implausible had they hated each other before it began. (This, incidentally, is one of the few times when Fitzgerald's use of "suddenly" is accurate: even in revising he overlooked its repeated misuse.) He found other errors that involved implausibility. Originally he had described Rose and Key as "ill-formed," but corrected this to "ill-nourished" (74.18). He wrote that the drunken Peter Himmel was "somewhat startled" to see the door opening, but in *TJA* Peter responds "calmly" (94.25), which is more likely.

This general tightening of relationships also led to the formation of three new metaphors that the *Smart Set* text had vaguely implied. The first had read, "Key's narrow brow was secretly forming a resolution . . ." which Fitzgerald developed into the clumsier metaphor, "brow was secreting a resolution" (79.15-16). A more successful change was from shadowy tombs of the "day's past splendour" to "late day's splendor" (103.6). In a third instance, "glittered" in the original implied the more fully realized yet more compact metaphor of the revision: in *Smart Set* he had written, "A bright sun had shot through two days' cloudiness and glittered . . ."; he condensed that to "The wealthy, happy sun glittered . . ." (70.20). But such revisions are rare, because the prose is seldom metaphoric in either text.

Most alterations in wording seem to have been judged on their sound rather than on the sentimentality, banality, wordiness, the imaginative obtuseness, vagueness, or implausibility that we have been discussing. And in his many revisings by ear, a few definite patterns can be seen. One tendency is to make the *TJA* text more conventionally correct, both in textual details like punctuation and spelling, and also in diction. Consequently, there is a very noticeable elevation of tone throughout the text, even though at the same time Fitzgerald makes his tone more harsh and potentially offensive when he needs to. The latter observation is the one to begin with. Clearly Fitzgerald had reason, after the success of *This Side of Paradise* in 1920, to write more confidently than he could have written at first. This, I suspect, accounts for his willingness to toughen up some of the bland dialogue in the *Smart Set* text: "darn" became "damn"

(81.29), "damn" became "God damn" (64.33-34), and so on. Fitzgerald had originally hoped to publish "May Day" not in *Smart Set*, but in *The Saturday Evening Post*, where the editorial policy was to confine profanity to the mild language we find in the text that was eventually sold to *Smart Set*.

But his revisions show definite signs of self-consciousness, too—a product, one could guess, of his first encounters with celebrity and criticism. The results are generally good, as we shall discuss in connection with character development and theme. But a few consequences are less satisfactory. For instance, he makes this sentence grammatically correct but dramatically impossible, changing "That who you mean?" to "That whom you mean?" (64.5). He also assumes a rather transparent guise of worldliness and sophistication in two places: the first, where he changes "great paintings" to "bad paintings" (70.25); the second, where he alludes to the "latest cures for incurable evils" (86.23-24).

Despite these minor lapses, it remains true that the revised text *sounds* far better than the original. That much can already be inferred about the narrative persona, since he more than anyone stood to profit by the general tightening. But it is equally true for the characters. Dialogue is greatly improved, in two seemingly contradictory ways. The one is that it becomes more relaxed and natural. The characters speak at the level of language that suits them. So Key asks his brother for "booze," not, as originally, for "liquor" (80.28-29). Where in *Smart Set* Key remarks that "everybody'd think one of the guests had taken it," in *TJA* the line reads, "everybody'd think it was one of the college fellas" (83.1-2). Again, Key relaxes from "My idea is this" to "Here's what I say" (83.20). Drunken Peter Himmel, confronted by the mysterious opening of the door, gets rid of his weightless "Hm" in favor of "Peek-a-boo" (94.28), which fits the humorous scene much better. Fitzgerald also eliminates most, though not all of the embarrassingly stiff lines that emerge anonymously from the mob scenes.

Paradoxically, however, the dialogue is also better because Fitzgerald became reluctant to let it govern itself and relax too much, as it did most noticeably in all the drunken scenes of the *Smart Set* text. Words too often lost their first or last letters, and articles were omitted to an extent that would have been believable only in men who were about to pass out from their intoxication. The effect was unduly degrading. In short, much of the original dialogue was unnaturally loose, even sloppy, just as other dialogue was too stiff. Fitzgerald revised both by ear, usually with success.

Indications of the tightening of the *TJA* "May Day" are numerically most evident in the punctuation, but these changes cannot be ascribed indisputably to Fitzgerald: Scribners may well have made "May Day" conform to house style in punctuation. There are 222 instances of punctuation either added or made more formal, as opposed to only 21 cases of punctuation deleted or loosened. Frequently the comma has been added between coordinated independent clauses. Also, commas were inserted after the penultimate members of series, and Fitzgerald's tendency to let parts of sentences run together with too little or no punctuation has been curbed. The dash in particular gave way to the period. Paragraphing was subjected to a similar scrutiny: revising got rid of 29 indentations but added only two new ones.

Thus far we have discussed revisions, the cumulative influence of which is great, but which are singly rather unimportant. We must turn now to the specific major changes he made.

The *TJA* text is prefaced by a paragraph that Fitzgerald included as the "May Day" entry in his annotated table of contents. I quote it here in full, mainly for his comment about pattern:

> This somewhat unpleasant tale, published as a novelette in the "Smart Set" in July, 1920, relates a series of events which took place in the spring of the previous year. Each of the three events made a great impression upon me. In life they were unrelated, except by the general hysteria of that spring which inaugurated the Age of Jazz, but in my story I have tried, unsuccessfully I fear, to weave them into a pattern—a pattern which would give the effect of those months in New York as they appeared to at least one member of what was then the younger generation. (*TJA*, p. viii.)

Fitzgerald thus invites examination of the "pattern" of the work, as he does also by his revision of the last paragraph of the untitled biblical prologue to Chapter I. Originally, that read: "So during all this time there were many adventures that happened in the great city and it is one of these that is here set down." This he changes, drawing attention to the question of unity by his own indefiniteness: "So during all this time there were many adventures that happened in the great city, and, of these, several—or perhaps one—are here set down" (62.9-11).

With his remarks in mind, we discover with particular interest a change in the chapter divisions of "May Day." Disregarding the *Smart Set* typesetter's errors in using "Chapter VII" as the heading for two successive chapters, and then skipping the number eight, we find nonetheless a new chapter division in the *TJA* text, occurring in the middle of what was Chapter VI of the *Smart Set* version. There appear to be two plausible explanations for the new division. First, the original Chapter VI was at least superficially disorganized. Edith dominates the first half of it, and at the juncture that was to become the new chapter division, she leaves Delmonico's and the chapter as well, passing Jewel (that is, Gloria in the original) on her way out. As she does so, Fitzgerald's attention shifts from her to Jewel, who dominates the latter half of the chapter. A closer look, however, will persuade us that this two-headed chapter was not as clumsily conceived as we might have thought. In it, the two very different women in Gordon Sterrett's life cross paths, Edith going literally and figuratively out the door as Jewel comes in. For Gordon it is the turning point in the story: by the end of the original chapter Jewel has convinced him to leave with her; the next morning, find-ing himself married to her, he buys a pistol and kills himself.

Structurally, then, this pivotal logic would seem to justify the original version of Chapter VI. Its revision is therefore only the more noteworthy. I believe that the structural consideration must have been subordinated at the time of revision to a dramatic one and, more suggestively, to a thematic one as well. In both texts the last line before the eventual dividing place reads: "She ran by a couple who stood at the door—a weak-chinned waiter and an over-rouged young lady, in hot dispute—and opening the outer door stepped into the warm May night" (100.21-25). The ending for the original Chap-ter VI, which was retained as the ending for *TJA* Chapter VII, con-sists of a similar exit, from the same door of Delmonico's: " 'All right,' he said heavily. 'I'll get my hat' " (102.35). If we now examine the other nine chapters (*TJA*), we find that all but two of them end, in good theatrical form, with the main characters leaving the respec-tive scenes. Moreover, the two exceptions occur at Delmonico's: Rose and Key settle in the mop room (Chapter III) with their bottle of stolen liquor, and later (Chapter V) they stay with Peter for still more drinking. I contend that these observations about chapter endings reveal two of Fitzgerald's plans for the novelette. The first was that he should keep each of the episodes in his "series of events" dramatically coherent. His revision of Chapter VI in *TJA* achieves this: having followed Edith's activities at the ball, we feel, when she exits, that a dramatic scene has been completed. Likewise,

Jewel's entrance and departure mark another coherent episode, beginning to end. The compound chapter was therefore divided in two.

But this matter of chapter endings also helps us account for Fitzgerald's allusion in the prologue to the unity (or lack of unity) of his novelette: "several—or perhaps one." The many episodes and characters do not readily conduce to a sense of unity in the work, and for us to tie the many strands together, we are always forced, sooner or later, back to Delmonico's. That, I think, is what unifies "May Day." Delmonico's represented a height of romantic expectations for Gordon and Edith, both of whom hoped to meet the other there; Peter Himmel, too, expected to find there the romantic culmination of two months "on special delivery terms with Edith"; and Dean looked forward to the dance as a high point in his "vacation," just as the many debutantes and Yale men did. Even Rose and Key turned up at Delmonico's looking for liquor, and Jewel went there to reclaim Gordon. Among the main characters, only Henry Bradin never appears at Delmonico's, but Edith thinks of him there and then leaves to visit him.

Delmonico's is an ironic center of unity, however. All the romantic optimism that the ball inspired in Edith, Gordon, and Peter is quickly dispelled. It is true that the sub-plots converge at Delmonico's, but only to go elsewhere, headed toward variously *unromantic* resolutions. With this pattern in mind the significance of Fitzgerald's division of Chapter VI becomes more apparent. It would be a mistake to assume that mere dramatic neatness governed the revision. By closing *TJA* Chapter VI with Edith's exit, he draws attention to the exit because she, like the other characters, has arrived only to leave again, restless and still not satisfied. The entire shifting world of "May Day" lacks an effective center of stability, including the romantic Delmonico's despite its glittering lights, elegant women, and rows of bottles. Thus, we can see that in revising Chapter VI Fitzgerald was working to *emphasize* the sense of hectic coming and going that at first inspection would seem to be a defect of the novelette. The restlessness and instability of the new-born Jazz Age is a major theme in "May Day," one which is epitomized in the next-to-last chapter, in the much reiterated symbol of Mr. In and Mr. Out.

Fitzgerald revised the names of many characters, both major and minor, for the *TJA* version. The effects of almost all these revisions is to emphasize either the grotesque or ironic nature of his materials. "Philip Cory" and "Peter Barton" are names with no very definite connotations; they were revised to "Philip Dean" and "Peter

Himmel." "Dean," of course, is cognate with "dean," a high official
in a school, cathedral, or loosely, in any field—"the dean of American journalism," for instance. In German, *"Himmel"* means
"sky," "heavens," or "Heaven." Thus, both these new names connote
exaltation, grandeur, of the sort one might have expected to find
at a Delmonico's ball. In their antics as Mr. In and Mr. Out, however,
we see Himmel and Dean stripped of everything but the drunken
illusion of their own exaltation. Fitzgerald stresses their anonymity
in the opening paragraphs of *TJA* Chapter X: "Mr. In and Mr. Out
are not listed by the census-taker" (117.1), and so on. The irony is
even more plain in the closing lines of the chapter, when the idea
of exaltedness is reduced to drunken jokes in the ascending elevator.
Fitzgerald ends the chapter with a pun on Himmel's ironic name:

> "Top floor," said Mr. Out.
> "This is the top floor," said the elevator man.
> "Have another floor put on," said Mr. Out.
> "Higher," said Mr. In.
> "Heaven," said Mr. Out. (*TJA* 124.25-29.)

Similar irony is achieved in revising the slatternly girl's already rather
grandiloquent name from "Gloria" to "Jewel," which connotes
materiality as well as beauty and value. And a man with prominent
teeth is named "Prominent Teeth" in the revised text, much the way
the man in Gatsby's library would be called "Owl Eyes" three years
later.

   In other ways, too, Fitzgerald's revisions affect our understanding
of individual characters. They are, in general, made to seem more
mature and imposing in the *TJA* revision. Edith, for instance, was
originally described as "laughing, debonnaire, rambling on in her
inconsequential chatter," but Fitzgerald resketched her to eliminate
some of the implied ungainliness of manner: she becomes "poignant,
debonnaire, immersed in her own inconsequential chatter" (72.26).
And more important to the soundness of the plot, in the later version she is no longer declared to be "in love with Gordon Sterrett";
rather, she was "falling in love with her recollection of Gordon
Sterrett" (85.1-2). Later the uncompromising assertion that "she
wanted Gordon more than she wanted anything in the world" is
modified to the more probable and more adult "unguessed desire
to see him again" (86.15-16). Her anticipation of the Gamma Psi
ball is still romantic, but not girlishly excessive. Moreover, there is
an increment of hardness in her personality as drawn in *TJA*, which
makes her subsequent behavior more plausible: the *Smart Set* text

had included a revealing comparison, for instance, between Edith and her brother, which is later modified in her favor. The original read: "Ostensibly, brother and sister had no more in common than a beaver and a peacock; at heart the springs of Harold's [sic] idealism were twin to the motive power of Edith's fancies." Fitzgerald deletes this passage and instead remarks, after an allusion to Henry's reforming zeal, that Edith, "less fatuously, would have been content to cure Gordon Sterrett" (86.26-27). So in comparison with Edith, Henry Bradin is somewhat fatuous, yet there is also in *TJA* the tendency to make him *more* sophisticated, less trite, and less vehement than he was originally. In short, both characters have been toned up in the revision.

We observe a similar maturing, for better or worse, in all the principal characters. When Gordon comes to the hotel room to borrow money from Philip Dean, Fitzgerald subtly redefines the relationship and makes Dean seem less friendly, more conscious of his own power in the transaction. At one point the *Smart Set* text shows Dean questioning, and advising sententiously, but then waiting for Sterrett to respond. Fitzgerald changes this passage to one unbroken and rather lordly speech: " 'Why didn't you? You've got to buckle down if you want to make good,' suggested Dean with cold formalism" (66.23-25). Originally he had suggested only "coolly." Similar revision occurs later, when instead of counting out the seventy-five dollars "hurriedly," Dean does so "deliberately" (73.30). And when he, Sterrett, and a third man are shopping at Rivers', his questions are no longer impartially phrased as "did they think"; rather, "did he think" (72.14), meaning the third man, but not Sterrett. Fitzgerald's revised portrayal of Dean is thus distinctly less ambiguous and less sympathetic than the original was.

But by far the most thoroughly revised character is Sterrett himself. Like the others, he is made to seem more mature, more complex, and therefore less easy to dismiss with hasty judgments. It is safe to assume that if Sterrett is still a weak and self-pitying character in the *TJA* text, it is because Fitzgerald wanted him just that way: the very consistent pruning of maudlin speeches by and descriptions of Sterrett indicates beyond doubt that Fitzgerald recognized the excessiveness of his first protrayal and knew how to correct it.

In the revisions, one very persistent pattern is to avoid references to Sterrett's drinking. From many possible examples, one will suffice: in *Smart Set* Dean tells him, " 'I'm hanged if I'll help you to

79

make a drunken bum of yourself.' " The line (wonderfully ironic, as it turns out) is dropped from *TJA* (69.7-8). The truly revealing change, though, is in the consistent substitution of women for liquor as the mark of Sterrett's weakness and deterioration. Dean challenges him, for instance, saying " 'How do I know you wouldn't use it to get drunk with?' " but Fitzgerald revises this to read, " 'How do I know you wouldn't use it on some other woman?' " (68.21-23). Similarly, Dean's remark that " 'If you haven't got money you've got to work and stay away from liquor and women,' " is changed to " 'stay away from women' " (67.26-28).

This shift from liquor to women prepares for the one major change in the plot of "May Day." In the *Smart Set* version, Sterrett is unmistakably very drunk at the Delmonico's ball even as early as his encounter with Edith, who cannot help but exclaim bluntly, " 'You're drunk' " (90.30-31). His extravagantly slurred speech is ample proof that she's right. But in the revision we see him in better control of himself and less sloppily intoxicated, only "a little drunk" (90.7); and Edith's exclamation is accordingly modified to " 'You look like the devil' " (90.30-31). Later on, therefore, when Jewel summons Sterrett to the side door, Fitzgerald can say that he was "drunker than he had been earlier in the evening" (101.28).

The difference is important in understanding the change in the ensuing scene, which must figure prominently in our thoughts about Sterrett. In the original version, Jewel has been entreating him to leave with her: "With a glance around him in which relief and despair were mingled, Gordon hesitated and then suddenly pulled her to him clumsily and kissed her soft, pulpy lips." The moment is entirely reimagined in *TJA*: "With a glance around him in which relief and despair were mingled, Gordon hesitated; then she suddenly pulled him to her and kissed him with solf, pulpy lips" (102.32-34). By making Sterrett's drunkenness at Delmonico's seem circumstantial rather than habitual, and by transferring the dominant role in the above scene from him to her, Fitzgerald successfully redefines Sterrett and his fall. He is no longer seen as simply weak and self-indulgent; rather, he is presented as being also a victim whose fate is decided by Jewel at a time when he is not fully capable of determining it for himself or of resisting her.

It remains for us to consider the two endings of the novelette. In bringing the plot to a conclusion, they are virtually identical insofar as both of them come to Gordon Sterrett's suicide, the original version indirectly, the *TJA* revision explicitly. But beyond that there are only incidental similarities, and the drastic rewriting allows us one last look at Fitzgerald, the maturing artist.

The original ending was ironic to the point of being glib. The characters—J. C. Fowler and his clerk "in charge of the fishing tackle trade"—are completely new to us, as is the sporting goods store. One reason for this choice of ending, we can suppose, was that Fitzgerald wanted to emphasize the human detachment and unconcern that are the setting for Gordon's intensely felt personal crisis, not only here at the conclusion, but throughout the novelette. The irony of the last scene taking place in a sporting goods store, added to the purely financial motivation of J. C. Fowler, do in some ways sum up the "May Day" view of the dawning Jazz Age. And like the last words of the preceding chapter, when Mr. Out's exuberance in the elevator finds expression in his unintentionally religious metaphor (" 'Heaven,' said Mr. Out" [124.29]), here too, the last words of the book convey religious as well as profane connotations: " 'Business is bad enough, God knows!' " If Fitzgerald was actually working for ironic contrast between the worldly and the divine, he may have even selected the other rather hackneyed details—the initials "J.C." and the allusion to fishing tackle—with conventional symbolism in mind. But for us the important fact is that this ending is discarded. If these were his intentions, he eventually thought the better of them.

One defect of the original ending was that a little too much was left to be inferred. We didn't even know positively that Sterrett was the "fella" who bought the automatic, though we assumed that much. His reason for buying it, however, could still have been misunderstood, and evidently Fitzgerald did not want to take the chance. The revised ending thus keeps Sterrett before us and shifts the conclusion from the impersonal surroundings of the suicide, to the man committing it. The irony of the sporting goods store is retained but not emphasized; characteristically, Fitzgerald also discarded the superficial religious overtones, which the novelette had never prepared us for. He gives us instead a more explicit ending, written more tersely and without the last-minute confusion and disunity of new characters being introduced. In the revised ending, the prominent detail is the "table that held his drawing materials." The revision no longer exaggerates those conditions which surround Sterrett's failure but are not solely responsible for it. Rather, the revised ending forces our attention back to the man himself, and to his awareness of personal failure—a failure that is, perhaps, symbolic of a society's failings as well.

[1] F. Scott Fitzgerald, "May Day," *The Smart Set*, LXII (July 1920), 3-32. In my collation I am indebted to Professor Matthew J. Bruccoli for use of his copy of *Smart Set*, which is now a rather scarce item. The present study is, in fact, a product of the graduate seminar on Fitzgerald and Hemingway that Professor Bruccoli offered at Ohio State University, 1968.

[2] Arthur Mizener, *The Far Side of Paradise: A Biography of F. Scott Fitzgerald* (Boston: Houghton Mifflin, 1951), p. 86.

[3] *Ibid.*, p. 104.

[4] New York: Scribners, 1922, pp. 61-125. All subsequent line references will be to the *Tales of the Jazz Age* page and line as listed in the collation appended to this study.

The following is a single collation of F. Scott Fitzgerald's novelette, "May Day," as it was first published in *The Smart Set* (July 1920, pp. 3-32), in contrast with its revised text in Fitzgerald's second published collection of short stories titled *Tales of the Jazz Age* (New York: Scribners, 1922, pp. 61-125). In the collation, the *Tales of the Jazz Age* reading appears to the left of the square bracket. The numbers in the margin designate the page and line in *TJA*. All marks of ellipsis, all brackets, slashes, and paragraph symbols are mine. The three-dot symbol of ellipsis is used regardless of paragraph indentations that intervene in the text between the words cited before and after the symbol. After the first notice of a change in a proper noun (e.g., Philip Cory to Philip Dean, 62.15), I have recorded only those places in the text where the corresponding name cannot be correctly inferred from the revision (as when "Philip Dean," the full name, is the revision of "Cory," the last name only, 63.1). I have recorded all changes in paragraphing, but changes in spelling, typography, and punctuation are reproduced only when incidental to substantive changes. If, however, a change in spelling alters the meaning or pronunciation of the original word (e.g., "wha's" revised to "what's"), I have entered the change as a sub-stantive variant. Also included are obvious errors in the *TJA* text that seem to have passed unnoticed from *Smart Set* and that might create confusion if omitted here.

SUBSTANTIVE VARIANTS IN "MAY DAY" BETWEEN THE *SMART SET* AND *TALES OF THE JAZZ AGE* TEXTS

TALES OF THE JAZZ AGE] *SMART SET*

61.17-19	varicolored . . . So gaily] vari-coloured slippers of silk, satin, and marvelously-wrought leather. ¶ So gayly
62.10-11	city . . . here] city and it is one of these that is here
62.15	Mr. Philip Dean] Mr. Philip Cory
62.17	well-cut, shabby] well-cut but quite shabby
62.18	was small, slender] was slender
62.31	certainly was] sure was
63.1	later Philip Dean] later Cory
63.2	his door and . . . greeted] the door and they greeted
63.3	exuberance.] exuberance still vaguely collegiate.
63.7	about him radiated] about him from his firm step as he moved about the room to the hard grip of his hand radiated
63.12	Going] I'm going
63.18	soft] soft-ribbed
63.19	rose and] rose nervously and
63.28	interest. His tie, of] interest. His suit had once been excellent; at present it shone with use; his tie, also of
63.34	body.] body with hearty metriculousness.
63.35	he remarked.] he commenced jovially.
64.5	whom] who
64.7-8	mean: . . . smear."] mean: 'if you touch her she smears.' "
64.10	mirror, smiled] mirror and smiled
64.14-15	know . . . Gamma] know there's a Gamma
64.19-20	in . . . lit] in B.V.D.'s, Cory lit
64.20	down by] down in a big chair by
64.21	knees . . . morning] knees carelessly in the morning
64.27	spiritless.] spiritless, a picture of utter misery.
64.33-34	"Every . . . "I've] "Everything," he said miserably, "every damn thing in the world. I've
65.6	a hell] one hell
65.11-12	trouble . . . a little.] trouble ruffled him a little, exasperated him.

65.29-30	in mild difficulty] in some sort of difficulty
65.35	Dean resolved that] Cory made a quick resolution that
66.2	he'd . . . Gordon.] he'd just have to see less of Gordon—that was all.
66.3	Jewel Hudson] Gloria Hudson
66.4	"She . . . I] "She—used to be decent, I
66.8	that everybody began] that all my friends and acquaintances began
66.14-15	listlessly. "I'm] listlessly, "but everything seemed to go wrong. I'm
66.16	poor. Then] poor. I'd get a few drinks in me and somehow, somehow the struggle'd seem a little more dignified. Then
66.18-19	involved . . . run] involved, whenever I'd get a little tight I'd run
66.20-21	people—of course] people—sometimes I'd come that office white as a sheet without even having closed my eyes all night. Of course
66.23-26	you? . . . "I tried] you?" ¶ "Why, I never seemed to get around to it." ¶ "You've got to buckle down if you want to make good," suggested Cory coolly. ¶ "I tried
67.4	pause. Gordon] pause. ¶ Gordon
67.5	side.] side, his eyes showing up large and dark in his feverish face.
67.9	three hundred] five hundred
67.10	been patting] been absently patting
67.10-11	ankles . . .quiet—] ankle, suddenly stopped—
67.12	taut and strained.] strained and taut.
67.14	ask for] ask 'em for
67.28	from women] from liquor and women
67.33-34	it." ¶ He raised] it." ¶ Gordon laughed bitterly. ¶ "I don't know," he said, "maybe you're right. But it just seems as if everything had combined against me—everything. I didn't want to get stewed most of the time, but I got so damn lonely and before I knew it I'd be thinking what's the use, why not be happy this evening anyhow." ¶ Cory raised
68.1	went on deliberately.] said deliberately.
68.2	like pleasure—] like a highball—
68.2	lot of it] lot of 'em

68.4	before. You seem] before. There's an air about you of– of weakness." ¶ "I know." ¶ "You seem
68.10-11	air of . . . said Gordon] air of poverty and sleepless nights and too much liquor," said Gordon
68.21-23	use it . . . "Why] use it to get drunk with?" ¶ "Why
69.2	A new hardness] Some new quality of hardness
69.7-8	wonder." ¶ "Do you] wonder. I'm hanged if I'll help you to make a drunken bum of yourself." ¶ "Do you
69.16-17	three hundred] five hundred
69.20	clothes carefully] clothes very carefully
69.26	tie precisely] tie carefully
69.28	teeth with solemnity] teeth with an air of critical solemnity
69.32	demanded.] demanded, turning to Gordon.
70.3	You've got nothing] You've nothing
70.17	quite . . . hated] quite definitely and completely hated
70.19	Fifth Avenue . . . swarmed] Fifth Avenue, Forty-fourth Street and Madison Avenue swarmed
70.20	crowd . . . sun] crowd. A bright sun
70.20	sun glittered] sun had shot through two days' cloudiness and glittered
70.23	pearls in] pearls laid in
70.25	bad paintings] great paintings
70.25-26	and . . . furniture] and period furniture
70.28	Working-girls] Gossiping shop-girls
71.3	cloaks; meanwhile] cloaks; most of them meanwhile
71.4-5	sundaes . . . lunch] sundaes that had comprised their lunch
71.8-9	to California] to Maine
71.10	thoroughly fed up] perhaps a little fed up
71.11-12	uncomfortable under] staggering under
71.15-16	latter . . . often] latter morose, blind to all except the ugliness that, to him, lay just beneath. He could not enjoy this crowd on the Avenue. Too often
71.21	greeted . . . Dean] greeted Cory
71.21-22	vociferously . . . in a] vociferously, and sitting around in a
71.24	Gordon found] Gordon, who took nothing to drink, found

71.29-30	some one . . . "Didn't] someone, and turning to Gordon he added, "Didn't
72.1-2	sister . . . coming] sister, eh?" ¶ "No." ¶ "Well," continued his eager informant, "she's coming
72.2	with . . . Himmel."] with some undergraduate named Barton."
72.4	meet Jewel Hudson] meet Gloria
72.6	four] four o'clock
72.9	But as] But to Gordon's great dismay, as
72.9-10	joined . . . dismay.] joined them.
72.13	long consultations] long deliberation and consulta- tions
72.14	Did he] Did they
72.17	the "Covington."] the "Livingston."
72.19-21	money . . . He] money right away. A vague idea of attending the Gamma Psi dance was becoming inter- mixed with his misery. He
72.22	romantic night] fairy night
72.23	The affair] Somehow the affair
72.26	her . . . immersed in] her, laughing, debonnaire, rambling on in
72.26-27	her own inconsequential] her inconsequential
72.27-28	chatter . . . and] chatter, flashed before him and
72.28	a hundred] a dozen
72.32	golf, swimming] golf, in bathing
72.33	arresting profile] kindly profile
72.33-34	eyes shut. ¶ They left] eyes shut. ¶ Yes, if he could get this money he could buy the essentials that would enable him to go to the dance and talk to her. That was what he needed after all, he thought—a good woman. But he must first have his dinner coat pressed, buy a dress shirt and some dancing slippers, redeem his pawned studs—and before all, he must settle with Gloria. ¶ They left
72.34-35	a moment] a minute
73.8	out, "Go] out a "Go
73.12	alive with] gay with
73.13	girls . . . the stellar] girls; Western girls with high colour and erect bodies, Southern girls with soft voices and limpid intriguing eyes, Eastern girls, bored and fash- ionable, and around them all stood the men, very well set up and correctly dressed for the parade of beauty.

For these girls were in a measure the pick of East and South, and West, the stellar

73.15	university. But]	university. ¶ But
73.25	Gordon . . . why]	Gordon was watching him dully, wondering why
73.26-28	projected. ¶ "—I'm]	projected. If he hit him now he would catch him just on the point of the two center ones. ¶ "—I'm
73.30	deliberately counted]	hurriedly counted
74.5	get . . . shop."]	get shaved now."
74.18	ill-nourished]	ill-formed
74.20	brings]	may bring
74.20	color into life]	colour to the struggle of life
74.22-23	friendless; tossed]	friendless and, tossed
74.23	births, they would]	births, would
74.30-31	blood . . . potentiality.]	blood of distinguished forbears.
74.34	resourcefulness.]	intelligence.
75.8	and complete]	and an air of complete
75.11	surprised if]	surprised or opposed if
75.13	"What you say]	"Whatcha say
75.14	liquor?" . . . The ginger]	liquor?" The ginger
75.14-15	the suggestion]	this suggestion
75.21-22	fella." . . . "He's]	fella. He's
75.23	"Maybe he]	"Let's us go there and maybe he
75.24	he can!"]	he will."
75.26	to-morra . . . again]	tomorra an' never get it on again
75.33-34	chuckling . . . high]	chuckles and mentionings of people high
75.34	biblical]	bibilical
76.2	an offended nasal]	a pessimistic nasal
76.3	upon the institution—]	upon the attitude toward them of the institution—
76.16-17	this . . . freedom.]	this complete and unquestioned new-found liberty.
76.22-23	chuckled . . . twinkled]	chuckled and broke into a run, his short bandy legs seeming to twinkle
76.31	but succinct]	but quiet succinct
76.34-35	their common consciousness]	their consciousness
77.5	find]	fin'
77.14	"God damn]	"The damn

77.14-15	soldier-blacksmith who] soldier with the arm of a blacksmith who
77.21	voices . . . minute] voices. ¶ "Too many of those damn suckers!" ¶ "We ought to kill the dirty bums!" ¶ "Damn filthy Russian Jews." ¶ In a minute
77.25-26	had . . . to] had swollen marvelously to
78.1	repeated . . . rapturously] repeated rapturously
78.15-16	on Tenth] in Tenth
78.22	on by.] on by them.
78.32	here. He] here and he
78.35	Key . . . inquire] Key inquired
79.1-2	waited . . . sidewalk.] waited outside.
79.3	Key emerging] Key as he emerged
79.15-16	was secreting a] was secretly forming a
79.16	ask . . . get] ask his brother about the profession and see if he could get
79.24	marvelous, hatless young] marvelous young
79.24	ladies, each] ladies in opera cloaks of blue and yellow and rose, hatless and elaborately coiffured, each
79.31	immediately, stationed] immediately, they stationed
80.1	emitting] emitted
80.25	news that] fact that
80.26	army. This disappointed] army, which latter fact disappointed
80.28-29	booze, and] liquor and
80.29	us none.] us any.
80.35	At this Rose started] He started
81.2	twelve o'clock banquet] midnight banquet
81.3	said Rose resentfully.] said Carrol.
81.16	stacks of scrubbing] stacks of used and unused scrubbing
81.29	"I don't] "Maybe they're there. I don't
81.29	damn] darn
81.35-36	it . . . inch.] it cautiously open an inch.
82.16	violins playin'?] violins startin' playin'?
83.1-2	think . . . fellas.] think one of the guests had taken it.
83.20	"Here's . . . said] "My idea is this," he said
83.25	nobody] no one
83.25	that there room] that room
83.29	sojers] soldiers

84.13-14	right arm] left arm
84.29-85.3	boy . . . ¶ So] boy and that she was in love with another man—a man she had not seen for three years. A man for whom she had so far only a sad-eyed, adolescent mooniness. Edith Bradin was in love with Gordon Sterrett. ¶ So
85.14	to be held.] to be.
85.20	black backs] black arms
85.24	carmine; the irises] carmine; her nose was pert; the irises
86.14	The twist] An unexpected, unexplainable twist
86.14-15	imagination . . . had] imagination two months before had
86.15-18	disclosed . . . For all] disclosed to Edith that she wanted Gordon more than she wanted anything in the world. ¶ For all
86.22	instructor in] assistant in
86.23	and had come] and came
86.23-24	pour . . . into] pour the dissatisfaction of his active mind into
86.25-27	newspaper . . . There] newspaper. He was managing editor of the *New York Trumpet*. Ostensibly, brother and sister had no more in common than a beaver and a peacock; at heart the springs of Harold's idealism were twin to the motive power of Edith's fancies. ¶ She was twenty-one, with a faint weariness. There
86.27-28	weakness in Gordon] weakness she had always seen in Gordon
86.29-30	a helplessness] a quality of helplessness
86.34-35	and this weariness] and, somehow, this tiredness
87.6	who presented himself] presenting himself
87.6	bowed] bowing
87.8	Peter Himmel.] Peter Barton.
87.16-17	to-night for] tonight, I guess, for
87.19	Was she rubbing] As if she was rubbing
87.22-23	forget . . . A few] forget it." A few
87.26-27	that . . . com-pan-ee!"] that if a saxophone is left alone it's more than enough for me.
87.28	a mustache] a light mustache
88.6-7	dancing and found] dancing; found
88.13	it," . . . "I] it—I
88.22	Howard Marshall's] Jim Marshall's

88.25	whiskey. She	] whiskey. It made her feel quite at home. She
89.6	a fat . . . hair	] a little man with black hair
89.19	called Edith	] said Edith
89.24	leave before long,	] leave long before,
90.6-7	pitiful . . . tired.	] pitifully and wretchedly drunk.
90.30-31	crying . . . devil."	] crying, "You're drunk."
90.34	trouble. Don't	] trouble. Just big mess. Don't
90.35	pieces. I'm	] pieces. I'm a mess. I'm
90.14-15	slam . . . "Thanks."	] slam." ¶ "You're a good woman," he repeated. ¶ "You're drunk, Gordon." ¶ "Thanks."
91.22-23	it?" ¶ "I'm	] it?" ¶ "What do you mean? I'm
91.25-26	Gordon?" ¶ "I'm	] Gordon?" ¶ "That's it—pretend not know me. I'm
91.26	you . . . unfair	] you—unfair
91.27	woman . . . Here	] woman—I'm a bad man. Now on we pretend not know each other. Here
91.32	crazy man	] drunken man
91.33	"I admit . . . Something's	] "Admit it. I'm drunken. I'm not worthy look at you. Something's
91.34	Edith. There's	] Edith, from bottom up. There's
92.2	little	] li'l
92.7	loony	] crazy
92.11	loony	] crazy
92.34-35	involuntarily she	] unconsciously she
93.11-12	saved . . . The new	] saved. The new
93.15-17	Peter . . . he was	] Peter Barton, unaccustomed to being snubbed, having been snubbed, was
93.25-26	the man . . . mustache	] the fair-haired man
94.3	bottles.	] bowls.
94.7	themselves, things lay	] themselves, lay
94.21	water. It	] water; and it
94.23	and that through	] and through
94.25	Peter calmly.	] Peter, somewhat startled.
94.28	"Peek-a-boo," murmured	] "Hm," murmured
95.33	brushes. And when	] brushes, when
95.35-96.1	Sunday . . . Rose	] Sunday?" ¶ Rose
96.1	vacantly. "Will	] vacantly. Key grunted. ¶ "Will
96.2	choose	] chose
96.9	these evening	] these mellow evening
96.22	lowly	] obscure

96.27-28	blue . . . say."] blue, so to speak."
96.34	"It's all] "S'all
96.35	A scrublady's] Scrub-/ lady's
97.1	Judy] Julie
97.2-3	skin.' " ¶ "Sure,"] skin.' One woman's as bad as another. Isn't she?" ¶ "Sure,"
97.5	that's] tha's
97.6	Refused] Refuse
97.7	whatsoever.] whats'ever.
97.9	What's the younger] Wha's younger
97.20	Kill the Bolshevik!] Kill Bolshevik!
97.24	Greatest] Greates'
98.7	habitual . . . débutantes] possible only to débutantes
98.8	glow . . . after] glow felt by a man after
98.13	many fragmentary subjects] many subjects
98.32-33	her, sublimely] her quite sublimely
99.3	doing—when] doing—to drink when
99.18	red-fat man] very dark man
99.21	red-fat man] very dark man
99.25	red-fat man] dark man
99.32	that her brother] that she had heard that very hour mentioned lately in some significant connection. Where? ¶ Then she remembered, her brother
99.33-34	in . . . until] in his Weekly office until
100.8	him, float] him up, float
100.9-10	cloak . . . It] cloak. It
100.18-19	peach . . . wrapped] peach. I'll meet you at the door of the dressing room in about fifteen minutes. Wrapped
100.26	VII] [no corresponding division of text]
100.34	I? Well] I? I'm not good enough, eh? Well
101.5	interrupted. "Oh] interrupted, mimicking him, "Oh
101.6	that one that] that little lady that
101.6	God knows] Lord knows
101.28	drunker than he] quite as drunk as he
101.29	and in a] but in somehow a
101.32	thickly . . . away.] thickly, "come righ' away.
101.33	that] tha'
102.2	very . . . Been] very drunk, Gloria. Been
102.4-5	bothering] botherin'

102.7	at all."]	t'all."
102.14	society friends]	débutante friends
102.20	your somebody else."]	your Yale girls."
102.22	come along," she]	come with me," she
102.33-34	hesitated . . . soft]	hesitated and then suddenly pulled her to him clumsily and kissed her soft
103.1	VIII]	CHAPTER VII
103.2	of the May]	of May
103.4	big shops]	great shops
103.6	the . . . splendor.]	the day's past splendour.
103.14	Avenue. She]	Avenue and hurried along Forty-fourth Street. She
103.18	a dog]	a big dog
103.21-22	building . . . upper]	building in the upper
103.24-25	window . . . *Trumpet.*]	window "The New York Trumpet."
103.29	occupants.]	inhabitants.
104.2	surprise,]	amazement,
104.5-6	person . . . talking.]	person he was talking to.
104.14	ought you]	had you
104.19	impression of]	impression, somehow, of
104.19	on a Sunday]	on Sunday
104.23	"How . . . said]	"Dropped in to see you, eh?" said
104.29	Edith]	Eleanor
104.33-34	bombs . . . good."]	bombs."
105.2	seat beside her.]	chair beside her and produced his pipe.
105.3	asked, absent-mindedly, "how]	asked, "how
105.4-5	trip . . . I'll]	trip?" ¶ "Not bad." ¶ "How's your dance?" ¶ "Not bad, and, Henry, I'll
105.21	glances.]	glances and laughed.
105.26	said Henry.]	put in Henry.
106.6-8	yawned . . . "but most]	yawned. ¶ "There always have been a lot of fools," he said casually. "The human race has come a long way, but most
106.13	see."]	see—some sort of holiday."
106.33-34	more . . . work."]	more."
107.2	time?"]	time?"
107.20	paused. Bartholomew]	paused. Someone
107.21	that he]	that Bartholomew
107.24	"People," said]	"Some people," said

107.24-25	instant: "Whole] instant, "a whole
107.34-35	seat. ¶ "Hadn't] seat. ¶ "Simple apes," he com-
	mented contemptuously. ¶ "Hadn't
108.1	minute."] moment."
108.16	racket now] racket which had hitherto come
	through the front windows now
108.23	God damn] damn
108.23-24	Socialists!" ¶ "Pro-Germans!] Socialists!" ¶ "We'll
	go get those Bolsheviks!" ¶ "Pacifists!—Aah—h-h!"
	¶ "Pro-Germans!
108.24-27	Boche-lovers!" . . . The next] Boche-lovers!"
	¶ The next
108.31	the office.] the desk.
109.1-2	Bo!" ¶ "Up late] Bo!" ¶ "Hello you yellow Bolshe-
	vik!" ¶ "Up late
109.4	that two] that there were two
109.4-5	soldiers . . . —one] soldiers in front, —one
109.5	them was short] them short
109.5	other was tall] other tall
109.6	weak of chin] weak-chinned
109.21-23	shouted . . . A new] shouted, "Here's the greasy
	sheet!" ¶ A new
109.24	closing around] closing in around
109.25	pale little] little pale
109.26	tall soldier] tall man
109.27	short . . . had] little dark man had
109.31	a riot.] in riot.
110.6	window with a] window a
111.6-7	passionately . . . Did] passionately, "What's the
	matter! What's the matter! What's the matter! Did
111.8-10	up . . . "They] up complained dismally— ¶ "They
111.10-11	leg . . . "Here] leg, hell take their stupid souls!"
	¶ "Here
111.13	IX] CHAPTER VII
111.16	of . . . tables] of a marble table
111.16-17	the frying pans.] a frying pan.
111.25-26	of Broadway . . . Avenue.] of Broadway's evening
	population.
112.4-5	desperately out] quite out
112.19-21	doughnuts . . . All] doughnuts. ¶ So he walked in
	and sat down. All
112.22	laughter. At first] laughter. ¶ At first

112.28	chat, while excited] chat. Excited
112.29	at him . . . out] at them silently as they bumped them out
112.30	way.] way on their imperious course.
112.32	of beauty] of young beauty
113.6	"He's] "I'll say he's
113.6	a spree] some spree
113.14	dumbly] carefully
113.16	to . . . most] to the most
114.1-2	promenader . . . "Gordy."] promenaders, "Gordy."
114.3	"Hello," . . . thickly.] "Hello," he said thickly.
114.4	Prominent Teeth shook] The man shook
114.16	up, owlish] up, very owlish
114.31	"What'd] "wha'd
115.9	fiercely. "Nice] fiercely, "You're Mr. Phillip Cory, that's who! Nice
115.16	"What's] "Wha's
115.19	"Let's] "Le's
115.19-20	this waiter] the waiter
116.2	said to Peter.] said.
116.7	a short struggle] an instant struggle
116.20	resumed; he] resumed, when he
117.1	X] CHAPTER IX
117.5	grocer's] greengrocer's
117.5-6	them and] them a long year since and
117.6	is vague] is very vague
117.7	in a] on a
117.22-23	risers which] risers who
117.27-28	the . . . awakened] the blue dawn had awoken
117.29	vigorous] strong
118.4	aimin'!"] aimin' at!"
118.9	turned to Dean.] turned jubilantly to Cory.
118.17	That's] Tha's
118.21	Ne'mind.] Ne'min.
118.23	bear.] bear. I drink—therefore I am."
118.27	"What's] "Wha's
118.31	concentration, for if] concentration if
118.35	overcoat] coat
118.35	left] forgotten
119.1	Delmonico's.] Delmonico's when he left there about three-thirty.
119.18	dressed the same] dressed same

119.19	overcoat] coat
119.19-20	was hanging them] was about to hang them
120.6	In effect, the] The effect given was that the
120.15	get] got
120.31	the] th'
120.31	and] an'
120.32-34	both . . . It] both 'em!" ¶ "Both 'em!" ¶ "Both 'em." ¶ It
120.35	curious eyes on] curious glances at
121.7	but startled] but quite startled
121.8-9	them an] them to an
121.14	"Repeat,"] "I repeat,"
121.14	with patient tolerance] with a sort of forced tolerance
121.16	upon bill] upon this bill
121.17	let me] Lem-me
122.14-15	brilliantly absurd.] brilliantly ironic.
122.26	walking fast] walking very fast
122.26	standing unnaturally erect] standing very erect
123.29	"I'm . . . he] "I' Mr. Out," he
123.31	said Peter] rejoiced Peter
123.33	infinite speck] infinite speck
124.13-14	spring . . . and then] spring and then
124.30	XI] CHAPTER XI
124.33	He looked at] He saw
125.1-2	room . . . raw] room, a raw
125.4	on . . . and] on all the chairs and
125.4	smelt stale cigarette] smelt cigarette
125.5-6	shut . . . bright] shut—outside a bright
125.14-15	before that he] before he
125.16-17	[no corresponding division of text]] ⊕ ⊕ ⊕
125.17-22	He went . . . the temple.] ¶ The clerk in charge of the fishing tackle trade at "J. C. Fowler's, Sporting Goods and Accessories," entered the little back room where they count the money, and going up to J. C. Fowler himself, addressed him in a low tone. ¶ "There's a fella out here just bought a automatic—an' he wants some forty-four ammunition." ¶ J. C. Fowler was busy. ¶ "Well, what about it?" he said. "Sell it to him. Business is bad enough, God knows!"

Ohio State University

95

Some Biographical Aspects of
This Side of Paradise

By

Susan Harris Smith

Biographical research on F. Scott Fitzgerald has revealed new facts that have led to new interpretations of his work. Thus I feel that my interview with Norris Jackson may help point to a better interpretation of Fitzgerald's *This Side of Paradise.* Mr. Jackson's early acquaintance with Fitzgerald,[1] his knowledge of St. Paul and Princeton, his lack of interest in self-aggrandizement through literary connections, all have permitted him a clear-sighted yet affectionate recollection of his boyhood friend.

Concern for social recognition dominated Scott's activities his first two years at Princeton. It is interesting that Amory Blaine is a synthesis of the superficial social qualities that Fitzgerald longed for, the personal haughtiness and literary interests that were not his, as well as the frivolous humor and weak character that were his own. Furthermore, Fitzgerald eliminated many of his own fine qualities and replaced them with less desirable ones in Amory, apparently to produce a character who needed the world's approval less than he did. Amory Blaine is a result of some self-understanding and a catharsis for Fitzgerald's unfulfilled dreams.

At Princeton Scott was "alert, cheerful, and bright, in general; he was entertaining and never dull." If he was moody, he never showed it when with others. In this he was unlike Amory who shares his worries with his closest friends. Fitzgerald does not present Amory as one whose ideals were ridiculed but rather as one who is accepted as an intellectual by his peers. But many times during Scott's own Princeton career he would come down to Norris Jackson's room to talk after "he had had a beer or two." Jackson's roommate, Henry

Donne, from Jacksonville, Florida, was working his way through school and didn't have time to listen to Scott "sound off." He, irritated by Fitzgerald's often empty verbosity, would turn to him and say, "Scott, you're a damn fool!"

What aggravated Scott's classmates was his analyzing people's characters, basing all his judgments on their extra-curricular abilities, for unlike Amory, he was not yet concerned with intellectual prowess. All Fitzgerald's subjects were low in his opinion until he discovered their social rank, popularity, or position on the football team or class council. "He pegged everybody on a thermometer scale." This intense categorizing, analyzing, and grading of social ability was not limited to others, however, for Fitzgerald carefully calculated his own behavior to complement the situation. Oddly similar to Amory's hopes to be accepted by the Cottage Club, Fitzgerald once revealed his personal concern for these matters: one Sunday afternoon of his freshman year, Joe McKibben asked Scott to join Norris Jackson, Henry Donne, himself, and another young man for a walk along the canal. The next day, when Scott discovered that the stranger was George Phillips, varsity football tackle, he burst into Jackson's room, visibly upset that he hadn't conducted himself well. "I behaved like a chump, sort of kittenish," he moaned.

Amory Blaine does not suffer such an ignoble loss of dignity, for he is careful to maintain a pose, his favorite being that of Rupert Brooke. For Amory, posing well proves one's talent as a "slicker." Scott, however, was a more likeable person and would play such a game for his own amusement with students who didn't know him well. He never seriously adopted a pose as he was too well aware of himself; it "wasn't really his nature, Scott was more genuine than that."

Amory also differs from Scott in that he is totally absorbed in various literary interests, whereas the Triangle Club is but a passing fancy. Amory writes much poetry; Jackson knew of nothing but "clever lyrics" and certainly not "long and serious poems." *Ha-Ha*! *Hortense* is a mock title for the original *Fie! Fie! Fi-Fi*, one of the best Triangle shows ever produced. "Scott had much more interest in Triangle than he did in the 'Nassau Lit'—he devoted all his time to the effort for that kind of work."

It was his friend, Walker Ellis, who helped Fitzgerald prepare his script for the review and who later gave himself credit for the book, indicating that Scott was responsible only for the lyrics. Jackson remembers Walker Ellis as an "aristocratic type, a bit of a snob, but a pleasant person." But Ellis did not remain only in Fitzgerald's personal life, he was also incorporated into the character of Amory Blaine. His personality is revealed as:

> ... unscrupulousness ... the desire to influence people in almost every way, even for evil ... a certain coldness and lack of affection, amounting sometimes to cruelty ... a shifting sense of honor ... an unholy selfishness. ...
>
> Vanity, tempered with self-suspicion if not self-knowledge, a sense of people as automatons to his will, a desire to "pass" as many boys as possible and get to a vague top of the world.[2]

Fitzgerald may have used Walker Ellis as a model for Amory Blaine, but he was unable to exclude his own dominant trait:

> There was, also, a curious strain of weakness running crosswise through his make-up ... he was a slave to his own moods and he felt that though he was capable of recklessness and audacity, he possessed neither courage, perseverance, nor self-respect.[3]

Fitzgerald had little of the fierce drive he attributes to Amory: "Scott may have wanted to succeed, but not at the expense of others; he was not a mean or vindictive person." Later in life Fitzgerald wrote that his friends "probably didn't recognize the child-like simplicity behind his petty sophistication and lack of a real sense of honor at Princeton."[4] This statement is qualified by Jackson's recollection that "Scott was weak and young, but he had a highly developed sense of honor." This does not reflect any lack of Fitzgerald's self-awareness, but rather it is another example of his need to recreate himself as the dashing, independent, dissolute young man he sought to be. Fitzgerald does not, however, endow Amory with a tenderness that was his—possibly because he knew his weaknesses made it ineffectual. Scott was sympathetic, but not to the point of identifying with or of helping a despondent person; "he was not sure enough of himself to have that ability."

The greatest difference between author and character is a matter of fine distinction between their idealistic attitudes. Amory calls himself "a cynical idealist," one who is motivated by self-interest and by a belief that his virtue can only be maintained through self-control and independence. It is impossible to read such descriptions as representative of Fitzgerald, for they would indicate an aloofness of which he was incapable. A disillusioned idealist, he was not able to maintain the standards he saw others failing to attain. "Scott didn't have that kind of earnestness, he was too easily turned off his basic track." Furthermore, he was very dependent on others and "believed enough in others to be very concerned for their welfare." Even after Ernest Hemingway turned on him, Scott remained loyal though he was deeply hurt.

Amory states that the two rewards which attract humanity are money and honor.[5] As with almost all of Fitzgerald's fictitious men, Amory has an inherited income which frees him from the daily pressures of existence. Not so Fitzgerald, for he acquired "a vivid, almost trained realization of what money would buy him." He later wrote that the realization of his dream resulted in "the conviction that life is a romantic matter." But his frivolous attitude toward life was a façade, for those who knew him well realized that the pressure from the basic need to acquire money was constantly upon him. Jackson recalls a letter he received from Scott telling him of the twenty thousand dollars a year he was earning as a writer. "He was not just boasting," it was more a matter of sharing his good fortune with his friends. They were "afraid it wouldn't do him a lot of good, he spent it so fast."

Fitzgerald also gained some self-assurance by imitating the men he most admired. What Amory says of himself is also true of Fitzgerald: "It was always the becoming he dreamed of, never the being."[6] Because of his phlegmatic nature, he was unable to attain any of the innumerable goals he set for himself. During his sophomore year, on his way home for Christmas vacation, there is an example. Norris Jackson, Joe McKibben and Fitzgerald had gone to the Blackstone Hotel in Chicago for some ice cream during the train layover in the station. On the way back to the train, Fitzgerald surprised his companions by stating that "he wished he had five good principles he could put down and live up to." Jackson recalls thinking that "Scott was a little bit like a ship without a rudder or a compass; that he succeeded as well as he did was amazing."

As Amory sought guidance from Monsignor Darcy, Fitzgerald as he grew older remained insecure and turned to those he respected for his values. In "Handle With Care" from *The Crack-Up* Fitzgerald describes the nature of his dependency on one of his old friends:

> . . . another man represented my sense of the "good life," though I saw
> him once in a decade, and since then he might have been hung. He is in the
> fur business in the Northwest and wouldn't like his name set down here.
> But in difficult situations I had tried to think what he would have thought,
> how *he* would have acted.[7]

Mr. Jackson assured me that this refers to Joe McKibben, an outstanding person whom Fitzgerald greatly admired.

Fitzgerald submerged himself in an imaginary world which he as its creator could control. Amory feels that he is "preserved to help in building up the living consciousness of the race,"[8] but Fitzgerald's aims were less noble. He wrote to be published, for "he wanted the admiration and respect which would come from something which would be accepted." As his living expenses and earnings increased proportionately, he also wanted as much money as possible for his writing. It is true that he also loved to write, for it "clarified his thinking," but "it became a chore later on when money became a necessity." During these concentrated efforts to write, Fitzgerald shut himself off from any distractions to spend months reworking his penciled manuscripts. He admired those who could write as he wanted to—especially Sinclair Lewis and Grace and Charlie Flandreau. He was never satisfied with some of his work, the "pot-boiler short stories," but recognized the worth of his own good writing.

Fitzgerald identified so closely with his work that his amusement about aspects of his own character portrayed in his novels was only possible after later reflection and detachment, thus when speaking he had a "spontaneous humor, but his wit in writing was forced." Fitzgerald's writing was a defense against the world and his own inadequacies.

Just as Amory disguised his insecurity with social bravado, so Fitzgerald's ambivalent attitude towards himself and the strength of his literary reputation was often covered by a relaxed sense of humor. The following inscribed in Mr. Jackson's copy of *The Beautiful and Damned*, reflects the youthful charm which was the essential Fitzgerald:

For the W. K. [well known] / Norris Dean Jackson / (herein called "Anthony Patch") / this story of his life / as he told it to / F. Scott Fitzgerald.

---

[1] Mr. Jackson first met Fitzgerald when they were both in elementary school—the former at Summit, the latter at Western. They were at Princeton together in the class of 1917. They were together after the war, in 1919, when Fitzgerald was beginning *This Side of Paradise*. Mr. Jackson saw Fitzgerald for the last time shortly after Scottie's birth, at the White Bear Yacht Club in St. Paul. All factual information and quotations, unless otherwise noted, are drawn from my interview with Norris Jackson (July, 1966).

[2] F. Scott Fitzgerald, *This Side of Paradise* (New York: Scribners, 1920), pp. 20-21.

[3] *Ibid*.

[4] F. Scott Fitzgerald, *The Crack-Up* (New York: New Directions, 1945), p. 252.

[5] *This Side of Paradise*, p. 294.
[6] *This Side of Paradise*, p. 19.
[7] *The Crack-Up*, p. 79.
[8] *This Side of Paradise*, p. 285.

Six Letters to the Menckens

From

F. Scott Fitzgerald

The following Fitzgerald letters to the Menckens are in the
Goucher College Library and the H. L. Mencken Room of The Enoch
Pratt Free Library. They were called to our attention by Betty Adler
and are printed here with the permission of the copyright holder,
Frances Fitzgerald Smith.   —M.J.B.

[ALS, 1 p. Enoch Pratt.]

c/o Guaranty Trust
4 Place de la Concorde
Paris, France

Dear Menk and Sarah:

    Excuse these belated congratulations, which is simply due to illness.
Zelda and I were delighted to know you were being married + devoured
every clipping sent from home. Please be happy

Ever your Friend
Scott (and Zelda)
Fitzgerald

Oct 18th, 1930

[TLS, 1 p. Enoch Pratt.]

La Paix, Rodgers' Forge,
Towson, Maryland,
October 5, 1933.

Dear Sarah:—

        didn't
Hope I ⟨don't⟩ give the impression of being callous about Anne Duffy,

102

on the contrary, I sympathize with them terrifically in their trouble. I was avidly absorbed by my desire to get some intelligent reader to listen to my completed novel—and as you may have guessed, I was taking it big alcoholically.

So, lovely and statuesque one, Venus of Cathedral Street, accept this correction.

Best wishes always,
F. Scott Fitzgerald

[ADS, 1 p. Baltimore, 1933. Enoch Pratt.]

+ one other

Recieved $100 for painting "Mourning" ∧ by Zelda Fitzgerald—with stipulations in my possession

F Scott Fitzgerald
(for Zelda Fitzgerald

[ALS, 2 pp. Letterhead of Grove Park Inn, Asheville, N. C. 1935. Goucher.]

Dear Menk: I'm sorry as hell about all this nuisance to Sara. That's the hell of getting older. It occurred to me the other day that I'm never in a group any more without their being one deaf person——

——My God! There is a convention of laundrymen here + a party next door has been telling for 10 minutes how a man named Bill vomited on his two long-haired dogs.

Anyhow you shouldn't have gone to that trouble of writing me about Gertrude Stien though your conclusions interest me. I remember the contradiction in sense—somebody is dead + then alive again, in *Melanctha*, I think. But I believe you would have felt the book more remarkable had you read it in 1922 as Wilson + I did. She has been so imitated + thru Ernest her very rythm has gone into ⟨ ⟩ the styles of so many people. I agree that Carl is too inclined to rapture on his Ronald Firbanks ect. but I still believe Gertrude Stien is some sort of a punctuation mark in literary history.

I am here resting, very bored + rather uninspired by my surroundings but here I stay another month by Doctor's orders. So I wont be able to have an evening with you, much as I'd like it. Saw George a moment in New York—he looked handsome + young for his years. He was with the embryonic ⟨ovarian⟩ Tully.

With Warmest regards to you both

Scott Fitzg

There hasn't been a novel worth reading in one solid year, English or American.

[ALS, 1 p. Letterhead of Grove Park Inn, Asheville, N. C. 1935.
Goucher.]

Dear Menk:

That's terrible news—I hope for the best. I wish to God that I ⟨ ⟩ or
anybody could help you both. It's so damn sad.

Scott Fitzg—

Saturday

[ALS, 1 p. Letterhead of Grove Park Inn, Asheville, N. C. May 1935.
Goucher.]

Dear Menk:

It is so terribly sad. Sara's fine life was all too short. My thoughts are
all with you tonight

Scott Fitzg

Will You Let These Kiddies Miss Santa Claus?

By

Ernest M. Hemingway[1]

They call it the ante room to the court of dead dreams. And it is the saddest room in the world.

In it you will see blank looking girls, holding babies in their arms. Standing a little away will be a sullen-faced man looking at the floor. He twirls his cap in his hands and with downcast eyes reflects that this is the end of the passage of Romance.

You will see young girls holding babies that look as if they might be their baby sisters. You will see middle-aged women with a whole brood of wide-eyed children climbing about them. It is the waiting room for the Court of Domestic Relations of Chicago and four thousand women for whom the Romance of life is a finished story go through it every month.

But it isn't the women with the dumb despairing look of lost illusions in their eyes that are the saddest thing about the room. The cheerful kids who are looking forward to a Santa Claus who will never come are what make the onlooker feel that lump in his throat.

To save Christmas for these children is the work of the Fund for The Court of Domestic Relations. James A. Kearns, clerk of the Municipal Court, is in charge of the fund.

"All of these families are here because they do not co-operate," said Miss Irene Inderrieden, Director of the Social Service Department of the Court.

"The wives come here because the husbands refuse to support

---

[1] *The Co-Operative Commonwealth*, II (December 1920)—the only Hemingway contribution that has been identified. Courtesy W. Jones.

them. The court makes an allotment out of the husband's wages. This goes to the wife. But still many of them are destitute. This is because of the lack of co-operation in the family. While the husband and wife and children could live together in comparative comfort the husband's salary when split will not support two homes."

A pitiful example of this is the case of a Polish woman, Mrs. Steve Prsybylski. Prsybylski is a funny name—but it is the only funny thing about the story.

Mrs. Steve, who lives at 2447 W. 46th Street, Chicago, has seven children. The oldest is ten years old. The court can only allot $16 a week of Steve's earnings to his wife. Figure out how much Christmas the seven little Polish kids will receive on sixteen dollars a week.

Then there is Mrs. Vasil Warwoszymak of 1514 Wabansia Avenue. That is another funny name. It would take something more than a humorist to find anything funny in the situation. Vasil refused to support the children. His wife has tuberculosis and there are three suspiciously bright-eyed, more than normally red-cheeked, pinch-faced little children—five years, four years and three months old. And there won't be any Christmas for them either, unless you give to them.

One family more out of a thousand that might be mentioned is the Olenski family of 2166 Elston Avenue.

It isn't nice to think about Mr. Olenski. He is employed at the Devoe and Reynolds paint factory. His family are destitute.

Mrs. Olenski is not employed. She is dying of cancer. Here is a list of the children: Martha, 12 years; Lillian, 10; Frank, 8; William, 7; Annie, 4; Marie, 2, and Raymond is 8 months. Wonder if Santa Claus gets the letters that Frank and Bill and Annie and the rest send him?

By the Kiddies' Fund all these families are listed and catalogued. If enough food and gifts are contributed every child of the Domestic Relations Court will have a Christmas party. A tree is to be set up in one of the court rooms and all the grim panoplies of justice are to be draped with holly and Christmas decorations. This room will be Christmas for the children for an entire week until all the seven hundred court kiddies have received their gifts.

It is planned to give each child a box of candy, a toy of some kind, an apple, an orange and some useful article like a sweater or a pair of shoes. Baskets will be sent to the homes of the destitute families but the Christmas Court Room will be an exclusive kids' feature.

Co-operators who want to aid this fund and bring Christmas to the ones who need it most should buy groceries, oranges, apples or anything they wish to contribute from their district Co-operative Grocery Store and take or send them to James A. Kearns, clerk of the Municipal Court. The Municipal Court is located in the City Hall, in the loop.

April 8, 1955 with Hemingway: Unedited Notes on a Visit to Finca Vigia

By

Fraser Drew

[These notes were scribbled on a pad in Havana's Rancho Boyeros Airport and on a Delta Airlines plane and then typed the same night on a borrowed typewriter in my room at the Hotel Monteleone in New Orleans. I was spending a week in New Orleans en route back to Buffalo State College from a four-day lectureship at Baylor University in Waco. Except for occasional bracketed comments, notes are in their original rough form.]

Letter from Mary Hemingway waiting when I reached Hotel Monteleone on 3 April, suggesting that I come to see them, sending their Havana phone number, saying that they would "be delighted to see me. Ernest says so specifically." I find that I can fly to Havana on Delta Airlines 8:45 Royal Caribe Thursday evening and return on 2:55 to New Orleans Friday afternoon.

Wednesday night I telephone Cotorro 154 and talk with both Hemingways. EH tries to get me to reverse charges on $10 call. They are having guests Friday afternoon but want to see me Friday morning. EH says that I am to go to Ambos Mundos Hotel where he will make reservations for me as his guest and that chauffeur Juan will pick me up there Friday morning at 9:00 and bring me to the Finca.

Plane flight delayed twice Thursday night, finally gets off at 1:30 a.m. CST and reaches Havana shortly before 5:00 EST. Customs procedure uncomplicated except for a woman just ahead of me who is caught smuggling a boxed live rabbit into Cuba, unacceptable behavior I judge from the gestures and the torrents of Spanish [I speak a little French and a little Irish, but no Spanish]. I have no trouble with my almost empty briefcase and climb aboard the one bus headed for the city. I ride it to the last stop, having no luck in communicating my destination to the driver, and then find a cab driver who takes me to the Ambos Mundos.

EH's old friend Manuel Asper, the proprietor, still waiting up, takes me with some ceremony to "Ernest's Room," unchains and unlocks it, admits me to the high-ceilinged room and bath, and opens a casement window. It is now well past 6:00 and I am to be picked up at 9:00. I go to the window and look out at dawn breaking over the old city. To my left is very old Columbus Cathedral, where the remains of the discoverer rested for many years, and straight ahead and to right the very beautiful harbor of the city, with Morro Castle in the distance. A trumpet begins to sound at ten-minute intervals from an army barracks across the harbor. I cannot sleep but watch the old city rouse to life and the first people come out on the streets—an old woman, a squad of soldiers. It is cool but there is promise of a hot day (it did go over 90).

I bathe and shave and am about to dress when the antiquated telephone rings. It is the proprietor, asking that I join him at 8:00 on the roof-garden for breakfast. I go up and look at a breath-taking panorama of the city and sea, while Manolo points out special things and then shows me his magnificent garden with its open-air dining-room. On the roof grow royal palms and flowering shrubs and vines. There is a shrine to the Blessed Virgin with more than one hundred flowers and plants which take their names from her. We have breakfast: a beaker of orange juice, fresh pineapple, hot white rolls, a pot of coffee—no meat because it is Good Friday. Manolo tells me of his long friendship with the Hemingways, how EH wrote *A Farewell to Arms* and some of *Death in the Afternoon* in the room in which I had stayed, how the three Hemingway boys have made the Ambos Mundos their headquarters as they grew up.

At 9:00 Juan arrives and we drive through the city to the suburb of San Francisco de Paula. Traffic heavy because it is Good Friday and people are going to the churches and the beaches. We stop at a small church. Finally we come to the Hemingway finca and the house may be seen, a sprawling white house on a hill with much land around it. Juan unlocks the gate, drives in, relocks, and we drive up a road between rows of grapefruits, avocados, palms, and strange trees which I do not recognize. Mary is on the terrace with a great armful of flowers and comes to greet me. She is most cordial and apologizes that she cannot spend much time with me because of guests who are coming later in the day. EH appears with the gardener (who is a cross between Robinson Jeffers and Gary Cooper in appearance).

EH is a huge man, dressed in khaki shorts and an old shirt, with gray hair and a gray beard and a ruddy complexion. He shakes hands and welcomes me and seems shy at first, as if I, not he, were the important man. He shows me the house. As one enters, the dining room is straight ahead. It has a long table and on the wall to the left hangs Miro's "The Farm." I recognize the Miro and EH is pleased. He is sure that he likes it for he has looked at it across his table for more than twenty years. I like it, too.

The main room is very long and has tables and chairs and bookshelves and the heads of beasts shot by EH, mainly in Africa. I recognize kudu, eland, and think that I recognize oryx and make a mental note to ask about them later. I forget. To the right of the long room is the library with thousands of books in ceiling—high shelves—natural history, military history, modern literature, here and there a Hemingway. These books were in good order once, said EH, and then there were hurricanes and moves and reorganizations and my boys rearranged them all once according to size and color, not subject. Straight ahead of the long room is the one where Hemingway works much of the time. Most of his work he types, standing, on a typewriter which rests on a bookshelf. There are also a bed, a large table covered with books and unanswered correspondence, and everywhere bookshelves and pictures, including a very good Klee which I do not know by name. Out of all these rooms are French doors to terraces.

Mary comes through the long room. She is 46, the magazines say, but does not look 46. She is blonde and slim and very suntanned and very pretty. EH is 55, will be 56 in July, and looks his age because of the beard and the many accidents he has had. He suggests that we go down by the swimming pool and talk—"Mary will be glad to get us out of the house." A servant brings a glass and a bottle of beer to me and another glass to EH containing "something supposed to be good for my insides," and we walk slowly down the hill to a bench and chairs in a grove beside the pool. EH walks slowly and volunteers the information that he is feeling better but has had some trouble. I've gained too much weight, he adds, but if I exercise enough to keep down the weight it's bad for the vertebrae injured in the crash. He had many injuries in that crash in Africa and in the one that followed it.

It is cool down by the water, a large square blue pool, fourteen feet deep. Across from where we sit is an opening in the trees through which we have a long view of Havana and the sea. There is a breeze, but it is a hot day and Cuba has had no rain in weeks so that trees are less green than they should be. Two dogs accompany us and lie down quietly; they are mongrels and seem intelligent and good-tempered. Cats are all over the place. One kitten kept following me and crying, so that I picked him up and carried him during our look at the house. Nearby I see a small green lizard the color of a lime lollipop and translucent and crystalline in appearance. We sit here and talk for more than two hours, although I make one apologetic move to go which is denied, "unless you have to get back into the city for something."

By this time EH is speaking freely and easily and I feel no awe or self-consciousness. He is a very easy person to be with, slow-moving and slow-speaking, and with the gentle manner which sometimes characterizes the large man and the great man. His voice is quiet and low and his laugh, which comes increasingly as we talk, is genuine and quiet, also. He is very kind and modest and unassuming and much impressed that I should "take so much trouble and come so far" just to see him. When I try to speak of my appreciation for his willingness to see me, he interrupts. I am very grateful for your interest and all you have done, he says. There is something which makes me sure that he means what he says. I think at the time that he always means what he says and says what he means.

Did you bring any books for me to sign? he asks, and I admit having a few in my briefcase. I'll be glad to sign them, he continues. It is very difficult to receive books by mail and return them because of customs and postal regulations, but I am happy to sign any that come here with friends. We'll save time for writing in them when we go back up to the house. I feel brief guilt for six books I had sent him several years before and for the six of his own copies that he had sent back with them as an "act of contrition," he had written, for his delay in returning my copies.

So we go on talking and he talks very well. He speaks often of his wife and is worried about her. Was Mary nice to you when you got here? he asks. I know that she wrote you a nice letter. I read it. But she is not feeling well. And she is worried about these people who are coming this afternoon and about my book. Then, too, her father died a few weeks ago in Gulfport. He had a long and painful death and it was very hard for her. She had to go over there often, of course. I want to take her out in the *Pilar* very soon and get her away from everything for a while. She's sore at me right now, he added, but it's because of all these things.

[Here my notes shift, most of the time, from present tense to past. I'm not sure why. Perhaps because in the brief interval between note-writing at Rancho Boyeros and note-writing on the plane the experience moved across the thin line

111

[dividing the present from the past. I also seem to be moving into more complete sentences. The English professor taking over again?]

I asked Hemingway if he was troubled by many visitors. I'm always glad to see friends like yourself and my old war friends and hunting friends, he said, but there are a lot of crazies too. There was a student from New Jersey, one of John Ciardi's boys from Rutgers. I try to be good to students but this one wanted to live here. He is going to be a writer and I had to read three of his stories. They were bad stories. I gave him some criticism that pleased him because it was the opposite of what his teacher had told him in New Jersey. EH went on to say that the boy did not have "basic command of the language," which is necessary before one can "try tricks." EH spoke freely of Mary's father who wanted to write, too. He got all sorts of free advice from me but wouldn't take it, of course. Mary wrote a fine story about him in which he appeared very human but not noble enough to suit him. Attitude of friendly humor toward Mary's father, but no superiority or meanness.

We talked of the books written about Hemingway, the critical studies by Baker, Atkins, Young and Fenton. He was inclined to feel that books should not be written about living men. He was amazed at Atkins' writing his book in Khartoum, far from libraries and primary sources; Atkins did not even have some of the Hemingway books about which he wrote and relied on a *New Yorker* article and what few books he did have. EH did not like Young's book, for the major thesis was that the Hemingway books derive from trauma, hurts experienced from Northern Michigan to Northern Italy, and EH found that silly. EH does admire Baker and Baker's "big book." Baker is a nice fellow, said Hemingway, but it is a hard book and makes too much, as so many critics do, of the symbolism. A digression then on the matter of symbolism—"No good writer ever prepared his symbols ahead of time and wrote his book about them, but out of a good book which is true to life symbols may arise and be profitably explored if not over-emphasized." Back to this later. The Fenton book he finds over-done. Fenton is a "disappointed creative writer and a disappointed FBI investigator." He belongs to the "laundry-list school" of literary criticism, over-investigating and then over-interpreting. Fenton, for example, over-emphasized the influence of Moise, a *Kansas City Star* editor during EH's apprenticeship there. Moise was a bad writer who wrote a long poem that he was always inflicting on people, said EH. It was no good, but how can you tell an old man his poem is no good?

112

EH asked about my trip to Baylor and I told him that there was great interest among the students there in his work, much more than in the work of Masefield, about whom I had also lectured at Baylor. EH wanted to know if Masefield was still living. He must be a very nice guy, he said, and he wrote some good adventure stories as well as good poems.

Tell me about teaching, Hemingway asked. He wondered why I had gone into teaching, if I liked it, and if the theme-reading got me down. It must be hard work, he said, but it is very important. The corruption of youth is the greatest crime and the good teaching of youth a tremendous responsibility. He then told me that he much appreciated my teaching of his books. I don't teach them, I said. I don't have to sell them. I merely suggest them, along with other books; they always sell themselves and the great majority of students like them. Which one do they like best, he wanted to know. I answered that their first choice was probably *A Farewell to Arms.* When I added that my own favorite was probably *The Sun Also Rises*, he said that it was the most moral book he had ever written, a sort of "tract against promiscuity." You don't look like a teacher, EH said. You have the face of a doctor. He asked if I had ever thought of being a doctor, and I admitted that I had and told him why I had become a teacher instead. I like to think that his remarks implied a compliment, remembering his love for his father, who was a doctor, and remembering the attractive figure of Rinaldi in *A Farewell to Arms.* I told EH how much I had liked the Ambos Mundos and Manuel Asper. He talked of his long residence there and long friendship with Manolo, but he had not written all of *Farewell* there, as Manolo believed.

Somehow we got back onto the subject of the critics and literary criticism, and Hemingway spoke of the great amount of adverse criticism he had received in recent years, particularly between the time of much-damned *Across the River and Into the Trees* and the appearance of the much-hailed *The Old Man and the Sea.* He spoke of the tendency of critics to over-identify him with the characters of his books and spoke at some length on the subject in connection with Jake Barnes of *The Sun Also Rises.* It is true that I got the idea when I was in the hospital in Italy after I had been wounded, he said. I too had been wounded in the groin and there had been wool infection there. I was swollen up like footballs, he gestured dramatically, but I was not made impotent like Jake Barnes, obviously. I was put into a so-called genito-urinary ward where there were many guys with groin wounds, and it was pretty bad. That is where I got the idea for Jake, not from myself. But of course people thought that he was a self-portrait. Once, EH said, the photographer Man Ray took a trick nude picture of him in which a gaping wound appeared in the front of his body. The picture was apparently shown to a writer-friend whose wife, not widely celebrated for her good sense, met EH a few weeks later at a cocktail party. After a few drinks, she suddenly rushed over to Hemingway, threw her arms around his neck, and cried, "You poor darling. Now I understand about Jake Barnes and I know what they mean by a fate worse than death." The laugh was hearty when he told the story, but there was an edge of exasperation on it. Continuing with the critics, he commented on their willingness to publish extravagant theories about people. They've said everything about me except that I'm homosexual, and that will be the end, and he laughed again. But he launched into an attack against irresponsible biography and criticism, citing particularly a recent book on Lawrence of Arabia. The book's presentation of Lawrence's illegitimacy and his sexual proclivities infuriated Hemingway, especially since Lawrence's mother and other members of the family were still living.

I spoke of its being Good Friday and recalled Hemingway's early *Today is Friday.* He then asked me if I went to church and I told him that I am a Roman Catholic, though originally a Congregationalist. This interested EH. He said, I like to think that I'm a Catholic, as far as I can be. I can still go to Mass, although many things have happened—the divorces, the marriages. He spoke with admiration of Catholicism and then of his friend, the Basque priest whom he had known in Spain and who now lived in San Francisco de Paula. He comes here a great deal, said EH. He prays for me every day, as I do for him. I can't pray for myself any more. Perhaps it's because in some way I have become hardened. Or perhaps it is because the self becomes less important and others become more important. But that *Time* article was bad. He referred to a recent article in *Time* which had commented that he had been born a Congregationalist, had become a Roman Catholic, and now no longer went to church. This conversation with EH confirms my earlier feeling that he is a religious man with respect for the religions of others.

Now I mentioned the time, fearing that I would complicate his schedule for the rest of the day. He said, Let's go up to the house and sign those books of yours. We walked slowly up the hill to the house, where we saw Mary and I thanked her for putting up with my intrusion. She was very gracious. EH then asked for the books. I had not brought any on my trip from Buffalo, for I had not expected to go to Havana. I wished that I had with me my copies of *Three Stories and Ten Poems* and *in our time*, his first two books. In New Orleans I had ransacked the bookshops for Hemingway firsts as soon as I knew that I was going to Havana, but I had found only one, a second issue of *A Farewell.* This I took along, as well as copies of *A Farewell, The Sun,* and *The Old Man and the Sea* for my three best students at the college, a *To Have and Have Not* for my colleague, Professor Conrad J. Schuck, and an *Old Man and the Sea* for George A. Drew, my father. EH inscribed the books for their recipients, asking for information about each, and also a photograph of himself for me. Then he said, I want to give you two or three other things. He brought back to the table a first issue of *The Spanish Earth*, a book which I did not have in my collection, noting that it was the "author's copy," as well as a first Italian edition of *The Old Man.* These he inscribed, carefully and variously, and then he found an Italian edition of *For Whom the Bell Tolls* and a French edition of *Farewell* and inscribed them. I was delighted to stuff them into the briefcase which had been my only baggage from New Orleans, though wishing now that I had brought a suitcase.

With some inner conflict I declined an invitation to stay for late lunch because the about-to-arrive guests were friends of long standing and I had no wish to intrude upon what might have been an anniversary occasion of the type which my host cherished. We walked out onto the terrace and EH instructed Juan the chauffeur to stay with me for as long as I wanted him that afternoon. He may want to drive around the city and take a later plane from Rancho Boyeros, he said to Juan. Now I want you to come again, he said to me. This has been a pleasure for me and I hope that you are not too badly disappointed after coming so far and taking so much trouble. "Writers are always a disappointment when you meet them. All the good in them goes into their books, and they are dull themselves." I'm sure that I remember these words exactly as he said them. I assured him that he was wrong and that the visit had been all for which I had hoped and more. Next time, he said, give me longer notice and I'll save time for taking you out in the *Pilar* and for showing you the city. And don't call me "Sir," he said, shaking my hand and putting the other great hand on my shoulder. Mary came out again as I was getting into the car with Juan. "Goodbye," she called, "and excuse me for being so busy." "Good luck," called Hemingway, and we drove down to the gate and out onto the road for Havana.

It was blazing hot but Juan's speed gave us good breeze. I watched the houses and people and looked at the harbor and occasional land-marks pointed out by Juan in his very good English. But I kept thinking about the friendliness and the wisdom of the man I had been visiting. At Rancho Boyeros I found that the Royal Caribe from Caracas was very late. I passed the time by writing the first pages of these notes on a pad of paper I had stuffed into the brief-case and by watching arrivals and take-offs of other planes, especially one bound for Buenos Aires and another for Mexico City. There were others for Miami and Houston and Montego Bay and the airport was crowded and busy. The flight to New Orleans was as smooth as it had been the night before. Was it really only the night before? We flew so high that I could not see the Gulf at all, and I continued writing until we came down over the Mississippi Delta and flew low up the river's winding course for many miles. Then New Orleans Airport, the line-up at Customs and Immigration and Board of Health, and a car back to the Monteleone in time for a shower, a little time in nearby St. Louis Cathedral, and a late dinner in the Quarter.

[Epilogue note, 1970: A 1962 letter from Mary ends, "I am so glad that Papa had time to chat with you that day." So am I, needless to say. It was one of the four or five best days of my life.] *

State University College at Buffalo

---

*See also Drew, "Pupil, Teacher and Hemingway," *New York State Education* (March 1962), 16-17, 37.

Hemingway and the Autobiographies of Alice B. Toklas

By

Lawrence D. Stewart

When some Disraeli chronicles the *Calamities and Quarrels of Authors* for our century, he will undoubtedly give a chapter to the dispute between Hemingway and Gertrude Stein. Hemingway, from 1927 until his posthumous *A Moveable Feast* (1964), drew up varying explanations for the break;[1] and Gertrude Stein sprinkled hints and observations about it through her writings for the last twenty years of her life. But there was a third party to these difficulties, and no one seems to have paid attention to her role in these imbroglios. I wonder, therefore, if it is not time we consider the woman Hemingway originally called "Miss Tocraz"[2] (and eventually refused to give any name at all).

Late in 1960, when she was 83, Alice Toklas went to Italy for a prolonged stay. Eventually she took up residence in a convent near the Forum and in that atmosphere dictated her memoirs. When *What Is Remembered by Alice B. Toklas* appeared in 1963, it presented her final judgment of Hemingway—or at least as much as she would make explicit:

> Scott Fitzgerald was brought to us in Paris by Hemingway one evening in 1925, just after *The Great Gatsby* was published. Hemingway brought both Fitzgerald and Zelda. Fitzgerald brought a copy of his book.
>
> Scott, who was not averse to giving Hem a little dig, once came up to me and said, Miss Toklas I am sure you want to hear how Hem achieves his great moments. And Hem said rather bashfully, What are you up to Scotty? He said, You tell her. And Hem said, Well, you see, it is this way, When I have an idea I turn down the flame, as if it were a little alcohol stove, as low as it will go. Then it explodes and that is my

117

idea. Fitzgerald turned his back on this and I said, the retreat from Caporetto is well done. I did not say anything about the rest of the book and Hem was satisfied.[3]

In April of 1960 I had gone to Paris to make a phonograph album of Alice Toklas reading the now-familiar hashish fudge recipe, as well as selections from *The Autobiography of Alice B. Toklas*.[4] Since Miss Toklas had agreed to record some impromptu impressions of her life with Gertrude Stein, I summoned up sufficient courage to ask what the Hemingway-Stein quarrel had been about. "The quarrel consisted in Hemingway's not wanting to be a pupil any longer," she asserted. "And the only way not to be a pupil was to stay away. And if you stayed away long enough, a certain coldness came up." It seemed a plausible explanation, at the time.

When I asked her to tell something about Scott Fitzgerald, she replied:

I can't remember the year [that we first met Fitzgerald] but it was through Hemingway. We were at the Rue de Fleurus, of course, and Hemingway's book—the one about the war in Italy [*A Farewell to Arms*, I reminded her] that's it!—had just been published, and I don't know how Fitzgerald knew what I thought of the book, but he said to me, Tell him about the book. And I said, Oh no, I don't want to. I'll speak to him about it when I'm alone with him. He said, Hem, come here! She wants to tell you what she thinks about the book. I hadn't intended to—so quickly. And I told him. And he said, Well, you see how it is: You have an idea and you use it and *then* you want to put it through—and you do it as they do with [a] little gas flame—a little thing—and if you turn it down too low (which I tried to do) it explodes. And when it explodes, you've got your theme.

Miss Toklas was somewhat deaf. Later in the recording session she misunderstood an inquiry I had made and gave a somewhat different account. (I had asked her when Fitzgerald had first come to Paris.)

Oh, after *The Great Gatsby*. He may have come before, but we didn't know him. When we knew him he had already written *The Great Gatsby*. He had written *This Side of Paradise* when Gertrude Stein discovered him—in *This Side of Paradise*. She thought it was a *great* work and that he was a *great* writer. And then (I told you that story already. Didn't that go in?) Hemingway brought him to the house—with Zelda—and there was no Mrs. Hemingway at the time, as I remember—he had lost his first or second wife and there was no one. And Fitzgerald said to me, You tell him the story of—what is the novel? [*A Farewell to Arms*? I suggested] Is that it? It's the one with Italy. *A Farewell to Arms*! You tell him what you said of it, what you feel about it. And I said, Well, I don't intend to tell him publicly, and he said, Well you go on and tell him; he'll be pleased. And so he said, Hem, come here and listen to what she has to say to you about your book. And I said, I liked the retreat from Caporetto—that's all I said! I said, I think the retreat from Caporetto is *excellent*: it's *real*, it's *true*, it's *lively*. And I liked that. And Hemingway said [and Miss Toklas mimicked him] Well, you see how it is: You have a little flame. And you turn it very low—as low as possible—and then it bursts. And then you've got your theme. And that's the way I work.

The story improved in the retelling, but the time remained disordered: a conversation that could have taken place no earlier than 1929—after *A Farewell to Arms* had been published—had been moved back to a time (perhaps 1926?) when Hemingway was separated from his first wife, Hadley, but had not yet married his second, Pauline. (It was not uncharacteristic of Miss Toklas to remember an evening by the presence of wives, for they were the ones who stayed with her at one end of the salon. Had not Gertrude Stein written the *Autobiography* to fulfill Alice Toklas's promise to write *Wives of Geniuses I Have Sat With*?) Later, when Miss Toklas dictated her memoirs, she overcame some of these difficulties. *What Is Remembered* placed the "flame" conversation some time after the first meeting with Fitzgerald. And whereas in conversation Miss Toklas had taken on Hemingway all by herself, in her printed remarks she provided herself with an ally in Fitzgerald.

In 1964, when I was paying another visit to 5 Rue Christine, Miss Toklas confessed to me: "When I was a girl, I didn't remember anything. But once I came to Paris and met Gertrude, I remembered everything."[5] She may not have remembered every *thing*, if *things* are facts. But she did not lose sight of her undimmed antipathy for Hemingway. In 1960 I had asked her if she had liked *A Farewell to Arms*. "Very little of it," she said tartly. "What I liked of it was the retreat from Caporetto. I thought that was really well done—very well done. It was faithful. . ." and she paused for the word: "*reportage*." I remembered that Gertrude Stein had told Hemingway he could not be both a writer and a reporter, and she had urged him to give up journalism. Miss Toklas's praise, therefore, was faint and damning.

In that 1964 spring *A Moveable Feast* had just been published, but neither Miss Toklas nor I had yet seen it. "I have a young man who comes nightly to read to me," she told me. "And he said he would try to get a copy. I said 'Don't bother! I never liked Hemingway.'" Maybe this particular book would have more interest to her, I suggested. The first reviews had said that much of the book was about her and Gertrude Stein. "I can't believe that—he certainly won't be kind to us. . . . When I first saw Hemingway he was beautiful. He never looked so well again. I went through all four of his wives. The first [Hadley Richardson] came to see me after Gertrude died—or was it while Gertrude was alive—just after the war? I can't remember. Anyway, she had married a Chicagoan and had become very nice. She used to be very stupid."

Miss Toklas had guessed correctly: *A Moveable Feast* was not kind either to her or to Gertrude Stein. The hatred Hemingway felt for Miss Toklas had become so consuming that even her name had gone up in smoke and she was reduced to "the friend who lived with [Gertrude Stein]" or "her companion" or "a companion." The kindest mention was: "But we liked Miss Stein and her friend, although the friend was frightening." Hemingway thought he had clear reasons for acting as he did: to some, he insisted that it was Miss Toklas's aggressive lesbianism that offended him; to others, that it was the way she treated Gertrude Stein, especially at the last.[6]

I wonder, however, if the animosity did not stem from Alice Toklas's first "dictated" book, the *Autobiography*? The first of those rather pretentious "flame" anecdotes had appeared there: "Hemingway also said once, I turn my flame which is a small one down and down and then suddenly there is a big explosion. If there were nothing but explosions my work would be so exciting nobody could bear it." The *Autobiography* continued: "However, whatever I say, Gertrude Stein always says, yes I know but I have a weakness for Hemingway."[7] Earlier, in the same book, Miss Toklas had observed: "And then they both [Gertrude Stein and Sherwood Anderson] agreed that they have a weakness for Hemingway because he is such a good pupil. He is a rotten pupil, I protested. You don't understand, they both said, it is so flattering to have a pupil who does it without understanding it, in other words he takes training and anybody who takes training is a favourite pupil. They both admit it to be a weakness" (p. 266). Hemingway as "pupil," good or bad, seems to have been the prevailing attitude in the Stein-Toklas household—certainly in 1933, and so late as 1960.

Hemingway counterattacked in December of 1933. From Tanganyika he sent an "introduction" to James Charters' *This Must Be the Place*. He said nothing of those Montparnasse memoirs by his old friend, Jimmie the Barman, because apparently he had not read them. But he had much to say about Gertrude Stein:

> Once a woman has opened a salon it is certain that she will write her memoirs. If you go to the salon you will be in the memoirs; that is, you will be if your name ever becomes known enough so that its use, or abuse, will help the sale of the woman's book. . . .

> The best way to achieve an at all exhaustive mention. . .is to have the
> woman be fond of you and then get over it. The reasons for the getting
> over it may be many: you may be no longer so young; you may lose your
> teeth, your hair, your disposition, your money, your shoes, your shirts
> may not come back from the laundry; anything in fact. Or you may get
> very tired of seeing the woman or of hearing her talk. It may be that the
> getting over it is induced by domestic compulsion, or by the changes of
> the seasons, or it may be anything you say, but the memoir writer will
> usually prove that a lady's brain may still be between her thighs. . . .[8]

There was no mention of Gertrude Stein's name. There was no allusion to the existence of Alice Toklas. So far as Hemingway was concerned, the book had been entirely Miss Stein's.

What particularly annoyed Hemingway was Gertrude Stein's new
style, which he felt she copped from him.[9] Certainly it was not the
style one had become accustomed to expect from her. But as *Everybody's Autobiography* and *Paris France* and *Wars I Have Seen* appeared in the decade following, it became apparent that Gertrude
Stein's "readable style" never precisely duplicated the style of the
Autobiography. The latter was a remembered transcription by Gertrude Stein of the attitudes and remarks of Alice Toklas—told in
Alice Toklas's own voice. And the opinions, unless labeled Gertrude's, were Alice's. To believe that "Miss Stein has Alice Toklas say
such and such" is to misunderstand the book. Alice Toklas was not a
puppet but a vital person of confirmed ideas—and those ideas were
not always those of her biographer.

Consider the *Autobiography*'s version of Alice's continuing dislike
of Hemingway:

> And then we heard that he [Hemingway] was back in Paris and telling a
> number of people how much he wanted to see her [Gertrude]. Don't you
> come home with Hemingway on your arm, I used to say when she went
> out for a walk. Sure enough one day she did come back bringing him with
> her. (p. 270)

On April 29, 1960, she would tell substantially the same story:

> And one day I said to Gertrude Stein, If you come back from your walk in
> the Luxembourg with the dog—exercising the dog—with Hemingway on
> your arm, I go out! I won't stay here with him! And by Jove she came in
> with him one day.

A few months before she died, Gertrude Stein reiterated that the
Autobiography had not been the autobiography of Gertrude Stein:
"I made a rather startling discovery that other people's words are

121

quite different from one's own, and that they cannot be the result of your internal troubles as a writer. They have a totally different sense than when they are your own words. . . . I did a tour de force with the *Autobiography of Alice B. Toklas,* and when I sent the first half to the agent, they sent back a telegram to see which one of us had written it! But still I had done what I saw, what you do in translation or in a narrative. I had recreated the point of view of somebody else. Therefore the words ran with a certain smoothness."[10] Had there not been an essential weakness in her account of Alice Toklas's life? "If it is your own feeling, one's words have a fullness and violence," Gertrude Stein concluded.

However smooth and lacking violence were Alice Toklas's words (as narrated by Gertrude Stein), the words had sufficient fullness to enrage Hemingway. Eventually he sensed that it had been Alice who had mocked him. Gertrude had said and written withering remarks, especially about his bravery. And Alice's point-of-view might never have attracted public notice had not Gertrude posted it for all to see. Despite all this, late in his life Hemingway occasionally distinguished between the valuable and the destructive in Gertrude Stein. From time to time, a residual affection surfaced, and in the *Paris Review* interview he remarked: "it is simpler and better to thank Gertrude for everything I learned from her about the abstract relationship of words, [and] say how fond I was of her. . . ." Alice Toklas, however, came to embody all that he detested in the Stein menage and work. And so frightening was the continuing memory of her that even when in *A Moveable Feast* he spoke of that local habitation (at 27 Rue de Fleurus) he could not bring himself to speak her name.[11]

San Fernando Valley State College

---

[1] The *New Yorker,* Feb. 12, 1927, pp. 23-24 published Hemingway's parody of Frank Harris's *My Life.* Hemingway labeled the second of four sketches, "The True Story of My Break with Gertrude Stein." (Reprinted in *The New Yorker Scrapbook* [Garden City, N.Y.: Doubleday, Doran, 1931], pp. 156-157). This was a humorous anticipation of what might happen (and to some extent did). Hemingway's gradual disenchantment with Miss Stein prompted him a year earlier to title one section in *The Torrents of Spring,* "The Passing of a Great Race and the Making and Marring of Americans." For other remarks on the quarrel, cf. Philip Young, *Ernest Hemingway: A Reconsideration* (Penn. State Univ. Press, 1966), p. 71: "This famous quarrel is said to have been patched up in Paris in 1945 but if so, and if Miss Stein could read *A Moveable Feast,* things would assuredly unpatch." Cf. also p. 288.

[2] Carlos Baker, *Ernest Hemingway A Life Story* (N.Y.: Scribners, 1969), p. 86.

[3] N.Y. : Holt, Rinehart and Winston, 1963, pp. 116-117.

[4] Recorded April 29, 1960. Verve album MG V-15017. All of Miss Toklas's 1960 remarks are transcribed from tapes made that day.

[5] From my journal for May 9, 1964. All of Miss Toklas's 1964 remarks are taken from that journal. For a discussion of the reliability of Miss Toklas's memory at the end of her life, cf. Janet Flanner's obituary of her old friend: "Letter from Paris," *New Yorker,* March 25, 1967, p. 174.

[6] For the lesbian story, cf. Baker, p. 509, who reports Hemingway's telling this to Donald Gallup, Sept. 22, 1952. (Before one accepts Hemingway's explanation he should consider the number of lesbians among Hemingway's close friends in the 1920's. Even when mentioning some of them in *A Moveable Feast* Hemingway made no observations about their private lives.) For Hemingway's notion that Alice "was so cruel to Gertrude, particularly at the end," cf. Leonard Lyons, "The Lyons Den," *New York Post*, March 9, 1967.

[7] N.Y. : Harcourt, Brace, 1933, p. 271. Gertrude Stein also used the "flame" image in a 1929 conversation with Scott Fitzgerald and compared his "flame" with Hemingway's. For antithetical interpretations of that conversation, cf. Arthur Mizener, *The Far Side of Paradise* (Boston: Houghton, Mifflin, 1951), p. 212 (rev. ed., 1965, p. 233) and Andrew Turnbull, *Scott Fitzgerald* (N.Y. : Scribners, 1962), pp. 189-190.

[8] *This Must Be the Place: Memoirs of Montparnasse* by Jimmie The Barman (James Charters), ed. by Morrill Cody (London: Herbert Joseph, 1934), pp. 11-12.

[9] Ernest Hemingway, *Green Hills of Africa* (N.Y. : Scribners, 1935), p. 66. Cf. also Ernest Hemingway, "The Art of Fiction," *The Paris Review,* 18 (Spring 1958), 73. Young, p. 174 thinks "it is probably true, as he claimed, that Gertrude Stein learned to write conversation from him, and not the other way around."

[10] Taken down in shorthand and transcribed by William S. Sutton for Robert Bartlett Haas, "Gertrude Stein Talking—A Transatlantic Interview," *UCLAN Review,* VIII (Summer 1962), p. 11. The interview took place January 5 and 6, 1946.

[11] Some may wonder if Alice Toklas's name was not deliberately omitted from the lesbian anecdote in *A Moveable Feast* through fear of a libel suit. It is possible that her name had appeared in the original manuscript and then been cancelled by Hemingway or his executrix or his publisher. Legal considerations, however, would not explain Hemingway's omitting Miss Toklas's name in the two other Stein-Toklas chapters of that book. Hemingway's 1933 introduction to Charters' *This Must Be the Place* suggests that Hemingway's inclination, when angry, was to avoid any mention of the enemy's name. In *Green Hills of Africa,* pp. 65-66, when Hemingway lambasted Gertrude Stein for having called him "yellow," he again carefully avoided mention of Miss Stein's name. There was no problem about a libel action there. Hemingway's suppression of Alice Toklas's name seems, therefore, to have been in character.

A Wedding Up in Michigan

By

William B. Smith

Those who know the stretch of land and water that makes up
the Traverse Bay resort area will understand the phrase "a
typical Lake Michigan day." Of course, it embraces many localities,
many lakes and streams, blue waters and green water, sand dunes,
towering cliffs and deep woods. It means a special zest to
the air which you can almost taste and smell.

We had weather like that the day Hadley and Ernest were
married in a neat little white frame church at Horton Bay,
Michigan. The day was Saturday, September 3 and the year 1921.
The ceremony in the crowded Methodist Church was simple and
went off smoothly.

After the ceremony the bride and groom drove away, carrying several bouquets of flowers.

Those simple declarative statements are correct but they reveal
almost nothing about the real event or what preceded it.

Hadley had stayed with my sister Katy just before the event and
there were several tense discussions about the exact language of the
ceremony, especially the use of the word "obey." Mrs. Usher,
Hadley's sister, objected strongly to the word and for a time the
skies grew very dark. Hem was not even aware of this situation.

There were other items however that gave me real concern.
One in particular. I had discussed it with Hem when he first
told me about the engagement. "Hash," as we called her, was
eight years older than Ernest and though I was devoted to her,
that age gap worried me.

Not so with Ernest. He listened and then said, "Of course,

M.E. Ch. Hortons' Bay, Mich.

125

I disagree with you from head to toe, but in any event she will have seen the show." How right he was.

I do not recall many details about the wedding even though I was best man. Hem was wearing a dark blue coat and "ice cream" trousers. Probably my clothes were similar. Hadley who had gone for a swim earlier in the afternoon along with my sister Katy and several others, thus delayed the actual ceremony a few minutes in order to dry the bride's thick lustrous auburn hair. She looked lovely and utterly happy.

Because local talent was lacking, they had imported a minister from Petoskey. "Pick me a prelate who does not wear a celluloid collar or chew tobacco" Hem had specified to a friend. The ushers were almost entirely fishing companions of Hem's. Hadley's sister was maid of honor. Her other attendants were mainly friends from St. Louis.

After the service, people milled about and posed for pictures outside one of the Dilworths' cottages. Then as dusk began to gather, Mrs. Dilworth called them in for one of her famous chicken dinners.

Night had closed in by the time the newlyweds stowed their bags and set off for a two-week honeymoon at Walloon Lake.

Pauline Hemingway: In Tranquillity

By

Bertram D. Sarason

I met Pauline Hemingway about the time that her former husband
had published *Across the River and Into the Trees.* I knew nothing
about her except that she had once been Hemingway's wife. Had I
known, as I have since been told, that she never ceased to love him, I
might have speculated that the failure of Ernest's new novel did not
altogether displease her. She might have taken the failure as a symp-
tom that the latest wife, Miss Mary, was bringing him bad luck or was
a little short on inspiration. If so, there might be hope for Pauline.
Who knows what the years ahead might bring? But what brought the
memory back of our meeting was Hemingway's *A Moveable Feast.*
Pauline is depicted in that memoir as rich and forward, one not hesi-
tating to break up an idyllic marriage. Pauline "the other woman"—I
found that difficult to believe. She was a mite. You would call her
petite to avoid saying that there was nothing about her remotely suggestive of the voluptuary woman. In fact, I thought her bordering on
the epicene. How could that little thing have lured Ernest Hemingway? Yes, she was sometimes gracious, and when gracious you could
like her because she was a good sport. And she had moments of
generosity. But these very qualities increased your doubt that she
was predatory. Hadley Mowrer, the first wife, had told biographers Hamill and Aronowitz that Pauline was not much to blame,
that the marriage was already on the rocks when she appeared on the
Paris scene. Hemingway's version in *A Moveable Feast* was altogether
different. But the book could be taken as fact or fiction, Hemingway
had advised.

So one day I wrote to Hadley Mowrer and told her that I found

Ernest's version of Pauline very difficult to believe. She replied, "Everyone knows Pauline came to Europe to get a husband."

Well, she got her husband, and who was at fault must remain an open question. But according to her Key West neighbors, Pauline never wanted to give him up. I did not know that, as I have said, when I met her; otherwise, I would have understood more clearly why she wanted to be considered young, wanted to remain youthful, pushed decades ahead the possibility of dying.

It was through a friend named Alex that I met Pauline Hemingway less than a year before she died. Just before the Christmas of 1950 Alex asked me and Johanna (a former friend) to help him move from an apartment he had next door to Carnegie Hall, and during the course of the evening he spoke about going down to Key West for a vacation. He needed one. That was evident from the collection of pills he had in the apartment. We knew, of course, he had had a bad time. He was divorcing his wife, Theodore Roosevelt's grand-daughter. It had been a nasty situation. I acted once as intermediary so that Alex could see his child on visitation day. That was possible because I had told Miss Roosevelt not to marry Alex in the first place; she regarded me as a friend. But I was sorry for Alex, and friendless, he needed sympathy as well as assistance in dismantling his apartment. He had some unusual things: a bound volume of auto-graphed photos of movie stars, a ten inch hunting knife, and a table on the underside of which was a piece of parchment inscribed by the son of Reverend Gastrell. The inscription stated that the table-top was made from the floor of Shakespeare's bedroom and that the rest of the table was Shakespeare's very own. The table was probably authentic—it would have taken a very scholarly forger to have known that Reverend Gastrell had acquired New Place, Shakespeare's home, which he destroyed in the eighteenth century. I told Alex that he had a very interesting item there. My opinion seemed to lift his spirits and he suddenly asked if we would like to join him in Key West. He had a small home there with room enough for us. He would introduce us to John Dewey. And Ernest Hemingway's wife—the one by whom he had two children.

Alex had to get leave from the State Department. Once he did, we arranged to meet him in northern Florida where he would arrive by train. We drove down from New York non-stop and picked him up at the Jacksonville railroad station. By late evening we made Palm Beach and Key West the next afternoon. It was two days before Christmas and the houses in town were bedecked with cardboard

Santas and reindeer. Carols competed with each other through loud-speakers on the outside of frame dwellings. The "inner town" was all lit up at night. It was all bizarre, a sort of surrealist Christmas in the midst of upwards of 80 degrees heat.

Christmas passed without our meeting either John Dewey or Pauline Hemingway. Dewey was in Key West all right. Turning a corner one day, I had to step on the brake of our metallic blue convertible to avoid hitting him. He scurried quickly to the other side. I pretended not to recognize the figure as John Dewey; no point in raising an issue with Alex now that he was feeling somewhat better. We spent our days at the Sun and Sand Club and Alex took in the surf and the relaxations of the beach. He had been more upset than we realized. One morning we found Alex's hunting knife underneath his pillow. A refugee from Stalin's GPU, he lived in fear. (Years later, when he went to Germany, where he came down ill, he believed he had been poisoned by Soviet agents.) I thought at first he was name-dropping when he spoke about Dewey. But Alex was well-acquainted in Key West. He was addressed as General—he had been a Soviet General as well as a diplomat. He had written a book about his escape and he looked important. Over six feet tall, broad-shouldered, handsome but grave, he kept in trim. Before our morning dip, Alex went through muscle-tightening exercises, much like those recommended to women to slim after having had a baby. He did these exercises on the beach and people who knew him took these activities for granted. There was Arnold Blanch and his wife Peggy Lee who were about to have an art show in an improvised museum along the waterfront. There was a friend of Harry Hopkins who had brought large WPA bounties to Key West in the depression days but whom the native gentry still regarded as a foreigner. There was someone out of Vermont who had lately published in the *Saturday Evening Post*. There was a big-diamonded dowager out of Guilford, Connecticut who read Eliot evenings and who apparently went South in the winter. There was a retired naval officer whose training failed him in repelling broadsides from his wife. These two were friends of Tennessee Williams, clipped coupons, and said grace before meals. Almost all of these acquaintances of Alex turned up at the Sun and Sand Club. But not John Dewey. Not Pauline Hemingway.

By two days after Christmas the only formal invitation we had had was from the naval officer and his wife. They squabbled for the first hour of our stay. Then, as we sat down for lunch, the host bowed his head and thanked God for "all our blessings." Squabbling resumed with soup. The uncertainties of the stock market were commented on, and there were kind words for Tennessee Williams from the hostess. We left early. Alex went off by himself.

I guess he felt obliged to improve our social life. He had evidently gone to see Pauline Hemingway, possibly John Dewey, to arrange for our meeting them. After supper that evening he told us that John Dewey had gone away sailing, but that we were invited to Pauline's for the next afternoon. He reported this invitation with gravity. We had to be briefed as if we were going to a high-level conference. Johanna was not to wear a tight-fitting dress nor a dress with a low neckline. We were to be careful not to swear. Mrs. Hemingway was very proper, he explained; we were to watch our manners. Our first impression was that Alex was joking. But he was not. Alex rarely joked, and now, it was evident, he was quite serious. I wondered how Pauline Hemingway ever got through *The Sun Also Rises*. (I wonder if she ever read Ernest Hemingway's letters.) Could she have lived through the era of F. Scott Fitzgerald and expatriate years on the *Rive Gauche*? Besides, Alex's fears were groundless. We knew how to behave. I had behind me the discipline of faculty teas as well as that sound upbringing that comes from having taught at those boys schools where vestiges of Newport society and pretenders to European thrones called to see their children on Sundays. One learned to limit conversation to assurances that there were no dangerous snakes in the area but many more owls than one could imagine, an occasional one migrating from Canada. Johanna, born in Europe, knew her way in the world. She had been proposed to by a German Prince, she had once been toasted to by Ambassador Henri Bonnet, and just recently had been perfectly at ease with a Vanderbilt kin who visited us. Nevertheless, we gave Alex the necessary assurances. When we set out the next afternoon, it was with the idea of seeing not the former wife of a famous writer but an anachronism, a museum piece, a remnant of a former age, unaffected by our time and unchaffed by experience.

The Hemingway house was on the other side of town but not far from its center. My recollection of it is vague. I remember, enclosing the property, a dark red brick wall, about five feet high, that seemed to encompass the side of an entire city block. The entrance was half way down the street, and the house itself was set back about 25 yards. There were lawn and palm trees. To the left of us, and not far from the house, was a large swimming pool. It was painted a bright green or blue. Great floodlights were visible in the bottom corners and palm trees lined the borders of the pool. It was clean, so that it must have been attended to; but it did not appear to have been used recently. There were no books or newspapers lying around its edge, no empty cocktail glasses. Flamboyant, and about 100 feet in length and 40 feet in width, it suggested something out of Hollywood. It hardly suggested that its present owner was a lady of moderate manners and Victorian tastes. The house itself was more in keeping with the reputation of the proprietress. Set in so extensive a setting, it seemed rather small nor was it gay modern. We entered into a reception hall and were welcomed in a living room to the left by a short but pleasant lady with the smile of a young girl, with the vivacious spirit of a college senior, and with a touch of that insecurity associated with the provincial. She was gayer than her house and furniture which was neither new nor brightly colored. Her hair was soft and somewhat wavy. I don't recall the color of her eyes. Her body was slight, and she was dressed inexpensively. She introduced us in turn to a dark haired young man, her youngest son Gigi, his complexion swarthy, his eyes dark and large, his expression suggestive of controlled hostility. With him was a girlfriend of about seventeen, dressed in white, her brown hair pulled back tightly, her manners correct, her greeting cool. She was the daughter of the founder of Dianetics. Gigi was much interested in Dianetics.

Pauline hardly spoke to us. She was not being rude. Alex was her friend and she found it easier to speak to him. Moreover, she was somewhat shy. I don't remember who suggested that we play penny-poker, but we agreed it was a good idea. It brought us all together around a table in the far corner of the living room where a large window brought in the light. Alex looked at Johanna as if to caution her against swearing. Somebody dealt the cards. We played for awhile with due solemnity. Pauline was the only one who was enjoying the game to the hilt. When she failed to draw to a straight or flush or two-pair, she blurted out, "Damn," or "Oh Hell." Alex took the game seriously. Before he paid his penny or two or before he threw in his cards he studied his hand with all the grimness of a man about to make a crucial diplomatic decision. He was holding up the game, and Gigi was letting his girlfriend know that he was disgusted. We played for about an hour. Gigi and his friend left. And then Pauline told us of his passion for Dianetics. Yes, he believed one could recall embryo days in the womb. "Do you remember," Pauline had asked him, "the time when you were in your seventh month and I fell down the stairs?" Gigi said he remembered. A look of anguish came over his face. But Pauline told us he had forgotton one thing. Before leaving school for vacation he had made some recordings of memories he had elicited from his friends and classmates—intimate stuff. These he had forgotten to take home with him. Alex thought that Gigi had a good grasp of politics. Pauline was pleased. She had some hope that Gigi would go in that direction. But I can't recall that Johanna or I said much of anything. It didn't matter. The purpose of the afternoon was to break the ice. That evening we received an invitation for a cocktail party for the next afternoon.

Gigi was there with his girl, and his brother Patrick with his wife. Patrick, who had a slight limp, had his father's charm; Gigi, his father's toughness. There were also Oliver St. John Gogarty who was living in Key West and Alfred Kazin who had just done a review of *Across the River and Into the Trees.* His review fell in with the general lamentation the book elicited, and I wondered if he was invited for that reason. I never found out. Kazin and Gogarty paired off. I could hear that Kazin had recently "discovered Minnesota." Gogarty said nothing. The Hemingway boys were not saying much either. Nor was Alex. There was just the usual chit-chat with which cocktail parties begin, and we were just beginning. I had an instant ago taken a sip of my second drink, had accepted some hors d'oeuvres from one of the two female Blacks who were serving, when Pauline announced, "Out, all of you." I don't recall who led the sheepish procession. But they all left without protest: the critic, the ex-General, Joyce's Buck Mulligan, Johanna. The drink and an eighth I had had warmed me up. It was a pleasant feeling and I resented being given short shrift. Who did this woman think she was? I had an impulse to smack her in the face. The impulse was sublimated by my going straight for her and planting a kiss on her.

"Oh," she said, "You must come to breakfast."

So that was it. We were not paying enough attention to her at the party.

The breakfast invitation was cancelled in favor of a New Year's Eve party. That turned out to be somewhat complicated. Alex had accepted an invitation for an early evening party for that night from the *Saturday Evening Post* writer, and as neither Johanna nor I had the required formal gear, we could not go. Nor did he think to get Pauline an invitation. It was arranged that he would join us about 11 p.m. at the Hemingway house. We would in the meantime start the celebration on our own. Pauline invited her partner, a fairly tall, good featured brunette who helped her run the Caroline Shop. It was, as I understood it, a Gift Shoppe where one could get demitasse things and bric-a-brac. I couldn't visualize this as another Neiman-Marcus or Macy enterprise; the impression I had was that

132

Pauline was having trouble making both ends meet. This delusion was brought about by Alex's having told me that Pauline could have had a small fortune if she accepted Ernest's offer at the time of the divorce to take the income from *For Whom the Bell Tolls*. Instead, she took the Key West house.

The partner complained of a slight cold. She had not much to say. There were a few moments of dead silence while Johanna and I sat on a small sofa with Pauline sitting directly opposite us.

Then suddenly, Pauline to Johanna, "You have legs like Marlene Dietrich."

I thought that was very nice of Pauline to say. I was young then and did not know that women did not compliment each other out of pure loving-kindness. Had I read Lillian Ross' recent profile of Ernest Hemingway I would have understood instantly what was on Pauline's mind. Not Ernest's new wife, Miss Mary—but Marlene Dietrich. Ernest had talked to Lillian Ross about his friendship with the actress, and Pauline knew about it.

The phone rang, and some sort of strange conversation took place. Pauline's words were cryptic; her emotions, aroused. There was some reference to a book but otherwise her part of the dialogue made no sense. When the call was completed, she returned half delighted, half flustered.

"From California," she said. "I'm supposed to get a book. Gertrude Atherton. About transplantation."

Her little commentary that followed indicated that someone (no doubt her sister Ginny) had recommended having monkey glands transplanted. There was a book about the subject that she ought to read, and supposedly the heroine of it had undergone some miracle of surgery whereby she either looked younger or retained her present looks unto a ripe old age. I forget what the surgical outcome was supposed to be, but the emphasis was on youth. It sounded like nonsense.

Pauline suddenly appeared with a small crowbar.

"Help me," she said.

I followed her to a corner of the living room and into a walk-in closet. On the floor was a wooden box. She handed me the crowbar to jimmy up the boards of the box. It was a case of champagne.

We were alone, and she softly said, "I have a bad temper. Sometimes I say things I'm sorry for. I act like a bitch. I hope you'll forgive me."

I assumed she had reference to her bad behavior at the cocktail party the other day. I simply smiled to indicate there were no hard feelings. She seemed pleased and she was rather sweet as women are when they confess gravely to faults of little significance.

We began the champagne, but it was not much of a New Year's Eve party. One man, three women. We decided that we needed Alex. We were going to urge him to leave where he was at once because he was missing out on something here. I don't remember what it was we planned to tell him he was missing out on. Probably, one of the world's great parties. The champagne flowing. Fascinating people. Pauline telephoned him, and he arrived a half hour later. He arrived and sensed at once that we had put our heads together to lure him. From that moment on he gave out a strong scent of gloom and outraged pride.

He wanted us all to leave at once to go somewhere for a drink. Pauline mentioned a new night club reputed to have been opened by New York gangsters. I assumed the look of the underpaid assistant professor. Pauline understood. She offered to pay the cover charge. Alex would not hear of it. And that was the last he said for the rest of the evening. At the night club, Alex stared over Pauline's head. Johanna whispered to me, "Dance with her." We danced. I mean, I attempted to dance with her, but she was wood and steel. Her body was inflexible. She had no rhythm. I attempted conversation. This was a good moment to ask some questions about Ernest Hemingway. But nothing too personal.

"Oh, by the way, is there any truth to the story that Ernest used to study Stendahl for style?"

A small smile. It meant that she wasn't offended, but she didn't want the questioning to go much deeper.

"No. As a matter of fact, Ernest used to complain that he had no style. I don't think he ever studied Stendahl."

"Some people think that Ernest was better in the short story than the novel."

"I agree."

The orchestra stopped. We sat down. Johanna, Pauline, and I made small talk. When we each finished our one and only drink, Alex indicated he was ready to leave. The check and tip was $60 for the one drink each.

We drove Pauline home. Alex would not even say good-night to her. She must have been very hurt.

Early next fall I decided to return to Key West for the Christmas season. I wrote to Pauline to ask her to recommend an inexpensive place to stay. Everything was expensive at that time, she wrote. And she added, stay at my house.

But I never saw her again. A few weeks later I read her obituary in the *New York Times.* And when I finished reading it, a fragment of that New Year's Eve came back to me. It happened just before Alex returned from the first party he had gone to. Somehow F. Scott Fitzgerald's name had come up.

"Oh, Scott was wonderful," Pauline said. "Just wonderful. When Zelda wanted to run off with that French officer, it just about ruined him."

"Why don't you write about Scott?" I said. "In fact, you knew all the interesting people in Paris. Why don't you write about them?"

She froze.

And then she screamed, "I'll write my memoirs when I'm ready to die."

Which event, as you can see, happened not long thereafter.

Southern Connecticut State College

The Hyphenated Ham Sandwich of Ernest Hemingway and J. D. Salinger: A Study in Literary Continuity

By

William Goldhurst

In his influential book on Ernest Hemingway, Philip Young contends that "there is little in Hemingway—and next to nothing of ultimate importance—that has not its precedents" in Mark Twain's *Huckleberry Finn.* Young bases this claim on parallels that emerge from a comparison of Twain's boy-hero Huck and Hemingway's fictional heroes, but especially the prototype-hero Nick Adams as he appears in the story collection *In Our Time.* After a detailed and convincing presentation of similarities, Young concludes that Huck and Nick are "nearly identical persons" who are "very nearly twins." Furthermore, says Young, "the adventures of the generic Nick Adams are the adventures of Huckleberry Finn in our time," the main difference being only that "at the very point where Twain found the boy too complex, and let him go, Hemingway has exploited his condition, and raised him to complicated manhood."[1]

It is the purpose of the present study to show that the process outlined and clarified for us by Philip Young, whereby Hemingway· picked up and developed the life story of a runaway boy, retaining the basic character of Twain's original model but adding particular circumstances from the collective experience of his own generation—that this process did not terminate with Nick's convalescence on the banks of the Big Two-Hearted River, but was picked up and carried forward to its conclusion by J. D. Salinger, who added his own version of the hero to the composite created by Twain and Hemingway. By so doing Salinger rounded out the story of a sensitive boy-adolescent-young man growing up through three generations of American experience.

As Young points out, in general outline the stories of Huck Finn and Nick Adams reflect striking affinities. Both are sagas of initiation; they concentrate on high points in the education of the hero. Both boys flee respectability in the person of pious females; both start out on their journeys with good intentions and naive expectations; both are eye-witnesses to events—among them bloody death—that unsettle the nerves, depress the spirit, and haunt the imagination. Both wind up, in Huck's terminology, with a case of the fantods: they are sickened by the corruption, cruelty, and violence practiced in their respective eras; and they both develop an instinctive protective maneuver of retreat from society to a place of refuge where they can enjoy temporary peace and a feeling of security. "I was powerful glad to get away," says Huck soon after escaping his involvement with the bloody Grangerfords, "and so was Jim to get away from the swamp. We said there warn't no home like a raft, after all." And of young Nick, who has come home wounded from the war and has gone on a fishing trip in the Michigan woods, selecting his campsite with great deliberation, Hemingway tells us, "He was settled. Nothing could touch him. It was a good place to camp. He was there, in the good place." On this occasion Nick's solitude adds to the comforting sense of immunity from the horrors of experience, but at other times he will derive the same sort of contentment from skiing or fishing or drinking with a sympathetic companion. In sum, the place of refuge for both Nick and Huck consists of a retreat into nature, either alone or in the company of other innocents like themselves.

Hemingway's method of presenting the Nick Adams story is also relevant to our present purposes. In the collection entitled *In Our Time* there are seven stories that deal explicitly with this protagonist. They are "Indian Camp," "The Doctor and the Doctor's Wife," "The End of Something," "The Three Day Blow," "The Battler," "Cross Country Snow," and "Big Two-Hearted River, Parts I and II." In addition Nick appears in one of the sketches or interchapters which Hemingway interpolates among the stories in the collection.[2] Specifically this appearance is headed "Chapter VI," and it shows Nick in the midst of a battle scene, shortly after he has been wounded in the spine.

In the years following the publication of *In Our Time* Hemingway brought out several more Nick Adams stories which in retrospect fit logically into place in the sequence of the hero's biography. One of these stories, which Hemingway wrote for the collection *Winner Take Nothing* (1933), is entitled "A Way You'll Never Be." Here

Nick is shown carrying out an absurd and at the same time grotesque mission in the Italian trenches, in an episode that probably occurs sometime after the interchapter where Nick is wounded and sometime before his fishing trip back home in "Big Two-Hearted River." Other Nick Adams stories include "In Another Country," "Ten Indians," "The Killers," "Now I Lay Me," "The Light of the World" (possibly), and "Fathers and Sons."

The first six stories of *In Our Time*, concluding with the sketch headed "Chapter VI," present Nick's experiences in proper chronological sequence. In order to list subsequent episodes *as they occur to Nick*, we need to make a slight rearrangement of the later stories, as follows: 7. "A Way You'll Never Be"; 8. "Big Two-Hearted River"; 9. "Cross Country Snow." Thus reshuffled according to the logic of events within the stories themselves, the hero's biography is developed by way of significant episodes which clearly define his progress from boyhood and adolescence in mid-West America, to the Italian front in World War I, then back home again—somewhat the worse for his war-time experiences; and finally back to Europe again, where we see him contemplating some of the problems that come with maturity. Obviously at this point Nick has come of age; he has weathered some rather severe storms and has suffered agonies; but no doubt he will endure. Or will he?

Before we proceed to our main point of emphasis, we must pause to consider another story that appears in *In Our Time*—not a Nick Adams story, but one that focuses on a Nick Adams-like hero involved in a situation that we might easily work into Nick's history. This is "Soldier's Home," which concentrates on the problems of a returned veteran named Harold Krebs. Here Hemingway has created a classic of twentieth-century portraiture—man alone, the individual almost completely alienated, isolated, *unrelated* to his community and its values. Mother, Father, Companion, Sweetheart—all these Krebs finds either uninteresting or nauseating. But oddly enough, there is Kid Sister, whom Krebs likes. "Do you love me?" Kid Sister Helen asks. "Uh, huh," replies the hero. Not exactly wild passionate devotion. But Helen also wants to know if Harold will come over to the school later that afternoon to watch her play indoor baseball. And at the conclusion of "Soldier's Home," that is exactly what Harold does.

Now we are prepared to demonstrate our contention that the Saga of the Salinger hero is a latter-day recapitulation of the Adventures of Nick Adams.

II

Let us begin at the end, with the death of the hero, and work backward through earlier stages of his life story, more or less as Salinger himself has done in presenting his protagonist. Our point of departure, then, is the suicide of Seymour Glass, which occurs in "A Perfect Day for Bananafish," the lead-off story of the collection *Nine Stories* (1953). We can not overemphasize the importance of this story and its bearing on other episodes in the history of the Salinger hero. Almost all of Salinger's fiction, in fact, may be seen as Events Leading Up to Seymour's Suicide.

Seymour Glass is mentioned in one other story in *Nine Stories*; it is entitled "Down at the Dinghy" and concerns a family crisis in the life of Boo Boo, Seymour's sister, who is married to a man named Tannenbaum. Boo Boo's reference to Seymour indicates that he is already deceased. Seymour figures indirectly in another story in the same collection; Walt, Seymour's brother, plays an important posthumous role in "Uncle Wiggily in Connecticut." Admittedly these materials do not provide much in the way of information about Seymour's character—or the reasons for his suicide. But in the middle and late 1950's and then again in 1965 Salinger published several works which present episodes of Seymour's life story in considerable detail. These are "Raise High the Roof Beam, Carpenters," which shows Seymour on his wedding day in 1942, with several flashbacks alluding to significant episodes in his youth; "Zooey," in which Seymour is already deceased, but is very much alive in the memories of Franny and Zooey; "Seymour—An Introduction," which constitutes a loving portrait of Seymour as a boy and young man rendered by his brother Buddy; and "Hapworth 16, 1924," which takes the form of an interminable letter which Seymour at the age of seven writes from summer camp to the folks back home in New York City. Taken together, these stories represent a fragmented but fairly continuous and coherent biography of Seymour Glass from his early childhood to his death at the age of thirty-one. Traits of character—such as Seymour's extreme intelligence and sensitivity—are established and maintained throughout; significant events—such as Seymour's marriage to Muriel—occur in one story and are developed in another, etc.

Now if we return to the collection *Nine Stories* we see that Salinger has presented episodes in the lives of other boys and young men who might easily contribute their own experiences to round out and complete the biography of a composite Salinger hero. We must include in the total picture the adventures of Holden Caulfield, the adolescent protagonist of *Catcher In the Rye*. This is not to say that Holden or the others are Seymour, or even that Salinger always writes about the same character; but rather that the different heroes have several traits in common, and that their experiences occur in a chronological sequence that logically fits the pattern of a New York City boy growing up during the 1930's and 40's. Thus if the hero (Seymour in this case) is seven years old in 1924, in summer camp in "Hapworth 16, 1924," he is a few years older in the late twenties, playing baseball in Central Park in "The Laughing Man." If in "Raise High the Roofbeam, Carpenters" Seymour is twenty-five years old and a corporal in the Air Corps, then the hero (Sergeant X in this case) of "For Esmé—with Love and Squalor" is twenty-seven, stationed in Europe during the last year of World War II. If in "Bananafish" Seymour is involved with a shallow wife in a hopeless marriage, then in "Pretty Mouth and Green My Eyes" we see the hero a few years earlier (named Arthur in this particular episode) suffering psychological torment from his involvement with an adulterous wife in a similarly hopeless marriage. Furthermore if in the "Pretty Mouth" story Arthur is contemplating a move to Connecticut, presumably to give his marriage a better chance in a more serene atmosphere than New York City, then in "Uncle Wiggily in Connecticut" we see the hero (named Lew in this instance) trying exactly that scheme without success; the adulterous wife of "Pretty Mouth" has developed into the alcoholic and neurotic wife of suburbia.

These several episodes involving the not-Seymour but the Seymour-like Salinger hero accumulate in effect to give us a much fuller and clearer understanding of the Seymour-hero's suicide in "Bananafish." What I am suggesting here is a continuity and a coherence for the biography of the Salinger hero. In its total effect it represents a poignant comic-tragic record of the typical cycle of experiences lived by that generation of Americans who grew up in the 1930's and 40's—boyhood, service overseas during World War II, return, business, marriage, domestic troubles, suburbia, etc. But if the cycle is typical, the individual who lives through it is not; Salinger has created a unique character, as did Twain and Hemingway before him, as a reflector for the specific drifts of American life "in our time." Certain patterns of character and event recur in the Seymour stories as well as the non-Seymour stories and including *Catcher in the Rye*: the hero is extremely intelligent and sensitive; he takes things very hard; he relates in an easy and inspired sort of way to young children; he is a loving person, very much involved with others; but the milieu in general, and in particular the people *closest to the hero* all seem to suffer, in his eyes at least, from the same character defects: they are exploitative, they are shallow, they lack compassion. A point worth emphasizing is that Salinger, again like Twain and Hemingway, is interested in the reaction of the hero at least as much as or possibly more than in the events he encounters.

But this is an overview. Let us look very briefly into the exact progress of the Salinger hero's career. This may be accomplished by rearranging his appearances in chronological sequence and by providing descriptions of each successive episode in his biography. 1) "Hapworth 16, 1924": Salinger's most recent Seymour story, published in *The New Yorker* in 1965. Here we see Seymour at the age of seven, writing to the folks back home in New York City from summer camp. Seymour is extremely precocious, learned, and involved with others. 2) "The Laughing Man": here the hero (unnamed narrator) is nine, plays baseball in Central Park and is deeply affected by the misfortunes of hero-acquaintances, both imaginary and real. 3) "Seymour—An Introduction": here Seymour is deceased, but we are given details of his life when he is around ten. He plays games with his brother, writes *haiku*, and gives lessons in spiritual discipline to the Glass family. 4) *Catcher In the Rye*: the hero (Holden Caulfield) is sixteen, a prep-school drop-out on his own in Manhattan; he winds up physically and emotionally ill as a result of his experiences in the city. 5) "Raise High the Roof Beam, Carpenters": Seymour is twenty-five, on leave from the Army on his wedding day. His erratic behavior, past and present, is emphasized. He agrees tentatively to undergo psychiatric treatment. 6) "For Esmé—with Love and Squalor": the hero is twenty-seven, an Army sergeant stationed in Europe during the last year of World War II. He suffers a nervous breakdown as an aftermath of combat, and suffers further demoralization in contemplating a return to civilian life; is saved from despair by a compassionate youngster. 7) "Pretty Mouth and Green My Eyes": the hero (Arthur) is twenty-nine or thirty, has been discharged from the Army and is attempting to "fit in" in the world of business and married life, is miserable in both. Suffers a psychotic episode. 8) "A Perfect Day for Bananafish": Seymour is thirty-one, has received psychiatric treatment in an Army hospital. On vacation with his wife in Florida, stakes out an isolated position on the beach and has a curious conversation with a child; but finds that it does not provide the usual restoration of spirit. After thirty-one years of extreme psychological ups and downs, the Salinger hero gives up, commits suicide. 9) "Zooey": Seymour has been dead for seven years, but is very much alive in the memory of his brother and sister. Here

Salinger emphasizes Seymour's continuing influence over those sympathetic to his genius; at the same time he underscores the eternal recurrence of Seymour's basic problem—i. e., the spiritual hardships of living in a world filled with unloving people. The sister, Franny, is clearly another incarnation of Seymour himself.

Even in terms of the brief outlines sketched in thus far, we may perceive certain important points of similarity between the Hemingway hero, who usually goes by the name Nick Adams; and the Salinger hero, who most often appears as Seymour Glass. The method of presentation is one such area. Just as Hemingway initially portrayed Nick in his story collection *In Our Time*, then in later years filled in broad gaps in the hero's development by means of additional stories, so Salinger originally established Seymour Glass in the key story of *Nine Stories* and later rounded out the portrait in subsequent stories. A few individual examples at this point might clarify the procedure employed by both authors and strengthen the case for affinity. The content of "Big Two-Hearted River" is explained not by any Nick Adams story in *In Our Time*, but by "A Way You'll Never Be"—published some eight years later. The suicide of Seymour Glass in "Bananafish" is hardly explained at all in any of the stories in *Nine Stories*, but is much more comprehensible on the basis of information about Seymour in "Raise High the Roof Beam, Carpenters"; in fact in the latter story we are informed that Seymour has already made one attempt on his own life a few years earlier. Let me add the point that we also may obtain a clear perspective on Nick and Seymour only after we have rearranged and worked out the chronology of their lives, which has been deliberately obscured and presented in illogical or inverse order by both respective authors. In addition, both Hemingway and Salinger have added immeasurably to our knowledge and understanding of the hero, the kind of person he is and the sort of experiences he has lived through, by extending his career into Nick-like and Seymour-like characters—as in the case particularly of Harold Krebs of "Soldier's Home" and Sergeant X of "For Esmé—with Love and Squalor."

At the same time let us bear in mind the equally important matter of content. We have seen, at least in general terms, that both Hemingway and Salinger are telling the same story about a sensitive boy and young man who on his journey through life encounters various evils in human experience. We are told further how both heroes react in similar ways to these encounters: they are shocked and shaken up, indignant over life's injustices; they suffer physical and psychical injury; at certain points along the way they find themselves sick in body and spirit.

As we look more closely into the two cycles, we discover a surprising number of correspondences in the matter of details. Both heroes, for example, have middle-class family backgrounds and both go on the bum—Nick in "The Battler" and the Salinger hero (as Holden Caulfield) in *Catcher in the Rye*. Both get punched—Nick by the brakeman in "The Battler" and Holden by Stradlater and the animal Maurice in *Catcher*. Both are eye-witnesses to scenes of gruesome violence—Nick in "Indian Camp" and in various war stories; and Holden in *Catcher* when for example he observes the broken body of the suicide, James Castle. Both are permanently impressed by these scenes, and both find it difficult to erase them from memory. Both Nick and the Salinger hero (as Sergeant X in "Esmé") fight in European wars and suffer nervous breakdown following their exposure to combat. Both embrace the value of self-discipline and control in times of nervous stress. "He held on tight for a moment," says Salinger of Sergeant X, as he feels his mind "dislodge itself and teeter, like insecure baggage on an overhead rack." But "holding tight" is a familiar pastime of all of Hemingway's heroes; and the phrase, as well as the nervous condition, is as appropriate to Nick as to Sergeant X. Both heroes, having survived the war, view a return to civilian life with misgiving—Nick in "Cross Country Snow" and Sergeant X in "Esmé." Both have women trouble. Both get married. Both have difficulties adjusting to civilian life after their discharge from the army—see Krebs of "Soldier's Home" and Seymour in "Bananafish." And both turn to the company of children for relief from the pressures and incompatibilities associated with adult relationships.

This last named theme, the idea of the-child-as-refuge, is of course only a very minor element in the Nick Adams-Harold Krebs cycle. Hemingway's hero usually prefers solitude in the out-of-doors, or the company of a drinking buddy or fishing companion with whom he can relax and joke, etc. By way of contrast, Salinger has elevated this single theme into one of the most significant patterns in the life story of his hero. The-child-as-refuge idea occurs in "For Esmé," when the young lady of the title saves the sanity of Sergeant X; it becomes the paramount article of faith for Holden Caulfield in *Catcher*; it is the final, though unavailing recourse of the despairing Seymour in "Bananafish."

Thus Salinger has added a new point of emphasis to the Huck-Nick continuum and by so doing has contributed a fertile idea to American letters. At the same time the difference in emphasis in no way weakens the case for literary continuity urged here. In "Soldier's Home" Helen Krebs pleads with her brother Harold: "Aw, Hare, you don't love me. If you loved me, you'd want to come over and watch me play indoor." A generation later Phoebe Caulfield of *Catcher in the Rye* wants her brother Holden to come see her in the school play. "If you go away," she says, "You won't see me in the play." In her later appearance, apparently, Helen has dropped sports and gone in for public school dramatics. Possibly Hemingway's Helen, though herself quite undeveloped as a character, served as the model for Salinger's other fictional children—Esmé, Sybil Carpenter of "Bananafish," the little boy who limps along the gutter singing the title song of *Catcher in the Rye,* et al. Thus she may be said to illustrate the principle of the literary mustard seed; she demonstrates one way in which Hemingway touched a vital spot in the imagination of his true literary successor.

III

These parallels and elaborations indicate that Hemingway's influence on Salinger operated via the stories in *In Our Time.* Hemingway provided the later author with a general outline of the hero's adventures and reactions; on occasion he planted a small clue in the total pattern which grew into more fully developed characters and themes. But the "passing down" process involved in this literary transaction manifests itself in still another way, when Salinger takes certain stories from the Hemingway collection and alters them to suit his own purposes; the characters, settings, and events emerge subtly transformed, while the essential content of the original is preserved to glimmer under the surface. An example of this practice may be seen in the Salinger story "Uncle Wiggily in Connecticut," which derives from one of the more uneventful stories of *In Our Time,* "The Three Day Blow."

"The Three Day Blow" is a sequel to the preceding story in the collection, "The End of Something," in which Nick Adams breaks off an adolescent romance with his girl friend Marjorie. In the later story Nick and his friend Bill get together in Bill's cottage, get drunk on liquor unknowingly provided by Bill's father, and have a long discussion which ranges over such subjects as books, baseball, fathers, and fishing, but which eventually focuses on Marjorie and the ruptured relationship. Bill thinks Nick is lucky to be out of it, and he warns his friend to be careful not to get involved with Marjorie again. Ironically, this fear gives Nick some satisfaction; it has not occurred to him that he has the option of going back and picking up the thread where he has dropped it. "He felt happy now," says Hemingway of Nick near the end of the story. "There was not anything that was irrevocable. . . . It was a good thing to have in reserve."

In the Salinger story, "Uncle Wiggily in Connecticut," Nick becomes an unhappy housewife named Eloise, while Bill is transformed into a career girl named Mary Jane, who was Eloise's roommate at college. Mary Jane visits Eloise in the latter's home in Connecticut, and the two women get drunk on Eloise's liquor. They talk all afternoon—about books and movies and the good old days at school. But eventually the conversation concentrates on Eloise's lost boy friend (this was Walt Glass, Seymour's kid brother, who was killed in a freak accident while serving with the Army of Occupation in Japan). The gale in the Hemingway story becomes a freezing wind that is turning the recently fallen snow into ice outside, while the two women sit inside in Eloise's warm living room. Salinger has retained— or a better word perhaps would be *recreated*—the atmosphere of intimate talk exchanged between members of the same sex; and in a subtle way he has even preserved Hemingway's closing theme. In the original version, Nick is pleased to discover the idea that "there was not anything that was irrevocable." In "Uncle Wiggily" Eloise suffers emotional anguish when she begins to realize the exact opposite of Nick's discovery—that nothing at all can be or should be preserved from the past—that in effect, "there is not anything that is revocable." In fact, this yearning for the *un*recapturable past, for the fun she had at college and the affectionate banter she exchanged with Walt—this yearning and her refusal to accept present realities have made Eloise into the cynical and despairing person she is. It is as if Salinger had picked up the comforting reflection which Bill placed in Nick Adams's mind, and carried it through to an extreme expression of its pathetic implications. Thus we may conceive of "Uncle Wiggily in Connecticut" as an ironic and pessimistic continuation of "The Three Day Blow."

Finally there is the remarkable case history of a Salinger story entitled "Just Before the War with the Eskimos," which when seen in the light of its origin emerges as an astonishing and highly significant literary performance. "Eskimos" concentrates on a teen-age girl named Ginnie Mannox and her encounter with two boy-men in the New York apartment of Ginnie's girl friend, Selena. The first to appear is Franklin, Selena's brother. He enters nursing a cut finger which is still bleeding. He picks his teeth with his fingernail, scratches a sore on his ankle, and then offers Ginnie some lunch. "I got a half chicken sandwich in my room. Ya want it? I didn't touch it or anything." After Ginnie declines this offer, Franklin tells her that he has been rejected by the Army on account of a heart condition (details of which remain unspecified), and has been working for the past three years in an airplane factory in Ohio. A few minutes later, after some more talk about his cut finger, Franklin exits. In a moment he returns, carrying the half chicken sandwich, which he presses upon Ginnie. It was purchased the night before, he explains, in a delicatessen. Ginnie accepts it reluctantly; then as Franklin goes off to shave, she slips the sandwich into her coat pocket.

The second character to enter the scene is Franklin's friend Eric, a young man in his early thirties who engages Ginnie in conversation while waiting for Franklin to emerge from the bathroom. Eric has worked with Franklin in the airplane factory, though he does not, he says in answer to Ginnie's inquiry, have a bad heart. He notices Ginnie's coat. "It's lovely," he says. "It's the first really *good* camel's hair I've seen since the war." But soon he grows impatient waiting for Franklin. They will be late for Cocteau's "Beauty and the Beast," which he has already seen eight times. By this time the reader at least, if not Ginnie, has a fair idea of the grounds on which Eric has been deferred from military service.

At this point Selena enters with money she owes Ginnie. But Ginnie, who was insistent about the money a little while earlier, now refuses to accept it. In fact she is suddenly in a hurry to leave the apartment. Outside on the street she walks several blocks, dips her hand in her coat pocket to get change for the bus, and discovers the half chicken sandwich. She puts it back in her pocket. "A few years before," Salinger tells us in his closing sentence, "it had taken her three days to dispose of the Easter chick she had found dead on the sawdust in the bottom of her wastebasket." End "Just Before the War with the Eskimos."

Although we must avoid the error of drawing definite conclusions from mere parallels, all the evidence points to a certain Hemingway story as the highly likely source, model, and inspiration for "Eskimos"; and that story is "The Battler," in which Nick Adams encounters a punch-drunk, crazy ex-prize fighter named Ad Francis and his travelling companion Bugs, a soft-spoken Negro ex-convict. Philip Young has described the process by which Hemingway derived "The Battler" from Twain's *Huckleberry Finn*, incorporating various of the novel's details into his story, where they emerged in altered but recognizable form. Huck of course became Nick; the Duke and the Dauphin became Ad and Bugs, to the accompaniment of more sinister overtones. Jim the runaway slave metamorphosed into Bugs—both motherly and affectionate Negroes who watch tenderly over their respective charges, Huck and Ad. But "what was innocent affection in Jim has become something else in Bugs."[3] And Nick Adams, who senses the creepy implications of the relationship between Ad and Bugs, Nick expresses his reaction to these creepy creatures and to the entire episode by leaving the cosy twosome near the fire and walking along the railroad tracks for some time before realizing that he is holding a freshly made sandwich which the obliging and mannerly Bugs has placed in his hand just before his departure. Nick puts the sandwich in his pocket and moves on to other adventures. It was, just for the record, a ham sandwich.

The effect of Young's analysis is to suggest that we cannot read "The Battler" with complete understanding if we fail to take into account its source in Mark Twain. By the same token we cannot understand the full effect of Salinger's fiction unless we consider its double descent from Twain and Hemingway. In "Just Before the War with the Eskimos" we find a compelling example that illustrates the process in operation.

If Huck became Nick, then in Salinger's story Huck-Nick became Ginnie Mannox. This composite protagonist, Huck-Nick-Ginnie, runs into two curious characters named Franklin and Eric, who are clearly Bugs and Ad refurbished for their appearance in a later generation. Franklin's vaguely described heart condition dates back to its original appearance in Ad Francis. "You know how I beat them?" Ad asks Nick, referring to his successes in the ring. "My heart's slow. It only beats forty a minute. . . ." Bugs' generous offer of a ham sandwich becomes the half chicken sandwich, bought the night before in a delicatessen, which Bugs-Franklin gives to Nick-Ginnie in what is surely one of the most complicated alimentary transactions in the history of literature. In Twain's story, Huck's adventure takes place on the river; in Hemingway's, along the railroad tracks; in Salinger's, along the route travelled by taxicabs and buses. But regardless, it is still the mainstream of life down which all these heroes journey and bump into all sorts of creeps and weird-os. And the crowning touch, the thing to be stressed, is that the concluding point in both Hemingway's and Salinger's stories is identical: the ham-chicken sandwich is the vehicle by which each author expresses the shocked reaction of the hero to what he has just seen and heard.

Huck and Jim, the Duke and the Dauphin, Nick Adams, Bugs and Ad, Ginnie and Selena, Franklin and Eric—all of these fuse into each other, change places and switch around, play their roles sometimes merged and sometimes singly, we could trace all the changes and mutations and permutations involved, but believe me, it would take more hyphenated character names and ham-chicken sandwiches than any reader needs or should by right tolerate. But generally and briefly speaking: Bugs and Ad are creeps of a certain sort and they give Nick the creeps. Franklin and Eric are creeps of a similar sort, in the implied sexual relationship in both stories; but Franklin and Eric are creeps *sans* the violence and practice in hobo-living; but in any case they give Ginnie the creeps. And to top it off, Salinger adds another creepy touch to the story by making Ginnie a bit of a creep herself, as we discover in the last few creepy words concerning the dead Easter chick, the final creepy flourish of "Just Before the War with the Eskimos."

But now we must step back a few paces from Eskimos and Uncle Wiggilys, from Salinger himself and the Seymour Glass stories to attain a properly distant view of the composite hero I have here been describing. There are, first of all, obvious points of difference in the Hemingway and Salinger cycles. In the Nick Adams stories the emphasis is upon the hero's being hurt, physically and spiritually, by repeated exposure to episodes of violence, ranging in effect from painful to gruesome to horrible. In the adventures of the Salinger hero, although instances of physical violence are occasionally present, the author's emphasis is on the anguish the hero suffers in interpersonal relations. In addition, there seems to be a deepening pessimism, an increasing sense of nervous strain, alienation, and hopelessness as the hero is picked up and developed by Twain, Hemingway, and Salinger. Huck takes things hard, to be sure; but he always has the ability to bounce back. Nick, though he suffers more intensely than Huck, can always seek out "the good place"—which will provide nourishment and give him enough spiritual capital to carry on. But the Salinger hero from the beginning knows that there is no such place; Holden Caulfield says so explicitly in *Catcher in the Rye*: "You can't ever find a place that's nice and peaceful, because there isn't any." We might also point out that the idea of the-psychiatrist-as-a-possible-refuge (though Salinger obviously places no confidence whatsoever in its efficacy) comes into the cycle in its third phase, as the hero Holden-Sergeant X-Arthur-Seymour emerges into the mid-twentieth century, when so many spiritual problems are neatly assigned to the neurotic-psychotic categories.[4]

At the same time the element of humor, which animated Twain's version of the hero, then died down in Hemingway's, springs to life again in the exploits of Salinger's adventurer. This precious element reconciles us, to some extent at least, to the Salinger hero's predicament—and perhaps by extension to the melancholy situation of man in the modern era. We can't after all feel terribly *tragic* about Seymour Glass: we remember him with too much laughter.

I must stress in conclusion that I have no intention of suggesting here that any of the authors mentioned might be considered *less* original for having derived materials from their predecessors. Far from it! After Twain, the Adolescent Hero Wounded by Experience becomes in essence a literary convention to which subsequent fictionists contribute, in a highly creative and original operation, their own unique protagonists. Yet we can assume a profound indebtedness on the part of each successive author, an admiration for the artist who inspired his own efforts, that (fortunately for students in this particular area) has sometimes found direct expression. "All modern American literature comes from one book," Hemingway remarked in *Green Hills of Africa.* "It's the best book we've had." The reference is of course to Mark Twain's *Huckleberry Finn.* And we have a letter, summarized for us by Carlos Baker in his recent Hemingway biography, which J. D. Salinger wrote to Ernest Hemingway in 1946, advising Hemingway that he, J. D. Salinger, was extremely grateful for their get-togethers in Europe during the closing phases of World War II, and that the talks they had had were for him "the only hopeful minutes of the entire war"; that furthermore, he was hereafter in a frame of mind to appoint himself "National Chairman of the Hemingway Fan Club." Salinger goes on to mention something about the work he has been doing on a book about a youngster named Holden Caulfield and his kid sister Phoebe.[5] One cannot resist thinking of these meetings between Hemingway and Salinger as symbolic personal encounters reflecting the literary transactions herein considered.

Yet for this commentator at least, the most remarkable and vivid aspect of the entire process is the way in which Hemingway himself, in his own person, incorporated the complete Huck-Nick-Seymour adventure. From a Huck Finn-like childhood, to a Nick Adams youth, to a Seymour Glass conclusion, the Hemingway biography reflects, encompasses, and dramatizes a cycle covering almost one hundred years of American experience, lending to it a fascinating and fatal air of inevitability.

University of Florida

[1] *Ernest Hemingway*. (New York: Rinehart 1952), pp. 203-208.

[2] These sketches were originally published in Paris in 1924 under the title *in our time*.

[3] *Ernest Hemingway*, pp. 206-207.

[4] The cycle initiated by Twain and carried forward by Hemingway and Salinger by no means terminates with Seymour's suicide in "Bananafish," but has been developed by other American authors. The most recent reincarnation, and surely one of the most interesting, is Philip Roth's *Portnoy's Complaint* (1969). Here the relations-between-the-hero-and-his-parents comes in for far greater emphasis than it received in earlier phases; the refuge of the boy-hero is masturbation; the comic dialect of Twain and Salinger assumes the form of Yiddish phrases and dirty words; and the psychiatrist-as-refuge idea is advanced to an absurd extreme: all the episodes are evaluated within the framework of psychiatry, while the entire story is narrated from the couch in the psychiatrist's office.

[5] *Ernest Hemingway A Life Story* (New York: Scribners 1969), pp. 420, 646.

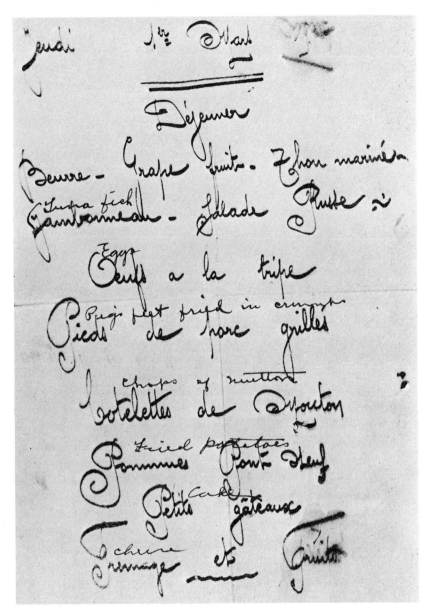

Menu from the *Chicago* for Thursday, March 1, 1917.   English translation by Col. Clark.

C. E. Frazer Clark and ambulance 35610 in the *parc* at 21 Rue Raynovard, Paris, April, 1917.

This is the Way It Was on the *Chicago* and At the Front: 1917 War Letters

By

Col. C. E. Frazer Clark, Ret.

The steamship *Chicago* was one of the many smoky, ungainly, un-glamourous war workships of France's Atlantic fleet of converted passenger liners. She had been built for something better, but the war had tarnished her brightwork.

Launched from the St. Nazaire ways in 1908,[1] this Cie. Generale Transatlantique ship was christened the *Chicago* with a covetous eye on the attractive American tourist traffic for which the French Line was ambitious. She was a coal-burning, twin-screw, steel-hulled steamer with a spar deck stem to stern for ocean watching, and three decks below. For her day, she was fast, 17 knots, middling-large at 10,502 gross tons, wireless equipped, and a tempting prize for the German U-boats.

The *Chicago* shuttled her zig-zag way between Bordeaux, her port of registry, and pier 57 in New York, making the round trip in a month of detour-slow travel. Hundreds of adventure-seeking young volunteers going in Belgian relief, American Ambulance Field Service, or Red Cross work took passage on the *Chicago* for France and the war—one such passenger in late May of 1918 was Ernest Hemingway.

Hemingway, Bill Horne, Fred Spiegel, Ted Brumback, among so many other young Americans before them, had decided that "going over" was the thing to do, something they wanted to do.[2] For all, it was an adventure in youthful idealism. Few were prepared for the grim realities.

From the seawater sloshing down the *Chicago* companionways to the leeching mud of the trenches, there was an unforgettable impact to those raw days where ideals met trudging fact in their own kind of

153

turmoil. It comes through in the letters written home, as it would in the literary work born of those times.

In special cases, like Hemingway's, where war, hero, agony, adventure, and disillusionment met at the crossroads, the experiences need to be remembered. They're important. The author tells us this: "I thought," wrote Hemingway later, "about what a great advantage an experience of war was to a writer. It was one of the major subjects and certainly one of the hardest to write truly of . . . ."[3]

Only those who were members of the clan will know and appreciate these experiences perfectly—it's a matter of clan principle. How it was driving an ambulance along the shell-ripped roads in the lee of Mort Homme or through the mud and wreakage of the Basso Piave, is a matter among the clansmen, and will remain so.

Many of the men who sailed on the *Chicago* and drove the Fords and Fiats are gone. Some who remain are patient enough to try and tell something of what it was like on the *Chicago* and at the front, although they know you can't really know exactly how it was.

Here are the war letters of one clansman—one of the young adventurers from up in Michigan who preceeded Hemingway over on the *Chicago*, took the night train to Paris, rendezvoused at 21 Rue Raynouard, and drove the Fords at the front.

Col. C. E. Frazer Clark, like so many of the young volunteers, paid his way to this adventure. He bought passage, steerage, on the *Chicago*, bought his uniform, paid duty on the cigarettes sent to the front from home, and donated his pay to the service. It was something they all believed in—this is the way it was.   —C.E.F.C., Jr.

ON THE CHICAGO

Pier 57
February 19, 1917

Dear Folks:

Just a line to let you know I am thinking of you as we pull out. A few more minutes now and we sail, so I must hurry. Will cable from Bordeaux when I arrive, so do not worry. There are almost 100 fellows here. Some going in Belgian relief, some in Red Cross work and some in American Ambulance, so the Dutch will not take such a chance. Well, God Bless you all.

154

Dear Folks,

This is the 6th day out and very rough. Everyone has been sick more or less, but I have continued very well. All I do is eat and sleep and it is agreeing with me. The damp salt air makes one very sleepy and we all take advantage of it.

This is a good, steady boat although not as fast as the "California" or "Olympic" upon which I last traveled, but I like its accommodations better. I have a stateroom by myself which is very comfortable and tidy and the meals are good but very long. You know it is the French custom to serve everything, no matter what, as a separate course—consequently our meals last very long. Petit Dejeuner (breakfast) at 8:00, Dejeuner at 11:30 and bouillion at 4:00, then dinner at 6:30. I'll add to this later. Pardon the writing but the boat pitches so it is difficult to do much.

All the ambulance fellows had gotten together and booked steerage. Since we were paying for our own passage we wanted to economize—we didn't have a lot of money and we would have to buy uniforms and whatnot in Paris—but we did want to stay together. None of us wanted to worry our families, so we wrote them the brighter side of things. Actually, the accommodations were fierce. Steerage was three decks down, well below the water line. The ventilation was bad and we spent a lot of time on our small deck at the stern, which shook all the time, being right over the screws. We had bunks and mattresses, no springs. The bunk frames were welded to the ship's hull and were in tiers of three. All the port holes were sealed and blacked out, so no light would shine out for the submarines to see. We had acetylene lamps, which were comparatively bright and not subject to the swaying of the ship, so there was no candle-like flickering.

We were issued a kind of mess kit—a cup-like bowl, a plate, a knife, fork, and spoon. We kept these for the whole trip, cleaning them after each meal in a big container of soapy water set out by the steward. We came to depend on our fingers and the bread that was served with every meal.

We'd line up for our meals—the steward, at breakfast, for ex-
ample, would put a big red cloth on a kind of buffet table.
Then he would set out a big bowl of a kind of porridge-like
gruel or a thick soup. We would all dip in our big cups and
pick up some bread. There were chairs with little arms on
them, like a classroom chair, welded to the deck around the
room and we would eat at these. Coffee would be set out in
another bowl following the porridge, and we would all go
help ourselves, using our same porridge cups.

A menu would be posted for lunch and dinner. I sent one
home. On the whole, the steerage food was horrible, but they
made it look good. This didn't bother us; we were young and
enterprising, and we soon found the steward most accommo-
dating. We would bribe him and he would disappear up to the
first-class kitchen, soon to return with many good things.

We also discovered that in the evening if we tipped our stew-
ard, he would let us go up the gangway into the first-class
area and mingle with the first-class passengers—and there were
some very nice young ladies of our own age, mostly nurses.
We would explain that we were third-class and ask them not
to tell their steward, or he would throw us back into steerage.
The gals thought it was a great joke and promised not to tell—
so all the way over we had the pleasant company of "first
class" ladies, but we had to eat and sleep in the bowels of the
ship.

2-10-70
cefc

On board "Chicago"
February 26, 1917

Dear Folks,

Several days have passed since I last wrote and we are now well
within the "danger" zone, only about 4 days separating us from the
coast of France. This boat has proved to be very slow, twelve days
enroute, and they are very monotonous. We travel slowly by day in
order to avoid smoking funnels, then by night we speed. Night is the

worst of all because you can't venture on deck safely, everything is shrouded in black, and we plough along in total darkness, every port-hole plugged and not a light showing. We haven't had a clear night yet, and you can't imagine how dark everything is.

We have had boat and life-preserver drills every day, but no one thinks anything about it. The lifeboats are ready to be launched at any minute. We'll be surprised at almost any time by the ship's bugle announcing a drill—the crew will tell us to take our positions in the lifeboats, so we all go to our boats and stand by. The boats are swung out from the davits, and we all get in, as if we were going to lower away. Then the boats are swung back in, and we get back out. It's all done very meticulously.

We passed an English freighter yesterday, the only sign of life yet seen. Day before yesterday we struck very bad weather—a real storm at sea which made us lose 125 miles in the day's run. I thought the boat was going to break in two. Waves dashed over us coming way up to the bridge, stoved in our railing and other damage. The wind was fearful, picking up what seemed waves and lashing them against us like bullets, just like some of those Hopkins seascrapes.

I guess I didn't tell you about our gun mounted aft. We have a long 75mm rifle on the stern which is all in readiness. It can be swung around completely 360 degrees for use against submarines, or ele-vated for protection against airplanes. The gun crew are all French marines and not part of the ship's crew. They practice every day, once in the morning and once in the afternoon, at regular hours, so we get used to the crash of the gun, I guess. They pick out a floating barrel or other piece of debris and register in on it. It certainly is a wicked-looking piece, and we all would like to see it in action.

We have a valuable cargo on board, seventy-five Ford chassis, air-planes, food, and munitions, plus horses in the hold, so I guess we're what the Germans would consider a valuable prize.

I surely do feel fine and hope you are all not worrying about me but I suppose you are over the extended length of this trip.

What we didn't write home about was the party we were hav-ing on about the sixth night out. We were making such a racket that the captain suddenly appeared before us. He was a small man with a mustache, but with all the braid and colored ribbons on his chest and with his cap on, he made an impressive sight. He was furious, so angry he could hardly speak. I'll never forget what he said—"I am ze captain of ziss ship and I'm trying my best to get ziss ship through zee zub-marine zone. The ship ahead of uz haz gone down, ze ship be-hind uz haz been torpedoed, and you men are making zuch a noize zat zee Germans can hear uz for miles in all directions. And you're going down unless you be quiet from now on. If you're not quiet, I'll put you in irons, I have zat authority." In the silence that followed, he turned and walked out. He had laid us all out, and from that night on we behaved. The next day, as if to emphasize his message, we were up on deck and here was all this wreckage floating by—bloated horses, barrels, crates, planks—which brought back to us emphatically what this captain was trying to impress upon us—that this was a most serious occupation that we were engaged in.

2-10-70
cefc

On board "Chicago"
February 28, 1917

Dear Folks,

Today everyone was on edge. All the boats are swung over and the gun crew is at its station. This is the real danger zone immediately off the coast, say 400 miles. Last night we remained practically sta-tionary, hardly moving. We presumed the captain wanted to make the run in daylight when the gun is effective.

We passed several barrels this AM and we all thought they were mines. Another dead horse floated by, tending to cheer us pilgrims up. I envy you people with newspapers. We are kept absolutely in the dark about news of any sort but it has been rumored that since we sailed they have got seventeen ships. Of course we don't know if that be so. I am in hopes of hearing the latest American news when we land, and I hope we are not at war.

We are due to land late tonight or tomorrow morning. It is now March 1. We are in the Bay of Biscay and tomorrow sail up the Gironde River. Bordeaux is in Gascony and I am going to take a train for the ten-hour run into Paris.

Hill 304
May 2, 1917

Dear Folks,

Spring has finally come. The weather is clear and the country beautiful. The topography reminds me much of Ann Arbor and if it were not for the guns and troops, I'd feel perfectly at home.

Do you remember teasing me about rats in our attic once? Well I had the real thing happen to me here the other night. I was aroused by some movement on my blanket and was startled to find a large rat enjoying himself there. You can imagine how long he stayed. I went back to sleep but he must have returned, as in the morning my neck was badly scratched by his claws. I figured that in crawling over me there, I unconsciously moved and he jumped, digging his claws into me. You can easily trace his feet on my skin. Believe me, the iodine I got in New York has been freely used and it is mending nicely. Now I have them fooled. I broke four wine bottles in half and inserted the legs of my cot in each thereby insulating myself. You would surely be surprised at what one gets used to here. Remember how I used to stand in horror of germs? Well, I'm on friendly terms even with them now—eating with my jacknife, etc.

I just thought I was killed. I'm writing with my back to a cloth-covered window, as glass will not stand the concussion. A big shell landed nearby and blew the cloth and dirt in on me, but I'm almost used to that now. The French have a saying that once one lets go near you yet touches you not, you are immune henceforth. I've had several such pleasant experiences and feel quite immune as a result.

This is a wonderful life, filled with the expected, yet never growing monotonous. Luck is no word for it. We have three postes de secours (Hill 304, Mort Homme, and Esnes) all of which have been given us by the French Ambulance, so you can imagine what that means. On one run we go parallel with the German trench in plain view. The road is wicked, so speed is impossible; but we enjoy it. Queer psychology! At the turn in the road lie three ambulances, all shot to hell as it were, yet we like it! You wouldn't recognize me. I'm fatter and beautifully tanned by sun, wind and rain—the very picture of health. After twenty-four hours of post duty and strenuous work with no sleep, of course one feels rather pepless, but a good day's rest back in Headquarters quickly puts you on your feet. Remember how we used to change tires in the basement? The other night I had to change one by light of star shells and speeded up by a few shells, etc. Believe me, I'm thankful now for that early training.

Everyday here is the same, and the end, as I said, seems at times almost beyond our horizon. We all do hope, however, for a speedy one as it is terrible beyond description, and one gets desperately sick of the continual slaughter. I am "home" now having but shortly returned from poste.

This part of France is beautiful. Of course everything is in ruins but even they sometimes seem beautiful. The apple trees in a little orchard back of us are in blossom now and with them and the birds one can easily forget the war. When we come in from duty we make out our reports on men carried, distance covered, gasoline used, etc., then get our cars in readiness, wash them, disinfect them and go "en repos". We usually have several days rest, unless an attack comes, in which case we are on reserve and then we write a letter or two and make up for lost sleep. You know we are in the French army and have a French Lieut. over us in command. They are always particular about the officer they give us as they know our peculiarities. Our French Lieut. is a "Count" and we rather like him. His English is fair, and he sees to it that we never lose out in our dealings. Occasionally when we have time he drills us in French salutes and etiquette as we are often reviewed by some General. The other day one dropped in on us and took us by surprise. We all lined up and he came down the line saluting and shaking hands with each of us. You know they are quite effusive; they salute, shake hands, then shake hands and salute, and one must be careful or he gets all mixed up. One of our fellows put his pipe in his pocket and burned his pocket out while going through formalities with the general. We do have some funny experiences. The other night one of the boys got lost on the road. You see we never use any lights so it is a simple matter. He made out a dim form by the roadside, drew up to it and got out. He next politely asked where he was and receiving no response, naturally thought the gentleman was deaf. He approached nearer and found it was one of these jackasses they use in carrying ammunition up to the lines. But that was mild to some of them. I have no trouble in changing Ford tires now; in fact, I can do it quite quickly—sometimes we use steel-studded tires and they skid terribly but they are good protection against hob nails in the road. The soldiers have big hob nails in their shoes, and when regiments continually pass over it, there are always chances for numerous punctures. My car runs like a charm and I have the best gas average in the section. That is very important as gas is very scarce. I average 10 kilometers to one litre of gas.

A funny thing just occurred. The boche planes have been flying over our heads this AM as it is very clear for observation. One just sounded particularly close so we all ran out to watch the shells from our anti-aircraft guns explode around it. They make white cotton puffs like this

O O O O O O O O O O O O O O

and although we get used to it, still it always makes a very pretty picture. We have never seen them hit one, altho two have been brought down recently.

We were standing under an oak tree watching when the shrapnel cases began to whistle down around us and you should have seen that crowd scatter! We have an abri or bomb proof here which of course we never use. It is about twenty feet below ground with a steel-vaulted roof covered with many layers of stone. The Germans are very prodigal with their ammunition and only send about one shell to every three or four of ours. So you see there is no danger. Last evening after supper Liddell and I took a walk down in the village and wandered thru the old battered church. Shells have come thru the roof even and have made a most desolate ruin. We climbed up into the belfry and sanctimoniously rang the chimes for the first time since the war began. When we came down I feared lest we be arrested, but they (the French troops) think that we Americans are crazy anyway, so humor us.

Argonne
May 24, 1917

Dear Mother,

Tomorrow I go up to a very quiet artillery poste. I say "quiet" in the sense of making "runs," but it is very noisy otherwise. I have found a young French Lieutenant up there whose mother is Scotch, and he naturally speaks English very well. He shows me his batteries and has let me fire them. They are so cleverly concealed that one can literally walk right over them yet never see them. Suddenly a shell comes whistling thru the air and explodes down on the hill shaking everything in the neighborhood. He points to his map of the boche positions and says "That's this battery of 150's—we'll throw a few into them." Then with a roar the whole battery in succession tears one—then silence reigns again. I have climbed an observation point and have seen the enemy thru the most powerful glasses way back of their own lines. I have taken quite a liking to the Artillery. Their secret is in remaining well concealed, as once the enemy airman finds them they are done for. It's all a great game.

Dombasle
June 10, 1917

Dear Mother,

This is one of a few Sundays I feel at all "dressed up." Lansing Paine, our Secretary of State's nephew, gave me a good hair-cut and then with a prehistoric bath by means of a stone basin and spring water, icy cold, I feel quite respectable. But I can't hand myself much credit for getting dressed on this day in particular as I only discovered a moment or two ago that it was Sunday.

We have just had our dinner—I'll send you the menu (Sunday noon).

1. Saummone—(Salmon or otherwise)
2. Rosbif—(We call it beef for decency's sake)
3. Pomme de terre puree (Potatoes twice weekly)
4. Salade (Garlic leaves and oil, from our garden)
5. Fromage Roqueforte (Phew!! Lord only knows how long course 5 had been dead!)

And then for drinking we have water and "Pinard" or red wine which helps sterilize the water. So you can see we are not starving by any means.

Mort Homme
June 21, 1917

Dear Mother,

The "boche" are laying in shells now back of us but at a safe distance. It is surprising how soon you get accustomed to them, providing of course that you know they are not getting too close. My car has been hit several times but not when I was in it. They usually give you about three seconds warning with their screech and I can usually manage to do many things in that short space.

162

I suppose you know that the chief of young Cliff Hanna's section, was killed day before yesterday. It is deplorable as it should not have happened. He was riding in an aeroplane with the French pilot when brought down.

I was almost lost last night on the road but a dead horse saved me. Said horse had been at this corner of the road for several weeks and somehow or other one always knew when he was in the vicinity. So when the "wind" mark was discovered I knew exactly where I was. For months now I have driven on the worst roads in utter blackness without a light and perhaps you can imagine what funny predicaments you get into. One of our boys pulled up beside a crowd of mules the other night and enquired the way before he discovered what congenial company he was in. Another of our boys went all to pieces and had to be carried in his own ambulance back to headquarters. He was sent home, poor devil, and none of us has ever heard from him. He cried all the time—couldn't talk even without crying— one of those queer cases known as "shellitis."

Jubecourt
August 3, 1917

Dear Mother, Father and Ci:

This is the 3rd anniversary of France's entry into the war, but as yet it is not a day for rejoicing. We are enroute back to the lines and are now resting in a little village quite near the old battlefield of the Marne.

It has rained the last three days. About the usual thing here, rain. I wear the heavy hob-nailed French army shoe and my feet do not get wet.

We have come slowly by day stages thru many ruined villages destroyed by the boche in the earlier days of the war. In some of these one sees signs of life springing up here and there amidst the ruins, but as a rule they are still deserted and present a desolate view even to an American. In most of these villages one can find no evidence of shell fire—just pure wanton destruction. We finally reached our present cantonment, after ploughing thru buckets of water and thru awful French mud, which lives up to the native characteristic for affection. We were a dreary crowd indeed—mud from head to foot and pretty well soaked thru. We found billets in what had once been a lean-to, one-horse hospital. Do you remember that picture on the pier just before sailing of the old *Chicago* crowd? Well I should never tell or even mention this to you but we take pride, we fellows, in the noble way some of our friends have gone and I know you will understand. Of course that crowd was split into several sections of which for some unknown reason we have been luckiest. Two sections in turn relieved us at Dombasle and four men were lost, where we only lost one and ours from shell shock. Now we are back in it once more and I know our old luck will hold. I shall stay the limit of my time and perhaps a few days over if the section be hard pressed, so do not expect me before September 1st and do not worry.

Two days ago I had a run to a large base hospital. A young intern strolled up to talk with me and display his English after we had unloaded. I asked him to take me through his ward which he was very proud to do. And here is one of those coincidences which one runs into so often. When we had finished, he suddenly beamed and asked me if I wouldn't like to visit a wounded comrade. Of course I was instantly interested when a nurse pardoned herself to tell us he had died that morning. I felt bad, but determined to find out who he was because we are all a big fraternity in this service, each section knowing and visiting with the other. I finally had to go into the morgue to find him. But such a wonderful attention! He lay in a closed casket with his name plate and legend over his head, and over his heart had been pinned the ribbons of the Croix de Guerre and Medaille Militaire—France's greatest honor. At the head of his coffin stood a little American flag and draped around the walls was the tri-color of our ally France. The next morning we drove over as a body to do him homage. There were only a handful of Americans there, naturally, but the French staff joined in, and it was a funeral which one could not have improved upon. A French priest delivered the sermon, a lovely one which inspired us all, even though we did not perhaps understand it all—and then the customary Croix du bois, a wooden cross which is France's tribute to private and officer alike. His name was John Newlin of S. S. U. 29 and was killed at the very poste from which I have written you so many letters.[4] Such is chance indeed.

Our shack is in the front yard, as it were, of an aviation park and every spare moment we fellows stroll up to watch them come in and go out. There are some very famous "aces" or "stars", as we would say here, and we see some wonderful flying. Last night I was talking with a Sargent and we spotted a biplane coming in; he was telling me of the tendency to fall of said machine, when away she fell. The pilot escaped uninjured but the machine was wrecked—all of which inspires one for aviation.

Rampont
August 11, 1917

Dear Mother,

For three weeks steadily now we have had nothing but rain which
makes us all feel pretty crabby. All night long and all day long and
the roads are terrible. Our cars sink right into the stuff and keeping
clean is well nigh impossible.

The boche have been making things interesting lately. They have a
new gas shell which we can neither hear nor sense. The effects become apparent about six hours after and are terrible. Yesterday we
evacuated 347 victims, some with arms and hands burned terribly
and faces discolored even though with masques on. They cough like
consumptives and if one touches them, it becomes contagious and
poisons your skin too. And also they have a new howitzer, two in
fact, the 88mm and 130mm (both Austrian) which throw shells at
incredible speed. They give no whistling warning, and it is nothing
but luck that will pull you thru. Last night our chief, Alec Hender-
son, was shot thru both legs and another one of the boys, Dominic
Rich, was hit in the arm. Luckily in both cases, however, we do not
think any bones were broken, although it is too early to be positive.
They had just pulled in at a new poste to look it over and had been
told to get into the abri but American like, had insisted upon turning
around first and getting ready to pull out when whiz-bang—and both
got it.

Lately I have been handling two cars, my Ford and the White
camion for emergency runs. She (White) is a wonderful car, powerful
and speedy and capable of handling 20 cases (sitting) in a pinch. My
Ford runs well but none too well. Number 2 pumps oil and forever
fouls the plug. We have no new piston rings so I trust to luck and
new plugs. We have been using Champion but have been having
trouble with them. I used to think I knew a little about my old Ford
but now after changing transmission bands, axles and a radiator, not
to speak of grinding valves, I realize how little I knew.

Rampont
August 18, 1917

Dear Father,

We are on the eve of a big French offensive and our section, or as I
can almost say, my section, is working the position known as "Mort

165

Homme" or "Dead Man's Hill." We worked Hill 304 and Mort Homme in the old days, so have the advantage of knowing the roads a great deal. By the time this reaches you, it will be all over, so no news will be good news.

I might add that Mort Homme lies on the west side of Verdun which is only a short distance away, say 8 or 10 miles.

The attack will begin soon, in two or three days and our section will be in the attack and again the counter-attack.

Mort Homme
August 23, 1917

Dear Mother,

Since my last letter I have been terribly busy and have had to postpone my letter writing. But now I have a breathing spell and shall try and describe my strange adventures. I have been through a big attack and no one could really give all the strange occurrences justice.

For five days and nights our artillery never ceased firing. One continuous roar, as the passing of many heavy wagons over a cobblestone road. At night the horizon was red with flashes of batteries, star shells, and signals from the trenches. For five days and nights we waited—that fearful suspense which tries your very soul, and then the day came. At dawn a few mornings ago the rumblings suddenly ceased. Then with a shout which we easily heard, our brave allies went over the top. We knew our work would commence and we were on edge, every car ready for action. I, as one of the officers, was so unfortunate as to draw the lot of staying at the base and directing things, so you can imagine how blue I felt. Away went the cars, everyone happy to be again in action and I left behind. But hardly had they gone when another call came in over our phone for every available car. I had my chance and soon was back in it, but so different! An offensive! The rest all seems so much like a movie drama that I can hardly realize that I was not an actor. I was so hard up for drivers that I pressed one of our French mechanics into service. After ten minutes driving we pulled into a poste slightly back from our advanced poste and discovered a spike in my rear tire. I told off the Frenchman to change tires while I took his car and went on. Over a road covered with debris of all sorts from dead horses on, I felt my way (5:00 AM), and finally, amidst all the din and confusion, found our *poste de secours*. From then on it was a case of load-ing, driving, and returning, and you should have seen the section go at it. As our general afterwards said, we drove so fast and made so many trips that he thought there were no other cars in France but Fords. During the heaviest fighting (five hours) we carried 750 wounded over a distance of 3290 kilometers, which smashes all American Ambulance records. It wasn't until afternoon that the Ger-man artillery made it particularly unpleasant for us and then the way the boys responded was magnificent. And for my own part I can easily say I never before faced such shelling. But the old luck hangs by us still and no one was even scratched. Just to show you, as I came up in the afternoon, shrapnel was bursting over a bad turn in the road. Just before me as in a play, a six-horse team was galloping, dragging along behind a 75 gun moving up. He turned off across a little valley giving me the road. A high explosive burst before me about 100 yards, overturning a wagon and freeing the wild horses but injuring no one. The question was, should I stop for a moment or shoot ahead. Well, to make a long story short, I gave my little car all she could take and we were at the poste in no time. There hun-dreds of boche prisoners were huddled together in a communication trench while others were helping the stretcher teams bringing in the French wounded. German wounded were everywhere and I admired the splendid attention the French gave them. The Germans were a queer lot, some very young and others quite old. They all seemed pretty forlorn and glad to be finished with it all. We took 400 un-wounded prisoners, and I have more German helmets than I can ever bring home. Never had I had such a conglomeration of sensations.

Bread and cheese were our rations and the dust was frightful! We are a red-eyed dirty crowd but very well satisfied with our record and now stand in order for a position of honor.

At night the boche bomb us or shell us, which makes it interesting. Five nights ago they dropped bombs on the nearby hospital of Vad-elancourt and killed twenty-seven and wounded forty-three. They call that fair play and try to make explanations but I have seen many, many "dirty tricks" as the saying is, done by these Germans and have gotten to hate them as the rest. Just think, they flew low and emp-tied their machine guns into the already wounded at a big hospital displaying the Red Cross!

Four days ago shrapnel brought down a boche plane near us here, and several of us chased over to view the machine. The pilot had been killed in air and the machine fell very freakily unguided and landed without injuring the observer. One of us in running was mistaken by some wild Moroccans as being the escaping observer and he escaped by leaving portions of his trousers behind. We have many such funny things which help to relieve the monotony. I was almost marched off in a group of Germans by mistake. Our uniforms when covered with dust much resemble theirs. The boche will not believe us when we say we are Americans, as they have been led to believe our entry was a big bluff.

August 26, 1917

Dear Mother,

I have a little secret for you which I know will make you and father feel pretty happy. Three other chaps and myself have been cited by the General of our division and in about a week your son will be decorated with a Croix de Guerre (War Cross) with a silver star, and for your sake I am very very happy. It should help to console you for all the worry that I have caused. It is too bad that you will not be able to see the ceremony, as it is always a wonderful sight. We lucky ones will stand with other soldiers before their regiments and band and will have them pinned on our palpitating chests by General Dedrain. It will be a great day for me truly. In a week or so I hope to be able to run home to see you for a short while. Don't worry—with love—FRAZER

---

[1] Data on the *Chicago* was supplied by Mr. Robert A. Cole, Librarian, Sociology and Economics Department, Detroit Public Library.

[2] Jay Robert Nash, "Ernest Hemingway The Young Years & The Chicagoans Who Knew Him," *ChicagoLand*, V (August 1968), 19-25. An excellent recollection of Hemingway in The War.

[3] *The Green Hills of Africa* (New York: Scribners, 1935), p. 70.

[4] John V. Newlin, Princeton '17, was on the *Tiger* staff with Fitzgerald.

"Over a road covered with debris of all sorts from dead horses on, I felt my way (5:00 AM) and finally, amidst all the din and confusion found our *poste de secours*."

When Ernest Hemingway's Mother Came to Call

By

Winifred Healey

The "north woods" was not just a pleasant descriptive phrase in our family. It meant a specific area near the top of the Michigan mitten where the piney air was deliriously lovely. We had a feeling, somewhere between arrogance and innocence, which gave us a sense of ownership of this section by right of living in it every summer and developing a passion for it.

Our frail little cottage on Walloon Lake had been built by a local handy-man with a talent for rough carpentry early in the first decade of this century. My father, a young doctor with a large family of red-haired children, bought several lots on the shore of Wildwood Harbor where the beach was smooth and excellent for children.

Ernest Hemingway's father, a doctor from Oak Park, settled diagonally across the bay about the same time. Sometimes we found ourselves on the same big boat, the *Manitou*, crossing Lake Michigan from Chicago to Harbor Springs. Everyone was at an explosive pitch of excitement, and when we got our first whiff of the wonderful aromatic piney air we filled our lungs with it as if we had never breathed before.

Dr. Hemingway was a distinguished-looking man with a well-trimmed dark goatee and sharp dark-brown eyes. He loved to make people laugh and was therefore sometimes surrounded by people who were expecting to catch him in one of his favorite antics such as piling several hats on his head on top of each other.

Mrs. Hemingway stood tall and straight like a true Brunhilde, and she had ruddy cheeks and vivid blue eyes that always seemed ready for laughter. She had a lovely, rich contralto voice.

In the evening, about sunset time, Dr. and Mrs. Hemingway loved to get out on the lake in their rowboat and glide quietly along the shoreline of Wildwood Harbor. Dr. Hemingway would do the rowing and Mrs. Hemingway would sing her favorite songs—Santa Lucia and others. And sometimes Dr. Hemingway would bring his bugle and accompany his wife or do a solo number. Whenever we heard them approaching we would stop whatever we were doing and come out on the porch and listen delightedly.

The families in our small group of cottages loved to sit around a bonfire on the beach in the evening. We had our dinner at noon and a light supper at night so we could hurry out on the porch and watch the sunset which was always a spectacular performance.

One evening as we were sitting around the bonfire, we suddenly observed a volley of sky rockets splintering into the dark sky from the direction of the Hemingway Cottage. One of the women said excitedly, "The Hemingway baby must have arrived." And sure enough, it had. So we threw another log on the bonfire and joined the festivities.

My grandmother loved all these Walloon experiences but she particularly enjoyed telling about the time when Mrs. Hemingway came over in her rowboat to call on us and had to stay for three days. Everything was calm when she arrived, but soon we noticed that the wind had changed its course and the waves were getting bigger. It was the beginning of a three-day-blow. Mrs. Hemingway looked anxious and bewildered. She knew she could not get back to her family until the storm was over, and of course there were no telephones at that time or any possible means of communication.

The waves quickly grew to enormous size and were pounding wildly on the beach. We rushed to get the bathing suits and towels off the line before they were blown back into the woods. We carried the rowboats up onto the grass. We shut the windows and the front door and put the two-by-four in place behind the iron rods that held it securely. We stuffed a small rug against the gap at the bottom of the door. The children were sent to fill the woodbox with dry wood for the kitchen stove and the pot-bellied stove in the living room.

Mrs. Hemingway was very uneasy as she watched the swelling waves mount and break into a spreading white foam. It would have been impossible for any boat to venture out on the lake. There was nothing to do but accept the situation and make the best of it.

My grandmother was a strong personality and I think she rather enjoyed the challenge of the elements. She and Mrs. Hemingway matched family stories and the little cottage rang with laughter.

Mother had been making her weekly batch of oatmeal bread that day. The atmosphere was full of the delicious aroma. And there was fresh blackberry jam made from wild blackberries picked by our children the day before.

No wonder everyone kept asking when supper would be ready. My brothers had been out fishing that morning and had brought back some fresh perch which was our main dish. Then there was corn on the cob from a nearby farm and new potatoes. For dessert we had stewed plums which my grandmother had cooked in abundance. Maybe it wasn't the best meal in the world, but we all thought it was.

After the dishes were done and the milk and butter were stored in the small pit which had been dug under the house to keep things cool we settled down around the stove for an evening of twenty-questions supplemented by pop-corn. Everyone was making an effort to be more cheerful than usual in order to keep up Mrs. Hemingway's spirits. Finally bedtime came and after the necessary readjustment of people to beds we settled down for the night and listened to the wind and the waves express their fury.

In the morning they were still spewing out their noisy discontent. Grandmother and Mother had been up early figuring out ways to stretch the food supply and meet the emergency, for there was no way to get more food until the storm was over. For breakfast we had bacon and eggs and a dish of stewed plums. There was a slight grumble of disapproval when the plums were dished out but Grandmother settled that in quick order. "We are going to eat plums at every meal from now on until they are gone. We are not going to waste good food during a three-day-blow. And that's final," she said. She looked as if she meant it, too. So every day, three times a day, a dish of stewed plums was passed to each person and no one was allowed to leave the table until his portion was eaten. Mrs. Hemingway would laugh uproariously and say, "Oh, thank you so much," when she was served. We all hated the sight of plums before the storm was over.

Finally on the third day the wind had run its course and the waves returned to their normal size. Walloon Lake was again its charming self. Mrs. Hemingway dumped the water out of her rowboat and prepared to leave. As she pushed her boat out in the water she stepped in regally and said, "I had a wonderful time. Thank you for everything—even the plums."

"Come again," we called out as she dipped her oars in the water. "I will," she said, "if you promise not to have any more plums."

Ernest Hemingway and Men Without Women

By

Robert P. Mai

In his fine study *Ernest Hemingway: a Reconsideration*, Philip Young argues that both the style and the thematic concerns that characterize Hemingway's fiction are psychological "adaptations" to experience that was largely traumatic. Likening Nick Adams' experiences to the many encounters with murder and unnatural death that led Huck Finn to repeatedly escape to the Mississippi, Young concludes that the Hemingway hero

> who—up in Michigan and then in a war—over-exposed to violence and death, became preoccupied with these things in an unhealthy way, and finally in idealized terms envisaged his end, the only escape left him being in the image of the force escaped from.[1]

Mr. Young's contentions are convincingly supported, and his reading of the early Hemingway stories collected in *In Our Time* is incisive and helpful. But his psychological diagnosis is technically faulty, and, more importantly, his hypothesis seems, perhaps even to him, somewhat reductive. Looking back on his study over a decade later, a decade which saw not only the death of his subject but also the publication of significant biographical works by Hemingway's younger brother Leicester and by A. E. Hotchner, Young asks himself in the "Afterword" of his revised edition how he might have rewritten instead of revised his book:

> For one thing he would deal at much more length with the writer's parents, who turn out to have been much more interesting and formidible people than their famous son made them out to be, in fiction or elsewhere. Their

Victorianism was so preposterous—so, too, their lack of understanding—
that as a context for his general rebellion the family now looks bigger than
the war.[2]

Helpful information concerning the Hemingway family was first
provided in the biographies by Leicester Hemingway and by Ernest's
elder sister Marcelline. More recently we have received Constance
Montgomery's book on Hemingway's experience in Michigan, and
the definitive biography by Carlos Baker. Both Baker's work and
brother Leicester's valuable book (which is notably less protective
towards the parents than his sister's collection of reminiscences) offer
considerable evidence to indicate that the war injuries were not the
only significant character-forming experiences the Hemingway hero
inherited from his creator.

A third major source of information is of course the Hemingway
fiction itself—in particular the Nick Adams stories and Robert Jordan's recollections of his youth in *For Whom the Bell Tolls*. The
following passage, for example, comes from the novel and gives what
is undoubtedly Hemingway's version of how things had stood between his parents, and what amounts to his harshest judgment on his
father's suicide. The reflections are Robert Jordan's.

> I'll never forget how sick it made me the first time I knew he was a
> *cobarde*. . . . He was just a coward and that was the worst luck any man
> could have. Because if he wasn't a coward he would have stood up to that
> woman and not let her bully him. I wonder what I would have been like if
> he had married a different woman?[3]

That the young Hemingway had well-defined feelings about cowardice and bravery is attested to by both family biographers, as well
as by Carlos Baker in *Ernest Hemingway A Life Story*. Leicester relates how when Ernest was beaten by a smaller boy, he promptly
undertook to learn how to box.[4] We can also surmise that another
reason for Hemingway's interest in self-defense derived from his
having witnessed, at the age of thirteen, an incident in which his
father refused to respond to the provocation of a hired man. This
anecdote readily calls to mind the dramatic crisis in the story "The
Doctor and the Doctor's Wife." It is perhaps most important here to
notice the same connection between cowardice and yielding to the
will of a woman that Robert Jordan recorded above. In just a few
lines of dialogue between the doctor and his wife, Hemingway frames
the principle events of the story in such a manner that the title of
the piece now seems appropriate in a distinctly insinuating way. One
feels at once that the doctor's uneasy adherence to the Christian

principle of turning the other cheek was somehow a capitulation to an insistently self-righteous wife. It is only after this new perspective has been provided that the boy's choosing not to go in to his mother, but off to the woods with his father, becomes significant.

Both Leicester and Marcelline admit that female "domination" bothered their brother. They describe Mrs. Hemingway as having been a particularly strong-willed person, who was considerably less disposed towards chores like housework and cooking than she was towards teaching music and voice. Since Dr. Hemingway often cooked and oversaw the washing and sterilization of clothes, we may presume that this reversal of roles might well have colored the son's estimation of his father. One example of some high-handed behavior by Mrs. Hemingway prevailing over the better judgment of her husband was especially decisive for Ernest, since it involved his summary dismissal from the Hemingway's summer cottage, and led to a real break from the family fold. It is in light of this kind of experience and the formative effects it had on an adolescent Hemingway that we must consider the various Hemingway heroes who stepped onto the battlefield of World War I and suffered "the big wound."

In Philip Young's theory, the infliction of the wound is the central psychic event of the hero's first adult confrontation with the world. But, like Huck Finn, he has previously been exposed to situations that contained a share of brutality and violence. To fit this early experience to his hypothesis that the shelling was for Hemingway and the Hemingway hero a traumatic shock, Young follows Hemingway's lead[5] and explains that the effect of being only a witness to violence and death is to generate in the mind an illusion of immortality. Then, during the shelling when the hit occurs, this illusion is rudely shattered. Young is now ready to invoke Freud, albeit with apologies, to lend to the analysis an official diagnosis of those symptoms he noticed particularly in the Nick Adams stories. But from the same essay (*Beyond the Pleasure Principle*) that Young finds his corroboration come statements that undermine his argument.

Young suggests that "the generic Nick" had been "thoroughly shaken" as a result of what he had experienced in "Indian Camp," in "The Battler" and in "The Killers" (or what Robert Jordan recalls in *For Whom the Bell Tolls*). Thus, he had "a high potential" for suffering traumatic shock—he was "properly constituted for it." These conclusions overlook, however, Freud's contention that rather than make the individual more vulnerable, these early incidents produce anxiety which then acts as a defense against the possibility of future encounters with experiences of similar content.[6] Furthermore, Freud says of so-called "war neuroses" that they "may very well be traumatic neuroses which have been facilitated by a conflict in the ego" (and with regard to the foregoing discussion of Hemingway's family relations, this speculation seems to me to be particularly relevant). Finally, Freud notes in the same paragraph that "a gross physical injury caused simultaneously by the trauma diminishes the chances that a neurosis will develop. . . ."[7] The point to be made here is that if we want to think with Young that "the explosion at Fossalta was the crux of that [Hemingway's] life," the experience must be considered in a wider context than the one which limits its significance to a reaction against violence and death.

Shortly after his knee had been operated on, Hemingway wrote his family a letter which gave the first detailed account of the shelling and the subsequent action that earned for him one of the highest military decorations that the Italian government could award. Here is the young Hemingway's vivid description of some common occurrences on the front:

> For example, in the trenches, during an attack, when a shell makes a direct hit in a group where you're standing. Shells aren't bad except direct hits: you just take chances on the fragments of the bursts. But when there is a direct hit, your pals get splattered all over you; splattered is literal.[8]

Despite the writer's inclination not to spare any of the details, the tone of this letter is almost cheery, and one cannot help noticing that the young man who has just narrowly escaped being killed now appears rather pleased with having gone through the experience. We also know that Hemingway had other reasons to be cheerful during this time, one of them being his love affair with Agnes von Kurowsky, who was a nurse at the hospital.

When Hemingway returned home after his discharge, he was greeted as a war hero. Chicago newspaper stories tended to lionize him as the "first American" to be wounded in Italy, and he was called upon to give several talks about his exploits. According to Leicester Hemingway's description of this period, Ernest quite enjoyed all the adulation that came his way, and frequently dressed up in his Italian army uniform when he took his walks around Oak Park. But there was another side to this extremely agreeable interlude: Hemingway was bothered by nightmares, his legs were often painful, and, perhaps worst of all, he received a letter from Agnes refusing his offer of marriage. From Marcelline's account we learn that Hemingway was deeply affected by this development. He became physically ill for several days, and it was probably his bitterness over the rejection which, more than anything else, caused his periodic sulking and gloominess during this period.

The wounded hero of Hemingway's fiction also gives us a picture of how Hemingway might have felt around this time. In "A Very Short Story," bitterness is hidden beneath a cynically matter-of-fact narration of a similar rejection and its sordid aftermath.[9] The story that follows this one in *In Our Time* is "Soldier's Home." Here a returned soldier, disillusioned with the war and disgusted with the lies he feels compelled to tell his acquaintances, mopes around the house, tells his anxious but sensitive mother that he doesn't love her, and then tries to assuage the hurt feelings that make him only uneasy and embarrassed. Though no direct mention is made of past unhappy love affairs, soldier Krebs has nonetheless adopted a rather self-protective attitude towards females that represents an important step in the evolution of what Philip Young calls the "code-hero," and of all the characters who emulate the code-hero in the later fiction. The passages quoted below tell how Krebs has thought out his position regarding girls:

> He did not want them themselves really. They were too complicated. There was something else. Vaguely he wanted a girl but he did not want to have to work to get her. He would have liked to have a girl but he did not want to have to spend a long time getting her.
>
> He did not want any consequences. He did not want any consequences ever again. He wanted to live along without consequences. Besides he did not really need a girl. The army had taught him that. It was alright to pose as though you had to have a girl. Nearly everybody did that. But it wasn't true. You did not need a girl. That was the funny thing.
>
> Now he would have liked a girl if she had come to him and not wanted to talk. But here at home it was all too complicated. He knew he could never get through it all again.[10]

The implication in the last sentence that something trying and unpleasant had happened before would indicate that there is a vital identification to be made here between Krebs and Hemingway, and we should be able to recognize in these reflections that psychological defense mechanism called rationalization. Furthermore, the deliberateness and the repetitiveness of this writing is remarkably similar to that of "Big Two-Hearted River." If we see in the prose of the latter, as most critics do, a reflection of the need of the hero to keep his disturbed mental apparatus under a strict and rigorous control, the thoughts of Krebs also indicate a need to develop a well-considered posture that would serve as a shield against "consequences."

Krebs would not be bothered with women because "It was not worth it. Not now when things were getting good again." Things are getting good now that he has begun to rethink his role in the war. If young Hemingway heroes have come out losers in their encounters with women (to the score should also be added the "betrayal" by Nick's nubile Indian girl that his father reports to him in "Ten Indians"), they have also reaped honors in the war. So Krebs finds consolation in the knowledge that "he had been a good soldier," and he looks forward "with a good feeling to reading all the really good histories" of the war. It is from these retrospective constructions which Krebs puts on the war that a new, more gratifying conception of the self can emerge. The achievement of these ruminations is such that the losses suffered on one field of battle are somehow voided by the newly-realized successes on another. It is as if the forces of a damaged ego managed to regroup in such a way that no one would be able to notice the actual wound. Furthermore, this strategic move also served to marshal an effective counterattack which, although never confronting the old enemy on its own grounds, would nonetheless be assured against any similar adversities. If a man is unlucky at love, he can still be lucky at cards—or at war, another man's game. Armed with these consolations, Krebs was able to "feel cool and clear inside himself," convinced that as a soldier "he had done the one thing, the only thing for a man to do."

During the year following his homecoming, after the shine had begun to wear off his Italian medal, Hemingway did some writing while living alone at his family's cottage, and then in the nearby town of Petoskey. Charles Fenton has tried to piece together various letters and descriptions relating to this period, and cites this comment made by a friend who visited Hemingway: "He seemed to have a tremendous need to express the things that he had felt and seen."[11] Fenton concludes that the stay in Northern Michigan provided Hemingway with a chance to assess his war experiences and to get them off his mind and onto paper. But Hemingway probably turned to writing at this time not just "to get rid of it," but because writing suggested a way to regain some of the self-confidence and peace of mind he had lost. If he wrote to purge his mind of disturbing memories, he also wrote to reconstruct, to cast his past experiences in different perspective, determined by new values and new standards for self-judgment. Leicester Hemingway remarks that the first summer his brother spent at home after his return from Italy "was a time of personal triumph and humiliation, one of violent emotion."[12] If the thought of humiliation was so unsettling, the obvious way to reduce its disturbing effects was to concentrate on the triumph. The problem here was that Hemingway's private opinion of his heroism was not so comforting as the unqualified admiration of his family and friends. For him, the real heroes were the fighting men who had actively challenged death, and whose wounds were not merely the "accidents" that led non-combatants like the hero of "In Another Country" to be decorated. The wounded American in this story quite enjoys the society of some Italian soldiers also recovering from wounds, but he acknowledges that "it had been different with them and they had done very different things to get their medals. . . . The three with the medals were like hunting-hawks; and I was not a hawk, although I might seem a hawk to those who had never hunted."[13]

The significance of the wound for both Hemingway and his fictional projections came to be how it tested their capacity to continue to take risks, to play the game and knowingly accept the consequences. "All matadors are gored dangerously, painfully . . ." Hemingway wrote in *Death in the Afternoon*, "and until a matador has undergone this first severe wound you cannot tell what his permanent value will be."[14] So too, apparently, for the writer. In the professional ethics of the good bullfighter, Hemingway saw standards he could extrapolate to his definition of the good writer. He felt an affinity for the bullfighter because the bullfight pits art against death, and Hemingway had already claimed his own encounter with death as a personal success of sorts. The good matador, like Pedro Romero in *The Sun Also Rises*, has the confidence to confront death without fear, and refuses to fake danger. Hemingway would constantly seek out ways to test himself against danger, and then write about them. He hunted big game in Africa, crossed behind enemy lines to report the progress of the Spanish Civil War, and led his own band of daring "irregulars" in the liberation of Paris from the Germans. He was not obsessed with violence. He was psychologically committed to act and write in such a way as to prove to himself that he was not a coward, that he could be "strong in the broken places."

Hemingway dedicated himself to the task of writing down what he knew in a way that would enable him to say to his readers, as he says in *Green Hills of Africa*, "There you can go as we have gone."[15] To achieve this goal, he establishes, in his introduction to *Men at War*, the following criterion for himself (and for all writers, since he needed to be judged as a writer in the same way that he judged bullfighters): the writer's "standard of fidelity to the truth should be so high that his invention, out of his experience, should produce a truer account than anything factual can be."[16] The permanent value of a matador, as Hemingway sees it, will be told by his ability to recover from a goring and continue to work close to the bulls. The permanent value of a writer will be told by his ability to adhere to his "one complete obligation"—to be "of as great probity and honesty as a priest of God."

All of Hemingway's more important heroes, with the exception of Santiago in *The Old Man and the Sea*, have suffered "the big wound."[17] Their scars, limps, deformities and missing limbs are like identification badges; the wound is a sign of initiation. The ways they have reacted to the wound are a measure of how far each has advanced in the process of becoming like the code-hero, a figure pre-eminently noted for inner strength and courage, and the ability to see things the way they are. The first stage of the reaction process is escape: Nick Adams and Lt. Henry both seek to get away, much as Hemingway did when he went off alone to Northern Michigan. Nick goes off fishing—trying to regain physical and mental equilibrium after his war experiences—but like Lt. Henry, he comes to realize that withdrawal into a cocoon of ease and pleasure can only be a temporary measure. Nick knows that the forbidding swamp in "Big Two-Hearted River" is there to be fished, and although he is not ready to go there at first, the closing sentence of this story states that "There were plenty of days coming when he could fish the swamp," indicating a time when Nick will quit "the good place" and take his chances again in a world of risks, where "fishing was a tragic adventure."

In *A Farewell to Arms*, Lt. Henry made a "separate peace" by leaving the fighting, but later on he "had the feeling of a boy who thinks of what is happening at a certain hour at the schoolhouse from which he has played truant." His hedonistic interlude in Switzerland is yet another escape, and the impossibility of sustaining this kind of existence is spelled out in terms of tragedy. If Nick must venture into the swamp, Lt. Henry must swallow his grief after Catherine dies in childbirth and go back out into the rain, and rain in *A Farewell to Arms* is an even more persistently ominous symbol than the swamp of "Big Two-Hearted River."

Jake Barnes is another escapist. An expatriate, he moves among that set of irresponsible, morally disillusioned people which came to be called the lost generation. But in an important way he is not like his companions, who are considerably more lost than he is. For Mike and Brett, pleasure-taking is an abandonment of responsibility. For Bill Gorton, it is the self-indulgence allowed by a comfortingly cynical attitude towards life, and for Robert Cohn, the necessary activity of a man who needs to fit in, to feel accepted. Jake, on the other hand, would like to come to terms with his responsibilities, but he is stymied because he is not sure where his responsibilities lie. Earl Rovit comments in his book on Hemingway that Jake is drained by pursuing the illusion that he can have Brett. At the end of the novel, he realizes that he has reached "the end of the line." His closing statement in the novel "commemorates Jake's separate peace with himself and his new determination to live his life by those passions which are within the scope of his powers and conducive to the possibilities of his self-realization in his pursuit of them."[18]

It is also in *The Sun Also Rises* that we get our first good look at the type of man who displays those qualities which render him invulnerable to the Circean designs of women, and which yield to him the respect and admiration of other men. Pedro Romero is the first fully-realized code-hero, and his strengths are twofold: he has the ability to be cool and controlled under pressure (that condition which is achieved by a dominating consciousness of craft that purges the mind of the emotion of fear) and he possesses an essentially narcissistic character which protects him against compromising his integrity in order to satisfy sexual needs. When Romero killed a bull for Brett, he maneuvered it near to the place she was sitting, but "Never once did he look up.

> He made it stronger that way, and did it for himself, too, as well as for her. Because he did not look up to ask if it pleased he did it all for himself inside, and it strengthened him, and yet he did it for her, too. But he did not do it for her at any loss to himself.[19]

And that is the essence of the code-hero: not to suffer "any loss to himself."

There is an analogy made in *The Sun Also Rises* between the impotent Jake and the steer who quiets and leads the bulls. If Hemingway meant us to follow the analogy through, it would lead us to this conclusion: if Jake is the steer, Cohn and Mike must be bulls, and the matador who "kills" them is Brett—the only one of Jake's friends who truly enjoyed the bullfight and who didn't "mind the blood" (Cohn identifies Brett with Circe, and Circe's pleasure is to make men cowardly and weak).[20] A priestess of the libido, Brett will not gratify the ego of any one man because her promiscuity denies that man his sense of power through possession. The way that Hemingway counteracts this figure in his fiction is to create the code-hero, who does not need a woman that badly since he has something better that no woman can take away. Such a character is an outgrowth of Krebs' rationalization that "You do not need a girl," and the progress of Hemingway's fiction from that point records the growing success with which the protagonists become more like the code-hero. The antithesis of the code-hero would be a man who needs to be recognized and approved by women, and such a man is Robert Cohn—appropriately the foil for Romero. Cohn is a boxer, but he boxes only to "counteract the feeling of inferiority and shyness." He is a writer, but he most admires fiction like W. H. Hudson's, and his own work will be as fanciful as his literary taste. And, he is a ladies' man, but is used and abused by each of the women he gets entangled with.

As with Romero, the identities of later code-heroes usually derive their core from professional standards. Robert Wilson, the white hunter in "The Short and Happy Life of Francis Macomber," is a perfect example. Wilson will serve his clients' desires "in all except the shooting. He had his own standards about the killing. . . . He knew, too, that they all respected him for this."[21] It is this commitment and self-discipline that make Robert Wilson so strongly independent, and the measure of his strength, as in many Hemingway stories, is the ability to prevail against overbearing women: Wilson remains as unimperiled by the ruthless egotism of Margot Macomber as Romero sleeping with Brett.

In *For Whom the Bell Tolls*, Robert Jordan also has to come to terms with a rather awesome woman. Jordan's behavior is considerably more complicated than Wilson's, but his effectiveness is still largely a function of his studied self-discipline, or "professional austerity"—a phrase Hemingway uses in *Men at War*. Jordan has only to go about his business to earn the respect of the formidable Pilar, whose emasculative potential is evinced in the rendering of Pablo. In contrast to Jordan, Pablo had proven unable to sustain his strength of character through situations where killing must constantly be an occupational ritual. Robert Jordan has a significant place among Hemingway heroes, because he is the first code-hero who is also the protagonist. Jordan marks the coming of age of the Hemingway tyro, who will no longer require a tutor.

Of all the novels in which the hero has reached a Hemingway kind of maturity, only *For Whom the Bell Tolls* portrays a hero who is not so ridiculous in his toughness as to undercut whatever his dramatic achievement may be. Robert Jordan strains our tolerance only in the scenes with Maria (and no more so than Lt. Henry did with Catherine). Love-making for the mature Hemingway here is plainly an activity to be engaged in only when it does not interfere with business, so Maria dutifully clears out of the sleeping bag before Jordan wakes up so as not to disturb the work schedule. Hemingway's earlier attempt at making a completely self-sufficient and resourceful protagonist failed precisely for the reason put forth in his criticism of a certain bullfighter in *Death in the Afternoon.*

> He laid his bravery on as with a trowel. It was as though he were constantly showing you the quantity of hair on his chest or the way in which he was built in his more private parts.[22]

When Harry Morgan announces in *To Have and Have Not,* "I got *cojones,* don't you worry about my *cojones,*" he is telling us not only of his courage but also of his sexual potency. Harry Morgan might be minus an arm, but he fulfils his responsibilities more than adequately, and his wife lets us know, following some vintage Hemingway love-making, that she has been "a lucky woman."

In the words of another outspoken Hemingway character, the man who takes risks, the "man who is a man," will always "bear some marks of past misfortune." The speaker is Col. Cantwell, and in *Across the River and Into the Trees* the visible sign of past misfortune is Cantwell's mutilated and deformed hand. It is his hand that his companion Renata likes so much to hold and fondle, and what she admittedly loves about Cantwell are the "wounded places." The wound once again has taken on an explicitly sexual significance, but instead of causing emasculation as it did for Jake Barnes, the wound has relocated itself anatomically and is now a rather unlikely sexual attribute.

In a sense, all of Hemingway's heroes suffered the same wound as Jake Barnes. That is, like the biblical Jacob, they have been touched in the hollow of the thigh because they have dared to wrestle with an angel. But Jacob would not cease his struggle until he gained the angel's blessing, and herein lies the model for the Hemingway whose fictional projections vowed to be "strong in the broken places," who would show their real mettle by continuing on after a "goring." *The Sun Also Rises,* probably Hemingway's finest novel, is a dramatization of Jacob's wrestling with the angel, and Jake's final statement is an indication that he has prevailed over his adversary. But whereas the wound has here a symbolic significance that is central to the form of the novel, in other instances it plays a somewhat less vital role. And in the two novels that are pronounced failures, the wound, rather than resonate within the structure of the fable, bleats out a rather flat, coarse note that is itself the most conspicuous measure of the artistic depth of these works. The wound in *To Have and Have Not* and *Across the River and Into the Trees* is displayed with so much sentimentality and self-pride that it ceases to function as an integrating element in the novel, and calls such attention to itself and its dramatic significance as to sabotage the project its earlier counterpart had so ably held together. The wound is finally no longer a symbol at all but merely a function in the equation: wound = *cojones*, and Hemingway's art suffers the obvious consequences.

When Lillian Ross interviewed him for her famous *New Yorker* "Profile," Hemingway said the following about his newly finished novel: "I think I've got 'Farewell' beat in this one . . . It hasn't got the youth and the ignorance."[23] Col. Cantwell has indeed lost his youth, and we are to presume that his persistent skepticism and self-criticism denote a wisdom that comes only through long experience ("Papa's delivery of hard-learned facts of life," Hemingway avers in the interview). The fecal monument Cantwell leaves at the site of his first serious wounding ceremonially buries one aspect of the youth and ignorance: the false sentiment, the meaningless decorations that attached themselves to an "accident" because people who had never hunted took him to be the hunting hawk he would only become later on. Indeed, there is a strategic retreat going on in this novel that discusses past military campaigns, but Col. Cantwell's self-redemptive gestures are not enough to efface the consequences of his "old wild-bear truculence." After each attempt to look objectively at his own behavior, past and present, he emerges a little more foolish-looking for his efforts. In retrospect, the project of writing *Across the River and Into the Trees* seems to have been in part as unsoundly conceived as the holiday of Col. Cantwell, the man with a heart condition in a city where "the current is not stable."

The Old Man and the Sea shows Hemingway on much surer ground. In fact, this last published novel provides the clearest expression of the author's most insistent personal commitment—the imperative to test oneself—as well as presenting the simplest, most compact statement of those values which Hemingway had assumed for the code-hero, then for his later fictional projections, and, just as deliberately, for himself. The hero whose identity had been founded on the manly virtues of courage, self-sufficiency, and integrity of vision, who would come to know strength of mind through an ethic of male solidarity, and who would seek to operate under such conditions where judgment is passed by men upon men, has made a final attempt to play out his drama—alone with his memories, fighting a fish in the open sea. By writing a story about an old man, a man truly without women, Hemingway has for once stayed completely clear of the pressing psychological issue that Nick Adams and Krebs and Robert Jordan were continually revealing, and that Harry Morgan and Col. Cantwell most grossly caricatured.

If Hemingway was an artistic success in his earlier attempts to resolve some of his anxieties through projection, the prospects for continued success were undermined by a crucial lack of psychological honesty in the themes that insisted themselves on his fiction. Krebs had not been truthful with himself, nor had Nick Adams addressed himself with candor and straightforwardness to the basic causes of his malaise, and subsequent heroes were forged on those lies. Hemingway's own life style, together with his sensitivity to criticism and his penchant for attacking other writers, are themselves reflections not only of his strengths but of his shortcomings as an artist. Unfortunately, the latter could only become more acute in time, given the fixed limits of his psychological perspective and the sexual self-defensiveness that lay beneath his bearishness and his courage.

---

[1] Philip Young, *Hemingway: A Reconsideration* (New York: Harcourt, Brace and World, Inc., 1966), p. 209.

[2] *Ibid.*, pp. 273-274.

[3] Ernest Hemingway, *For Whom the Bell Tolls* (New York: Charles Scribner's Sons, 1940), pp. 338-339.

[4] Leicester Hemingway, *My Brother, Ernest Hemingway* (Cleveland and New York: The World Publishing Company, 1962), p. 29.

[5] As he variously describes the experience of confronting death for the first time. Cf. the introduction to *Men at War* for one such instance.

[6] Sigmund Freud, *Beyond the Pleasure Principle* (New York: Bantam Books, 1959), pp. 59-60. On page thirty of this essay, Freud says, "I do not believe anxiety can produce a traumatic neurosis. There is something about anxiety that protects its subject against fright and so against fright neurosis."

[7] *Ibid.*, p. 62.

[8] Cited in Constance Cappel Montgomery, *Hemingway in Michigan* (New York: Fleet Publishing Corporation, 1966), p. 110.

[9] In *The Torrents of Spring*, Hemingway's early parody of Sherwood Anderson, the exploits of Yogi Johnson in Paris offer a burlesque of the disappointment-in-love theme. Yogi tells his Indian friends, "What I thought was a very

beautiful thing happened to me in Paris . . . . Well, it turned out to be the ugliest thing that ever happened to me." After having viewed the woman he thought he had been in love with in a rather risque situation, Yogi concludes, "Since then . . . I have never wanted a woman. How I have suffered I cannot tell. But I've suffered, boys, I've suffered." (Ernest Hemingway, *The Torrents of Spring* [New York: Charles Scribner's Sons, 1926], pp. 125-126).

[10] Ernest Hemingway, "Soldier's Home," *In Our Time* (New York: Charles Scribner's Sons, 1953), pp. 92-94.

[11] Charles Fenton, *The Apprenticeship of Ernest Hemingway* (New York: The Viking Press, 1960), p. 72.

[12] Leicester Hemingway, *op. cit.*, p. 60.

[13] Ernest Hemingway, "In Another Country," *Men Without Women* (New York: Charles Scribner's Sons, 1955), pp. 63-64.

[14] Ernest Hemingway, *Death in the Afternoon* (New York: Charles Scribner's Sons, 1932), p. 166.

[15] Ernest Hemingway, *Green Hills of Africa* (New York: Charles Scribner's Sons, 1935), p. 109.

[16] Ernest Hemingway, *Men at War* (New York: Crown Publishers, 1942), p. xv.

[17] Too young to have participated in World War I, Robert Jordan received a disabling wound only at the end of *For Whom the Bell Tolls*. And Santiago was still plagued by his perverse left hand, which never could be relied upon to function as well as the right.

[18] Earl Rovit, *Ernest Hemingway* (New York: Twayne Publishers, Inc., 1963), p. 158.

[19] Ernest Hemingway, *The Sun Also Rises* (New York: Charles Scribner's Sons, 1926), p. 216.

[20] Robert B. Lewis, Jr., in citing Hemingway's use of *Ecclesiastes* for the composition of *The Sun Also Rises*, refers us to *Ecclesiastes* 8:26, which he feels Hemingway must have considered: "And I find more bitter than death the woman, whose heart is snares and nets, and her hands as bands: whoso pleaseth God shall escape from her; but the sinner shall be taken by her." (Robert B. Lewis, Jr., *Hemingway on Love*, [Austin and London: University of Texas Press, 1965], pp. 33-34).

[21] Ernest Hemingway, "The Short Happy Life of Francis Macomber," *The Fifth Column and the First Forty-nine Stories* (New York: Charles Scribner's Sons, 1938), p. 125.

[22] Ernest Hemingway, *Death in the Afternoon*, p. 94.

[23] Lillian Ross, "How Do You Like It Now, Gentlemen?" in *Hemingway: A Collection of Critical Essays*, ed. Robert P. Weeks (Englewood Cliffs, N. J.: Prentice-Hall, Inc., 1962), p. 24.

Collection of C. E. Frazer Clark, Jr.

7 **LAWRENCE** (T. E.), The first eight chapters of "The Seven Pillars of Wisdom," with the printed note facing Chapter one "On the Foundations of the Arab Revolt," complete with all the headpieces. Enclosed in a white wrapper with the word "Proof" (in Lawrence's hand?) scrawled on it. From the library of J. C. Squire, very fine condition, exceedingly rare, in slip case $50.00

9 **HEMINGWAY** (Ernest) Three Stories and Ten Poems, Paris, 1923. His first book, only 200 printed, presentation copy to the editors of "This Quarter," "To Ernest Weld and Ethel Moorhead, with love from Ernest Hemingway," Paris, 1924, as new, also 17 pages of letters, one 4 pages long, replete with autobiographical and literary interest. It speaks of his early life, his desires, wishes, method of work, his abysmal poverty and joy of having his book "The Sun Also Rises" accepted by Boni & Liveright, and of his interest and devotion to Ernest Walsh, and desire to promote "This Quarter"; some of the passages are absolutely impossible to put into type. The letters are a complete revelation of the man as he really is; they are written in his own hand, and dated from 1924-1926. All of his later letters that I have seen are typed, but the above were written when he couldn't a machine. His story "The Up defeated," which appeared in "This Quarter," "put him on the map," 9 letters of 16 pages, to be sold as one lot $150.00 The following are some of the extracts:—

Feb. 28, 1925. AUSTRIA.
...A guide brought two cables up to the hut from N.Y. saying my book had been accepted by Boni and Liveright, so I guess its official. Wish one could open a bottle of something together to celebrate ...Am working like hell on one thing and another, and trying to get in shape to fight Friday. It's a job sweating the poison out. I'm in rotten shape. Have been going six rounds a day and have thumbed an ear, and unhooked my nose—good to be doing it again, but gawd how hard to get into condition.

January 29, 1925. AUSTRIA.
... As near as I can find out am 27 years old, 6 feet tall, weigh 182 pounds, born in Oak Park, Illinois, served in war on Italian Front, wounded, profession newspaper correspondent, married Hadley Richardson, Sept. 3, 1921, one son, John Hadley Manor, born Oct. 10, 1923, Author of Three Stories and Ten Poems, Contact Publishing Co., Paris, and In Our Time, Three Mountains Press, Paris, Edited Transatlantic Review, for Ford Madox Ford during latter's absence in America. Edward J. O'Brien dedicated Best Short Stories of 1924 to me. Amusements, Boxing, Trout Fishing, Ski-ing and Bull-fighting. Prefers to do the first three and watch the latter. State of health good. Very fond of eating and drinking. Lives in France for that reason among others. Believes Gertrude Stein to be a great writer. Friend of Ezra Pound. Believes Pound greatest living poet. Believes other great living poets would admit it. Few great living poets living. Fond of horse-racing.

July 20, 1925. MADRID.
..... It has been a hell of a wonderful trip—and I'm working hard. It is so tough and honest and crooked and pleasant and tough, tough, hard and beautiful. And the people are so damned nice. We travel 3rd class and coming down here there was a man bringing samples of his wines he grows near Tafalla—big 'jugs—to buy and sell wines in Madrid and we all got to offering each other drinks and he opened all the jugs and made the whole carriage, including four priests and the guard, and, I'm sorry to say, myself drunk. He said it was all right. He had plenty of money anyway. During the evening, it was just after sunset, I either gave away or threw away my tickets and the guard foxed it up for us at Madrid.

January 2, 1926. MADRID.
: .... The last day I was in Paris I went around looking for him intending, whenI found him, to beat him up, not regarding the transaction in any way creditable to myself, but because I figured that was the best way to show my contempt—that I wouldn't be ashamed of beating him up, even though he's half my size, any more than I would feel remorse at squashing a bed bug which is even less than half my size. An I suppose that had I found him—I wouldn't have had the guts to do it—being lousy with Christian precepts and inhibitions.

I've always given you my best stuff and always will. At present I'm trying the Fight Story, about 15,000 words on the big money market. It's come back from Hearst's. Ray Sarg said he would buy it if there was woman interest in it. They would pay me $1,200. I'm not pulling in any woman interest and not changing one word to suit anybody. But have to try it on the other 3 magazines. . . Needless to say I would prefer 1,000 times over to be published in this Quarter than in the Dial. I had an offer of several hundred dollars for the bull fight story from Scribners.

If I am anything I am a Catholic. Had extreme unction administered to me as such in July, 1918, and recovered. So guess I'm a Super-Catholic. It certainly is the most comfortable religion for anyone soldiering. Am not what is called a "good" Catholic. Think there is a lot of nonsense about the Church, Holy Years, etc. What rot. But cannot imagine taking any other religion seriously .. I may have to go to America in January. Hope to hell not steerage in thewinter. Still the sea is always worth it. Had a fine drunken New Year. I also won 1,230,000 kronen at cards. That's over 400 francs in French money.

11 **HERGESHEIMER** (Joseph) Three Black Pennies, N.Y., 1922. There is a slight water-stain on the top of the front cover, and stamp of a Chinese bookseller on title-page, otherwise as new, in original dust wrapper, rare $25.00

Collection of C. E. Frazer Clark, Jr.

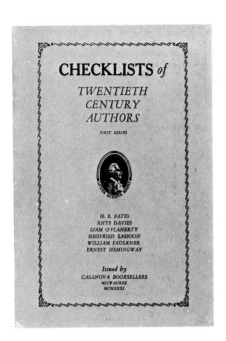

Collection of C. E. Frazer Clark, Jr.

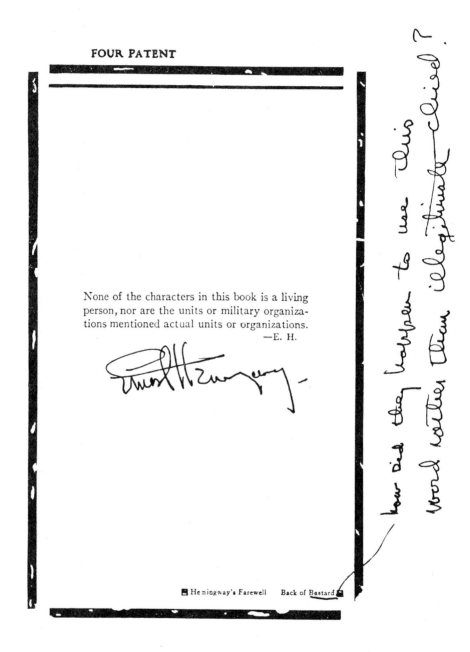

FOUR PATENT

None of the characters in this book is a living
person, nor are the units or military organizations mentioned actual units or organizations.

—E. H.

*How did they happen to use This
word rather Than 'illegitimate' chisel?*

■ Hemingway's Farewell   Back of Bastard ■

Bastard Note. Issued December 1931 by Louis Henry Cohn. Collection of
C. E. Frazer Clark, Jr.

The Beginnings of Dealer Interest in Hemingway

By

C. E. Frazer Clark, Jr.

Many authors escape collecting, but no great author has failed to
have his stature confirmed by the prices set in the rare book trade.
The auction gallery and the dealer catalogue arbitrate the market
value of a collected author, reflecting the scholar's critical appraisal
or anticipating the collector's determination.

Hemingway was elevated to prime collectible status in 1930, both
by auction and catalogue, both in America and in England. Hemingway first appears in American auction records with the sale,
March 10, 1930, at The Ritter-Hopson Galleries in New York, of a
fine copy of *in our time*. The buyer, at $160, a bold price at the
time, was Captain Louis Henry Cohn, who opened the House of
Books, shortly following the sale. The first Hemingway item to reach
auction in England was also a copy of *in our time*, sold May 8,
1930.[1]

The same year, English dealer interest in Hemingway was signaled
by the Ulysses Book Shop (Catalogue No. 1, March, 1930) offering
of an important collection of association material, including a presentation copy of Hemingway's first book, *Three Stories & Ten Poems*,
together with nine letters, all to Ernest Walsh and Ethel Moorhead.
The collection was described as a lot and aggressively priced at
$150.[2]

Emerging dealers traditionally take pains to make the best possible
impression with any *Catalogue No. 1*. A splash is called for, since
high visibility is sought. Good material is hoarded for a first catalogue, and often new territory is explored. Both factors are represented in the first Ulysses Book Shop Catalogue, which is an offering

in the budding field of *Contemporary American and English First Editions* with an impressive gathering of presentation copies and association material. The 1930 Hemingway market was being assayed by Ulysses with the $150 price asked for the collection—top price in the catalogue.

Significant (but inaccurate) extracts from four of Hemingway's letters were published in the Ulysses catalogue, and for this reason and because it has proved elusively scarce, the catalogue itself has become a minor collector's prize.

Dealers have special feelings about the importance of particular authors. Hemingway and Hemingway collectors benefited from such friendships. Sylvia Beach was Hemingway's first such friendship, with 12, rue de l'Odéon proving much more than a doorway just to Shakespeare and Company.

1930 saw the first of Captain Cohn's Hemingway publications with the effort, in August, to privately print ("for the prevention of piracy") four of Hemingway's early poems. Cohn had copyright difficulties with the New York Society for the Suppression of Vice, and *Four Poems By Ernest Hemingway* survives in galley proof only.[3]

In Chicago, in November, 1930, The Walden Book Shop published in leaflet form *Bibliographical Notes on Ernest Hemingway*. This prints an extract from a 1927 Hemingway letter recounting the publication history of his books as he remembers it, together with some brief Walden notes on Hemingway publication.[4]

What the Walden *Notes* tells us is that by 1930 more grist for the rare book mill was needed. Dealer, collector, and scholar interest had reached attractive proportions. Enough of a market had been established to warrant researching better information about first printings, as well as to justify uncovering other collectible Hemingway material.

This demand was met in the fall of 1931 by the publication of Captain Cohn's *A Bibliography of the Works of Ernest Hemingway.*[5] This immediately broadened the spectrum of Hemingway collectibility, and attractively so, not only by staking out fresh ground and differentiating printings and "points," but by identifying such rarities as the *Introduction to Kiki*, limited to a printing of twenty-five copies only.[6] As a practical matter, the Cohn *Bibliography* also appropriately identified House of Books as an essential stop on the Hemingway collector's path—a reputation to be entirely justified in the years following.

The *Bibliography*, appearing in August, 1931, spawned three months later the publication in limited quantity of a facsimile of the "bastard note"—the foundry proof of the legal disclaimer in the second printing of *A Farewell to Arms*—suitably inscribed and annotated by Hemingway.[7] Two years later, *God Rest You Merry Gentlemen* appeared as the second in the House of Books "Crown Octavo" series.

Early dealer interest in Hemingway bibliography is continued in the *Checklists of Twentieth Century Authors* published by the Casanova Booksellers, H. Warren Schwartz and Paul Romaine, in 1931. Hemingway is one of six authors included in the *Checklist*, with the Cohn *Bibliography* listed and credited as source for some of the information provided. The *Checklist* also notes the forthcoming publication by Casanova of Faulkner's *Salmagundi*, but notice of the inclusion of Hemingway's poem ("Ultimately") is left to the prospectus for *Salmagundi* which followed. The book was scheduled for March 15, 1932, but, according to Paul Romaine, the "prospectus sold every copy of the book before publication." This says something about Faulkner interest in 1932. Including the Hemingway poem can be argued as the consummation of a literary marriage celebrated by the joint appearance of "Ultimately" and Faulkner's "Portrait" on the same page in the June, 1922, *Double Dealer*.[8]

These beginnings of dealer interest saw the Hemingway boat well launched for the rare book trade winds, with new canvas being laid on all along the way. Notice that Hemingway had officially "arrived," as far as the antiquarian bookman's new world was concerned, was his inclusion in the revised and enlarged second edition of Merle Johnson's landmark *American First Editions*. Hemingway did not appear in the 1929 first edition of Merle Johnson's bookman's bible, so his inclusion in the 1932 second edition might fairly be considered the end of the beginnings of dealer interest in Hemingway—his future for the trade was assured.

---

[1] See Clark, "Hemingway At Auction: A Brief Survey" *(Fitzgerald/Hemingway Annual 1969)*.

[2] Hanneman F57.

[3] Hanneman F149.

[4] Louis Henry Cohn, *A Bibliography of the Works of Ernest Hemingway* (New York: Random House, 1931), pp. 75-76. Cohn points out that while the Walden *Notes* carries an October 1930 date, it was not issued until November, 1930.

[5] *Ibid.*

[6] Hanneman A9.

[7] Hanneman F150.

[8] Hanneman C91.

FOUR POEMS

By

ERNEST HEMINGWAY

On August 31, 1930 *There were printed privately for the prevention of piracy 12 copies of* FOUR POEMS, *for* E. H. *by* L. H. C. *This is Number*

THE AGE DEMANDED

The age demanded that we sing
and cut away our tongue.
The age demanded that we flow
and hammered in the bung.
The age demanded that we dance
and jammed us into iron pants.
And in the end the age was handed
the sort of shit that it demanded.

THE EARNEST LIBERAL'S LAMENT

I know monks masturbate at night
That pet cats screw
That some girls bite
And yet
What can I do
To set things right?

THE LADY POETS WITH FOOT NOTES

One lady poet was a nymphomaniac and wrote for Vanity
Fair. (1)

One lady poet's husband was killed in the war. (2)

One lady poet wanted her lover but was afraid of having
a baby. When she finally got married, she found
she couldn't have a baby. (3)

One lady poet slept with Bill Reedy got fatter and fatter
and made half a million dollars writing bum plays. (4)

One lady poet never had enough to eat. (5)

One lady poet was big and fat and no fool. (6)

(1) College nymphomaniac. Favorite lyric poet of leading editorial writer
N. Y. Tribune.

(2) It sold her stuff.

(3) Favorite of State University male virgins, wonderful on unrequited
love.

(4) Stomach's gone bad from liquor. Expects to do something really good
soon.

(5) It showed in her work.

(6) She smoked cigars all right, but her stuff was no good.

THE SOUL OF SPAIN WITH
McALMON AND BIRD THE PUBLISHERS

In the rain in the rain in the rain in the rain in Spain.
Does it rain in Spain?
Oh yes my dear on the contrary and there are no bull
fights.
The dancers dance in long white pants
It isn't right to yence your aunts
Come Uncle, let's go home.
Home is where the heart is, home is where the fart is.
Come let us fart in the home.
There is no art in a fart.
Still a fart may not be artless.
Let us fart and artless fart in the home.
Democracy.
Democracy.
Bill says democracy must go.
Go democracy
Go
Go
Go.
Bill's father would never knowingly sit down at a table
with a Democrat.
Now Bill says Democracy must go.
Go on Democracy.
Democracy is the shit.
Relativity is the shit.
Dictators are the shit.
Menken is the shit.
Waldo Frank is the shit.
The Broom is the shit.
Dada is the shit.
Dempsey is the shit.
This is not a complete list.
They say Ezra is the shit.
But Ezra is nice.
Come let us build a monument to Ezra.
Good a very nice monument.
You did that nicely.
Can you do another?
Let me try and do one.
Let us all try and do one.
Let the little girl over there in the corner try and do one.
Come on little girl.
Do one for Ezra.
Good.
You have been successful children.
Now let us clean the mess up.
The Dial does a monument to Proust.
We have a monument to Ezra.
A monument is a monument.
After all it is the spirit of the thing that counts.

Collection of Mrs. Louis Henry Cohn.

Hanneman Addenda

By

Audre Hanneman

Since publication of my Hemingway bibliography on December 18, 1967 (0 frabjous day!), I have frequently wished that I had inserted a note in my preface to the effect that I would be grateful for any omissions being called to my attention. The absence of such an appeal was not meant to be construed as confidence on my part that the bibliography was "complete." Quite the contrary. In 1966, I reluctantly faced the fact that one cannot ever expect to make a bibliography "complete" and sent my eleven-years' effort off to Princeton University Press. It contained everything by and about Hemingway that I had been able to assemble (with the exception of numerous articles in men's magazines, which were left out by intent).

Soon after publication day, the first of my sins of omission was called to my attention. Walter Goldwater informed me that *Fact*, the monograph published in London containing Hemingway's Spanish Civil War dispatches, was missing. After the initial shock, I realized that its omission was not completely inexplicable. It appears in the first and second drafts under periodicals, in Section C. I remember debating whether, in the third draft, to leave it there, since *Fact* was published monthly, or to list it under books and pamphlets, in Section A, since the whole issue is devoted to Hemingway. Unfortunately, due to my vacillating, I omitted it entirely. Since special Hemingway issues of other serial publications appear in Section C of the bibliography that is where I have listed *Fact* below.

A number of Hemingway buffs and interested persons* have very

---

*Including Mrs. Louis Henry Cohn, Charles W. Mann, George Hocutt, Matthew J. Bruccoli, C. E. Frazer Clark, Jr., William F. Nolan, Donald D. Teets, and Robert B. Carowitz.

kindly informed me of omitted items that were previously unknown to me. (As well as informing me of a few errors. While any errors are regrettable, I do not plan a corrigenda at this time.** I corrected some errors in spelling and punctuation for the second printing, April 1969.) Other omissions are coming to light, such as Hemingway's 1925 review of Sherwood Anderson's book, which was reprinted in the first issue of this *Annual*. And the emergence after a fifty-year interim of Hemingway's work on the *Kansas City Star*. We can only hope that issues of the *Co-operative Commonwealth* for the winter of 1920-1921, when Hemingway was responsible for much of the magazine's content, will be located.

I look forward to listing new items in the Hemingway canon and of Hemingwayana here in coming years. And I would welcome any items that I have missed being called to my attention.

PART ONE: OMISSIONS

Omissions to Section C: Contributions to Newspapers and Periodicals

Articles. For 12 unsigned articles in the *Kansas City Star* (1917-1918), see *Ernest Hemingway, Cub Reporter* in Part Two below.

Book review. Review of Sherwood Anderson's *A Story-Teller's Story*, Ex Libris, II (March 1925), 176-177. Reprinted in the *Fitzgerald/Hemingway Annual 1969*, pp. 71-75, see below.

Short story. "The Tradesman's Return," *Fiction Parade* (New York), II, v (March 1936), 567-574. Reprinted, see C241.

Dispatches. "The Spanish War," *Fact* (London), No. 16 (July 15, 1938), pp. 7-72. Nineteen of Hemingway's North American Newspaper Alliance (NANA) dispatches reprinted: Part 1. "The Saving of Madrid" (March 23 - May 2, 1937). Part 2. "The Aragon Front" (Sept. 14 - Sept. 30, 1937). Part 3. "Teruel" (Dec. 20 - Dec. 21, 1937). Part 4. "Franco Advancing" (April 3 - April 18, 1938). Part 5. "Last Despatches" (May 9 - May 11, 1938). The introduction, on pp. 4-5, states that no changes were made but that some abridgment was necessary.

**This addenda had already gone to the printers before I saw a copy of Keneth Kinnamon's review in the *Journal of English and Germanic Philology*, LXVIII (1969), 556-560, which includes a corrigenda and addenda to my bibliography.

"The omitted matter consists chiefly of descriptions of events which in retrospect seem unimportant and speculations on the future course of the war which have no interest now." Note: This issue was bound together with three others to form *Fact* (Second Series), published by Fact Publishing Co., London, (n.d.). Bound in blue cloth with a white paper label, lettered in black, on the backstrip.

Short story. "A Story from Spain," *Lilliput* (London), V, iv (Oct. [1938?]), 369-370. "Old Man at the Bridge" reprinted, see C296.

Short story. "La Dénonciation," *Volontaires* (Paris), I, i (Dec. 1938), 25-37. "The Denunciation" translated into French by Roland Malraux. See C307.

Short story. "The Killers," *Redbook*, LXXIV, vi (April 1940), 24-25, 80-82. Reprinted, see C172.

Article. "Remembering Shooting-Flying: A Key West Letter," *American Rifleman* (Washington, D.C.), XC, vi (June 1942), 11-12, 15. Reprinted, see C227.

Short story. "Une pêche à la truite," *U.S.A.* (published by U.S. Office of War Information), II, iv ([April?] 1945), 72-79. Part II of "Big Two-Hearted River" translated into French. Editor's Note on pp. 70-72. See C165.

Short story. "The Killers," *Ellery Queen's Mystery Magazine*, IX (June 1947), 54-61. Reprinted, see C172.

Article. "On the Blue Water," *Jack London Adventure Magazine*, I, i (Oct. 1958), 34-40. Reprinted, see C243.

Article. "Milan and the Mistletoe," *Topper* (Los Angeles), (Feb. 1962), pp. 8-10. "A North of Italy Christmas," reprinted from the *Toronto Star Weekly*, see C151[1].

Omissions to Section E: Anthologies

The Pocket Book of Short Stories. Edited with an Introduction by M. E. Speare. New York: Pocket Books, Inc., 1941. pp. 1-13: "The Killers."

The Avon Story Teller. New York: Avon Book Co., 1945 [New Avon Library.] pp. 11-23: "Che Ti Dice La Patria?"

Two-Fisted Stories for Men. Compiled by R. M. Barrows. Chicago: Consolidated Book Publishers, 1945. pp. 20-27: "The Killers."

The PL Book of Modern American Short Stories. Edited by
Nicholas Moore. London: Nicholson & Watson, 1945. [Editions
Poetry London.] pp. 81-87: "The Light of the World."

The Pocket Book of Adventure Stories. Edited by Philip Van Doren
Stern. New York: Pocket Books, Inc., 1945. pp. 1-27: "Fifty
Grand."

15 Great Stories of Today: The Avon Annual, 1946. New York:
Avon Book Co., 1946. pp. 172-186: "The Gambler, the Nun,
and the Radio."

A New Collection of Great Stories. New York: Avon Book Co.,
1946. [No. 33.] pp. 38-46: "The Three-Day Blow."

Midland Humor: A Harvest of Fun and Folklore. Edited by Jack
Conroy. New York: Current Books, Inc., 1947. pp. 237-244:
"The Light of the World."

11 Great Modern Stories: The Avon Annual, 1947. New York:
Avon Book Co., 1947. pp. 27-33: "Big Two-Hearted River:
Part I."

Champs and Bums. Edited by Bucklin Moon. New York: Lion
Books, 1954. pp. 69-78: "The Battler."

The Damned. Edited by Daniel Talbot. New York: Lion Books,
1954. [Lion Library Edition.] pp. 37-44: "Soldier's Home."

Omissions to Section F: Book Blurbs by Hemingway

Book band. *Nothing Is Sacred* by Josephine Herbst. New York:
Coward-McCann, 1928. White paper band, printed in black.
2-3/16 x 20. Reads: ERNEST HEMINGWAY—"A fine book by
an honest writer." Note: Blurbs by Ring Lardner and Ford
Madox Ford also appear on the band.

Dust jacket. *The Lincoln Battalion* by Edwin Rolfe. New York:
Random House, 1939. Blurb on back of dust jacket reads:
From a letter to the author. / "The galleys came. I think you
did a fine, fine job, Ed. It is a book to have. / Good luck and
congratulations." / ERNEST HEMINGWAY

Book cover. *The Professional* by W. C. Heinz. New York: Berkley,
1959. [Berkley Books, paperback edition.] Blurb on front
cover reads: ". . . the only good novel I've ever / read about a
fighter and an excel-/lent first novel in its own right." /
—ERNEST HEMINGWAY

Omissions to Section G: Books On or Significantly Mentioning Hemingway

Carlisle, Harry, ed. *The Legacy of Abner Green: A Memorial Journal.* Issued by the American Committee for the Protection of the Foreign Born, New York, December 1959. pp. 2-3. Relates how EH's reply to Abner Green's open letter in the *American Criterion* (under the pseudonym of Paul Harris, see H271) led to his becoming Co-Chairman of the Committee of Sponsors for the American Committee for the Protection of the Foreign Born (see H407). p. 3: Letter from EH to Green briefly quoted.

Collins, Larry, and Dominique Lapierre. *Is Paris Burning?* London: Gollancz, 1965. [New York: Simon & Schuster, 1965.] pp. 170-171, 196, 215, 233, 304, 326. Regarding Hemingway's intelligence efforts at Rambouillet and his participation in the Liberation of Paris in August, 1944.

Crichton, Kyle. *Total Recoil.* Garden City, N.Y.: Doubleday, 1960. pp. 157, 158-161. p. 159: Letter from EH briefly quoted, regarding anti-fascism in America. pp. 159-161: Letter from EH quoted, regarding the author's criticism of him in *Redder Than the Rose* (see G150), and his writing habits.

Dickinson, Asa Don. *The World's Best Books: Homer to Hemingway. 3000 Books of 3000 Years, 1050 B.C. to 1950 A.D.* New York: H. W. Wilson, 1953. p. 158: Five books by EH: *SAR, FTA, DIA, First 49,* and *FWBT.*

Hardy, John Edward. *Man in the Modern Novel.* Seattle: Univ. of Washington Press, 1964. pp. 123-126, 137-141, 197. pp. 123-126: Ch. 7: "*A Farewell to Arms*: The Death of Tragedy."

Linn, James Weber, and Houghton Wells Taylor. *A Foreword to Fiction.* New York: Appleton-Century, 1935. pp. 25, 36-37, 89, 90, 99, 109, 110, 112-113. Regarding Hemingway's style.

MacLennan, Hugh. *Thirty & Three.* Edited by Dorothy Duncan. Toronto: Macmillan, 1954. pp. 85-96: Ch. Eleven: "Homage to Hemingway." Previously unpublished.

Rolfe, Edwin. *The Lincoln Battalion: The Story of the Americans who Fought in Spain in the International Brigades.* New York: Random House, 1939. pp. 70, 111, 130, 236. Photograph. p. 130: EH dispatch quoted. Note: For dust jacket blurb, see above.

Schulz, Franz. *Der nordamerikanische Indianer und seine Welt in den Werken von Ernest Hemingway und Oliver LaFarge.* Munich: Max Hueber, 1964. 192 pages.

Smetana, Josette. *La philosophie de l'action chez Hemingway et Saint-Exupéry.* Paris: La Marjolaine, 1965. 182 pages. Preface by Edouard Morot-Sir, on pp. 1-6. A study of similarities and divergencies in the two writers.

Stewart, Randall. *American Literature & Christian Doctrine.* Baton Rouge: Louisiana State Univ. Press, 1958. pp. 120 n., 123, 134-137. pp. 134-137: Regarding the "virtue of ritualistic discipline" in "A Clean, Well-Lighted Place" and "Big Two-Hearted River."

Sulzberger, Cyrus [Leo]. *The Resistentialists.* New York: Harper, 1962. pp. 5-68: Ch. 2: "The Bravest Collaborator." The story of Hemingway's driver in France and Germany during World War II. He is called here "Michel Dupont." (Cf. Carlos Baker, *Ernest Hemingway: A Life Story*, p. 654, third note.) pp. 18-25: Three letters from Hemingway to Sulzberger, from Finca Vigia [ca. July 15, Aug. 10, and ca. Sept. 5, 1951] are extensively quoted. Note: This book was withdrawn by Harper's before publication day. The number of review and library copies distributed is not known.

[USIA]. *Ernest Hemingway: A Bibliography.* United States Information Agency, Office of the U.S. High Commissioner for Germany. Bonn, November 1954. Pamphlet. 18 pages. A listing of EH's novels and short stories, with the most recent German translations; anthologies containing his work; and biographical material and criticism in books and periodicals. In English.

Wilson, Colin. *Eagle and Earwig.* London: Baker, 1965. pp. 113, 115, 121-127. pp. 113-127: "The Swamp and the Desert: Notes on Powys and Hemingway."

Omissions to Section H: Newspaper and Periodical Material on Hemingway

"Dare Girls Rescued," *Oak Leaves* (Feb. 3, 1917). Describes how three girls who decided to ride the dumbwaiter in the high school lunchroom "were flying to destruction when Ernest Hemingway . . . saw and realized the danger. He grabbed the rope and was jerked off his feet and his bare hands engaged and blocked the pulley at the top" until four other boys ran to his assistance and pulled the girls to safety. Reprinted in *Trapeze* (June 9, 1967), p. 7.

Calverton, V. F. "Ernest Hemingway and the Modern Temper," *Book League Monthly* (New York), III (Jan. 1930), 165-166. The author differs with the claim that Hemingway "has already won a secure and lasting place in literature."

Harrison, Charles Yale. "Story for Mr. Hemingway," *Modern Monthly*, VIII (Feb. 1935), 731-737. A story by the author of *Generals Die in Bed*. The headnote, on p. 731, quotes Hemingway's reference to his book: ". . . writers are mistaken who write books called *Generals Die in Bed* . . . the titles of all such books should be *Generals Usually Die in Bed*, if we are to have any sort of accuracy in such things." (From "A Natural History of the Dead.")

Fagin, Bryllion. "The Psychological Moment," *Step Ladder* (Chicago), XXIV (May 1938), pp. 101-107. pp. 101-103: Discusses Hemingway's work.

"*Look* Examines: Ernest Hemingway," *Look*, V (April 8, 1941), 18, 20-21. Photographs.

Spilka, Mark. "The Necessary Stylist: A New Critical Revision," *Modern Fiction Studies*, VI (Winter 1960-1961), 283-297. pp. 289-297: Regarding Warren Beck's essay "The Shorter Happy Life of Mrs. Macomber," see H967.

Ledig-Rowohlt, H. M. "Der Tod am Morgen," *Die Zeit* (Hamburg), XVI, No. 28 (July 14, 1961), 9. Includes long excerpts from two Hemingway letters to Ernst Rowohlt, translated into German. Dated: Key West, Feb. 11, 1930; Montana, Nov. 30, 1930.

Krock, Arthur. In the Nation column, "Previous Veto of a Pulitzer Board Award," *N. Y. Times* (May 11, 1962), p. 30. Regarding the Pulitzer prize Advisory Board's recommendation of *FWBT* in 1941 and Nicholas Murray Butler's veto of their selection. (See W. J. Stuckey below.)

"50 Pounds of Hemingway," *Newsweek*, LXIII (Jan 6, 1964), 67. Photograph. Interview with Mary Hemingway regarding Hemingway's unpublished manuscripts.

Thompson, Hunter S. "What Lured Hemingway to Ketchum?" *National Observer* (Washington, D.C.), (May 25, 1964), pp. 1, 13.

Books and Pamphlets

Second paperback edition: *To Have and Have Not*. Published by Charles Scribner's Sons, New York, August 15, 1966, as No. SL132 in the Scribner Library series. viii + 262 pages. 8 x 5-3/8. $1.65.

Fourth pirated reprint: *The Collected Poems* of Ernest Hemingway. San Francisco, 1960. (Haskell House, New York, [1967?]. Monograph Series, MS44.) 28 pages plus 2 blank leaves. 9 x 6. Issued in gray stiff paper covers, printed in black. $1.95. See A26C.

First edition: *Two Stories: Fifty Grand and The Undefeated*. Edited by Aage Salling et al. Copenhagen/Helsinki/Oslo/Stockholm: Easy Readers, 1967. 108 pages. Paperback. In English. "Simplified for Use in Schools." Contains: pp. 7-54: "Fifty Grand." pp. 55-56: Questions. pp. 59-105: "The Undefeated." pp. 106-108: Questions.

School edition: *A Farewell to Arms*. Published by Charles Scribner's Sons, New York, February 2, 1967, at $3.60. School Edition. x + 358 pages. 8 x 5-3/8. Introduction, pp. vii-x, and Study Guide, pp. 333-358, by John C. Schweitzer. Map endpapers.

First edition: *By-Line: Ernest Hemingway*. Selected Articles and Dispatches of Four Decades edited by William White. Published by Charles Scribner's Sons, New York, May 8, 1967, at $8.95. xvi + 494 pages. Indexed. 8-3/8 x 5-1/4. Introduction by the editor on pp. [xi]-xiv. Contains articles and dispatches from the *Toronto Star Weekly* (15), *Toronto Daily Star* (14), *Transatlantic Review* (1), *Esquire* (17), NANA (9), *Ken* (2), *Vogue* (1), *PM* (7 plus Ralph Ingersoll's "authenticated interview," see H481), *Collier's* (6), *Holiday* (1), *True* (1), and *Look* (2). Paperback edition: Published by Bantam Books, New York, in July 1968, at $1.25. No. Q3788. 428 pages. English edition: Published by Collins, London, in 1968, at 45s. 479 pages. Foreword, on pp. 19-24, and Commentaries before sections by Philip Young.

First paperback edition: *The Short Stories of Ernest Hemingway*. Published by Charles Scribner's Sons, New York, August 15, 1967, as No. SL141 of the Scribner Library series. viii + 500 pages. 8 x 5-3/8. $2.95 pp. v-vi: Preface by EH, dated 1938, reprinted from *First 49* with references to *The Fifth Column* omitted.

Second edition: *Hemingway: The Wild Years*. Edited and Introduced by Gene Z. Hanrahan. "New edition" published by Dell Publishing Co., Inc., New York, September 1967, at 75¢. No. 3577. Paperback. 288 pages. 7 x 4-1/8. See A30.

First English separate hard-cover edition: *The Fifth Column*. Published by Jonathan Cape, London, in January 1968, at 18s. 112 pages. pp. 7-8: Preface by EH, regarding the play, reprinted from the *First 49*.

Second paperback edition: *The Old Man and the Sea*. Published by Charles Scribner's Sons, New York, January 18, 1968, at $1.20, as No. SSP6 in the Scribner School Paperbacks series. iv + 124 pages. 8 x 5-3/8. Text on pp. 5-94. Study Guide by Mary A. Campbell on pp. 97-123. See A24D. Cover painting by Victor Mays.

Large-type edition: *The Old Man and the Sea*. Published by Charles Scribner's Sons, New York, June 15, 1968, at $6.95. 140 pages plus 2 blank leaves. 11 x 8-1/2. Illustrated by Raymond Sheppard and C. F. Tunnicliffe. Text on pp. 11-138. Published as an aid to the visually handicapped.

Large-type edition: *A Farewell to Arms*. Published by Charles Scribner's Sons, New York, June 15, 1968, at $7.95. viii + 344 pages. 11 x 8-1/2. Text on pp. 3-[343]. Published as an aid to the visually handicapped.

First paperback edition: *Winner Take Nothing*. Published by Charles Scribner's Sons, August 15, 1968, as No. SL155 of the Scribner Library series. viii + 244 pages. 8 x 5-3/8. $1.65.

First paperback edition: *Death in the Afternoon*. Published by Charles Scribner's Sons, New York, January 20, 1969, as No. SL175 of the Lyceum Edition of the Scribner Library series. viii + 488 pages. 96 pages of photographs. 8 x 5-3/8. $2.95.

Third paperback edition: *A Farewell to Arms*. Published by Charles Scribner's Sons, New York, February 4, 1969, as No. SSP23 in the Scribner School Paperbacks series. 8 x 5-3/8. $2.36. x + 358 pages + 8 blank leaves. Cover design by Victor Mays. Study Guide by John C. Schweitzer. See "school edition" above.

First edition: *The Fifth Column and Four Stories of the Spanish Civil War*. Published by Charles Scribner's Sons, August 13, 1969, at $4.95. vi + 152 pages 8-1/4 x 5-3/8. Contains the play,

The Fifth Column, and four short stories collected for the first time: "The Denunciation," which first appeared in *Esquire*, X (Nov. 1938); "The Butterfly and the Tank," which first appeared in *Esquire*, X (Dec. 1938); "Night Before Battle," which first appeared in *Esquire*, XI (Feb. 1939); and "Under the Ridge," which first appeared in *Cosmopolitan*, CVII (Oct. 1939).

Second paperback edition: *Across the River and Into the Trees*. Published by Charles Scribner's Sons, New York, January 28, 1970, as No. SL202 in the Scribner Library Series. xii + 308 pages. 8 x 5-3/8. $1.95.

Ernest Hemingway, Cub Reporter. Edited by Matthew J. Bruccoli. Pittsburgh: University of Pittsburgh Press, 1970. xiii + 68 pp. Also a limited printing of 200 copies. Attributes twelve *Kansas City Star* articles to Hemingway: "Kerensky, the Fighting Flea" (Dec. 16, 1917); "Battle of Raid Squads" (Jan. 6, 1918); "At the End of the Ambulance Run" (Jan. 20, 1918); "Throng at Smallpox Case" (Feb. 18, 1918); "Laundry Car Over Cliff" (March 6, 1918); "Six Men Become Tankers" (April 17, 1918); "Big Day for Navy Drive" (April 17, 1918); "Navy Desk Jobs to Go" (April 18, 1918); "Would 'Treat 'Em Rough,' " (April 18, 1918); "Recruits for the Tanks" (April 18, 1918); "Dare Devil Joins Tanks" (April 21, 1918); "Mix War, Art and Dancing" (April 21, 1918)–plus list of stories possibly by Hemingway.

Contributions and First Appearances in Books and Pamphlets

El Gran Gatsby. Havana: Editora Del Consejo Nacional De Cultura Editorial Nacional De Cuba, 1965. Pirated. pp. 165-188: "Retrato de Scott Fitzgerald." The chapter on Fitzgerald translated into Spanish from *A Moveable Feast*, pp. 149-176.

Years of Protest: A Collection of American Writings of the 1930's. Edited by Jack Salzman. New York: Pegasus, 1967. pp. 191-195: "Dispatch from Spain," reprinted from the *N. Y. Times* (April 25, 1937). See C261.

Three Great American Novels: The Great Gatsby by F. Scott Fitzgerald, *A Farewell to Arms* by Ernest Hemingway, *Ethan Frome* by Edith Wharton. New York: Scribners, 1967. [Modern Standard Authors.] vi + 570 pages. Published October 9, 1967. *FTA* on pp. 189-471. Introduction by Robert Penn Warren on pp. 153-186, see A8L.

The Last Will and Testament. (n.p.): Robert A. Farmer & Associates, Inc., 1968. Paperback. 184 pages. [RAF Books, 103 N.] "Unabridged Historical Series." Includes the wills of 27 famous people from Shakespeare to John F. Kennedy. p. 51: "The Will of Ernest Hemingway." (Sept. 17, 1955.) Note: A facsimile of EH's will appeared in the *N. Y. Times* (Aug. 25, 1961).

Facsimile of *Ciao* (June 1918). 4 pages. 12 x 8-1/2. Issued on 11 November 1968, in beige paper covers, printed in brown. 200 copies were printed as a keepsake for the first exhibition from The Joseph M. Bruccoli Great War Collection, Alderman Library, University of Virginia. p. [2]: "Al Receives Another Letter." See C32.

New Masses: An Anthology of the Rebel Thirties. Edited with a Prologue by Joseph North. Introduction by Maxwell Geismar. New York: International Publishers, 1969. pp. 181-187: "Who Murdered the Vets?" Reprinted for the first time in book form. See C236. pp. 306-307: "On the American Dead in Spain." See C313. p. 308: Letter from Hemingway briefly quoted in the Editor's Note.

Contributions in Newspapers and Periodicals

Short stories. *Crest*, LXXIII, ii (Spring 1967) [A Literary Magazine published by the students of Oak Park-River Forest High School.] Cover drawing of EH by Jeff Varilla. pp. 12-13: "Sepi Jingan." Reprinted, see C10. p. 14: "Judgment of Manitou." Reprinted, see C3. Note: This "tribute" to EH also contains articles by Carol Coven, Ben Davenport, and Ralph Gottfried.

Article. *Playbill* (New York), IV, x (Oct. 1967). pp. [23]-[24]: "About Marlene Dietrich." Reprinted, see C367.

Articles. "Remembering Hemingway's Kansas City Days" by Mel Foor. *K. C. Star* (July 21, 1968), Sec. D, pp. 1-2. Photographs and drawings. Four unsigned articles attributed to EH: "Throng at Smallpox Case" (*K. C. Star*, Feb. 18, 1918, p. 3); "At the End of the Ambulance Run" (*K. C. Star*, Jan. 20, 1918); "Kerensky, the Fighting Flea" (*K. C. Star*, Dec. 16, 1917); "Mix War, Art and Dancing" (*K. C. Star*, April 21, 1918, p. 1). Reprinted in *Ernest Hemingway, Cub Reporter* edited by Matthew J. Bruccoli, see above.

Article. "Ernest Hemingway as Cub Reporter." Introductory note by M. J. Bruccoli. *Esquire*, LXX (Dec. 1968), pp. 207, 265. "Battle of Raid Squads," an unsigned article attributed to EH, from the *K. C. Star* (Jan. 6, 1918), p. 1. Reprinted in *Ernest Hemingway, Cub Reporter* edited by Matthew J. Bruccoli, see above.

Book review. "A Lost Book Review: *A Story-Teller's Story*," *Fitzgerald/Hemingway Annual 1969*, pp. 71-75. Introductory note by M. J. B. [Matthew J. Bruccoli]. pp. 72-74: EH's review of Sherwood Anderson's *A Story-Teller's Story* is reprinted from *Ex Libris* (journal of the American Library in Paris), II (March 1925), 176-177. Note: A companion review by Gertrude Stein is also reprinted.

Published Facsimiles of Hemingway's Manuscripts

Texas Quarterly, IX, iv (Winter 1966), pp. 66-101. "The Texas Manuscript of 'The Snows of Kilimanjaro' " by Robert W. Lewis, Jr. and Max Westbrook. Facsimiles of typescript with holograph insertions from the Ernest Hemingway Collection at the University of Texas. p. [69]: Facsimile of page 24, mentioning "poor Scott Fitzgerald." p. [73]: Facsimile of page 28, the last page. p. [97]: Facsimile of page 12.

Ernest Hemingway: A Comprehensive Bibliography by Audre Hanneman. Princeton: Princeton University Press, 1967. Opp. p. 51. Facsimile of a holograph manuscript page from *A Moveable Feast*.

Hemingway's African Stories by John M. Howell. New York: Scribners, 1969. Frontispiece. Facsimile of typescript with holograph insertions of page 12 of "The Snows of Kilimanjaro." (Also reproduced in the *Texas Quarterly*, see above.)

The Hemingway Manuscripts: An Inventory by Philip Young and Charles W. Mann. University Park: Pennsylvania State University Press, 1969. Following p. 18. Facsimile of last page of notebook draft of *The Sun Also Rises*. Facsimile of holograph first page of "Summer People," believed to be the first Nick Adams story. Facsimile of typescript of first page of "The Killers." Facsimile of typescript with holograph insertions of the original first page of "Fifty Grand," which was later discarded. Note: Facsimiles of pages two and three of "Fifty Grand," which were also later rejected, are reproduced in the limited edition only (see below).

N.Y. Times (Sept. 22, 1969), pp. 1, 36. "Hemingway Papers Yield Surprises" by Henry Raymont. p. 36: Facsimile of holograph first page of "Summer People." (Also reproduced in *The Hemingway Manuscripts*, see above.)

PART THREE: BOOKS ON OR SIGNIFICANTLY MENTIONING HEMINGWAY PUBLISHED SINCE 1966

Aaberg, Jean, and Judith Homme Bolduc. *Classics in the Kitchen: An Edible Anthology for the Literary Gourmet.* Los Angeles: Ward Ritchie Press, 1969. pp. 87-92: "October: Ernest Hemingway and Viands of Valencia." Includes short excerpt from *FWBT*, p. 85.

Arnold, Lloyd R. *High on the Wild with Hemingway.* Caldwell, Idaho: Caxton Printers, 1968. xvi + 344 pages. 11 x 8-1/2. 160 photographs. Foreword by John H. Hemingway on p. [vii]. A friend's account of the nine seasons Hemingway spent in Idaho, between 1939 and 1961.

Baker, Carlos. *Ernest Hemingway A Life Story.* New York: Scribners, 1969. xviii + 698 pages. Photographs. [London: Collins, 1969. 702 pages.] This full-length biography, authorized by Mary Hemingway and Charles Scribner's Sons, was the Book-of-the-Month Club selection for April 1969. Sources and Notes on pp. 567-668.

Baker, Sheridan. *Ernest Hemingway: An Introduction and Interpretation.* New York: Holt, Rinehart and Winston, 1967. [American Authors and Critics Series.] x + 150 pages. Photographs. A study of Hemingway and the "undefeated loser" who emerges in his work. Selected Bibliography on pp. 137-142.

Benson, Frederick R. *Writers in Arms: The Literary Impact of the Spanish Civil War.* New York: New York Univ. Press, 1967. pp. 60-63, 123-129, 292-296, and *passim.* A study of the impact of the Spanish Civil War on six writers: André Malraux, George Orwell, Gustav Regler, Georges Bernanos, Arthur Koestler, and Ernest Hemingway.

Benson, Jackson J. *Hemingway . . . The Writer's Art of Self-Defense.* Minneapolis: Univ. of Minnesota Press, 1969. x + 202 pages. A study of Hemingway's use of style and technique to express "the living experience in words." *SAR, FTA, FWBT, ARIT,* and *OMATS* are analyzed.

Brack, O M, Jr., and Warner Barnes, eds. *Bibliography and Textual Criticism: English and American Literature, 1700 to the Present.* Chicago: Univ. of Chicago Press, 1969. pp. 314-333: "The Text of Ernest Hemingway" by James B. Meriwether. Reprinted with revisions, H1474.

Bradbury, Ray. *I Sing the Body Electric!* New York: Knopf, 1969. pp. [3]-14: "The Kilimanjaro Device." The title of this short story was changed from "The Kilimanjaro Machine," see H1567.

Bridgman, Richard. *The Colloquial Style in America.* New York: Oxford Univ. Press, 1966. pp. 4, 5, 11, 12, 31, 62, 129-130, 137, 188, 195-230. pp. 195-230: Ch. Six: "Ernest Hemingway."

Brophy, Brigid, Michael Levey, and Charles Osborne. *Fifty Works of English [and American] Literature we could do without.* London: Rapp & Carroll, 1967. [New York: Stein & Day, 1968.] pp. 149-150: "Ernest Hemingway: *A Farewell to Arms.*"

[Brown, John, et al.] *Hemingway.* Paris: Hachette, 1966. [Collection Génies et Réalités.] 292 pages. Photographs. Photograph of EH by Karsh on endpapers.
  pp. [7]- 35: "Une vie légendaire" by John Brown.
  pp. [57]- 75: "Paradis perdu" by Marc Saporta.
  pp. [77]-101: "Un Américain à Paris" by Georges-Albert Astre.
  pp. [121]-131: "La fascination du néant" by Michel Mohrt.
  pp. [133]-149: "Solitaire et solidaire" by Michel del Castillo.
  pp. [169]-187: "Hommes sans femmes" by Roger Grenier.
  pp. [189]-201: " 'Il était une fois un vieil homme . . .' " by Jorge Semprun.
  pp. [221]-237: "Le style et l'homme" by Jean-Louis Curtis.
  pp. [259]-283: "Cours, cours chère légende" by Alain Bosquet.

Bryer, Jackson R., ed. *Fifteen Modern American Authors: A survey of research and criticism.* Durham, N. C.: Duke Univ. Press, 1969. pp. 275-300: "Ernest Hemingway" by Frederick J. Hoffman.

Cohen, Hennig, ed. *Landmarks of American Writing.* New York and London: Basic Books, 1969. pp. 303-312: "Ernest Hemingway: *The Sun Also Rises*" by Earl H. Rovit. Notes on pp. 313-314. Essays originally prepared for the Voice of America.

Considine, Bob. *Toots.* New York: Meredith Press, 1969. pp. 169-171: Regarding EH's inscriptions in books presented to Toots Shor, the restaurateur.

Cooperman, Stanley. *World War I and the American Novel.* Baltimore: Johns Hopkins Press, 1967. pp. 181-190: "Death and Cojones: Frederic Henry (Ernest Hemingway)."

Cowley, Malcolm. *Think Back On Us . . .: A Contemporary Chronicle of the 1930's.* Edited by Henry Dan Piper. Carbondale: Southern Illinois Univ. Press, 1967. pp. 219-225: "A Farewell to Spain," review of *DIA.* Reprinted, H196. pp. 310-314: "Hemingway: Work in Progress," review of *THAHN.* Reprinted, H337. pp. 361-364: "Hemingway's 'Nevertheless'," review of *FWBT.* Reprinted, H457.

Crane, R. S. *The Idea of the Humanities: and other essays Critical and Historical.* Vol. II. Chicago: Univ. of Chicago Press, 1967. pp. 303-314: "Ernest Hemingway: 'The Killers'." Previously unpublished. pp. 315-326: "Ernest Hemingway: 'The Short Happy Life of Francis Macomber.'" See E143.

Crothers, George Dunlap, ed. *Invitation to Learning.* New York: Basic Books, 1966. pp. 329-336: *"A Farewell to Arms."* Discussion by Carlos Baker, Philip Young, and George D. Crothers transcribed.

Cunard, Nancy. *These Were the Hours: Memories of My Hours Press, Réauville and Paris 1928-1931.* Carbondale: Southern Illinois Univ. Press, 1969. pp. 127-128: During a discussion about Ezra Pound, the author recalls that "Hemingway never spoke more charmingly and gently."

Davenport, Marcia. *Too Strong for Fantasy.* New York: Scribners, 1967. pp. 138, 175, 214, 298. p. 298: The novelist relates how Hemingway rudely ignored her when Max Perkins tried to introduce them.

Desnoes, Edmundo. *Inconsolable Memories.* New York: New American Library, 1967. pp. 55-73: A long scene in this novel takes place at the Hemingway Museum (formerly Finca Vigía).

Fallaci, Oriana. *The Egotists: Sixteen Surprising Interviews.* Chicago: Regnery/Reilly & Lee, 1968. pp. 116-130: "My Husband, Ernest Hemingway," interview with Mary Hemingway reprinted from *Look,* XXX (Sept. 6, 1966).

French, Warren G., and Walter E. Kidd, eds. *American Winners of the Nobel Literary Prize.* Norman: Univ. of Oklahoma Press, 1968. pp. 158-192: "Ernest Hemingway" by Ken Moritz. Includes EH's Nobel prize acceptance speech on pp. 161-162.

Gibson, Walker. *Tough, Sweet, and Stuffy: An Essay on Modern American Prose Styles*. Bloomington: Indiana Univ. Press, 1966. pp. 28-42. "Tough Talk: The Rhetoric of Frederick Henry."

Gurko, Leo. *Ernest Hemingway and the Pursuit of Heroism*. New York: Crowell, 1968. viii + 248 pages. [Paperback edition: Apollo Editions, A-211. 1969.] A study of Hemingway's "search for a relevant and sustainable heroism." Selected Bibliography on pp. 240-242.

Hovey, Richard B. *Hemingway: The Inward Terrain*. Foreword by Frederick C. Crews. Seattle: Univ. of Washington Press, 1968. xxiv + 248 pages. A partly psychological approach to Hemingway and his books. Bibliographical Note, with a Checklist of Selected Readings, on pp. 239-241.

Howell, John M. *Hemingway's African Stories: The Stories, Their Sources, Their Critics*. New York: Scribners, 1969. [Scribner Research Anthology.] x + 170 + x pages. Paperback. Frontispiece facsimile, see above.
pp.   1- 2: Introduction by John M. Howell.
pp.   5- 22: "The Short Happy Life of Francis Macomber."
pp. 23- 36: "The Snows of Kilimanjaro."
pp. 39- 42: Excerpt from *GHOA*.
pp. 43- 44: Excerpt from *AMF*.
pp. 45- 49: "Monologue to the Maestro: A High Seas Letter." See C237.
pp. 50- 51: Excerpts from *DIA*.
pp. 55- 59: "The Slopes of Kilimanjaro" by Carlos Baker, reprinted from *American Heritage*, XIX (Aug. 1968).
pp. 60- 62: "Asia Minor" by Charles A. Fenton. Reprinted, G143.
pp. 63- 65: Excerpt from *AMF*.
p.   66   : Excerpt from *DIA*.
pp. 67- 73: "Three Tanganyika Letters" from *Esquire*. See C218-220.
pp. 74- 88: Excerpts from *GHOA*.
p.   89   : Excerpt from EH's Introduction to *Men at War*.
pp. 93- 94: "Hemingway's Riddle of Kilimanjaro: Idea and Image" by Robert O. Stephens. Reprinted, H1181.
pp. 95- 96: Excerpt from *Across East African Glaciers: An Account of the First Ascent of Kilimanjaro* by Hans Meyer (London, 1891).

pp. 97- 98: Excerpt from *Snows on the Equator* by H. W. Til-
man (New York, 1938).
pp. 99-100: The Leopard of Kilimanjaro: Dr. Richard Reusch's
Letter to the Editor.
pp. 101-109: "Vivienne de Watteville, Hemingway's Companion
on Kilimanjaro" by Robert W. Lewis, Jr., reprinted
from the *Texas Quarterly*, IX (Winter 1966).
p. [111]   : EH's Nobel prize acceptance speech. See B56.
pp. 113-115: "Dangerous Game" by Carlos Baker. Reprinted,
G26.
pp. 116-118: "The Hero and the Code" by Philip Young. Reprinted, G460.
pp. 119-128: "The Shorter Happy Life of Mrs. Macomber" by
Warren Beck. Reprinted, H967.
pp. 129-136: "Ernest Hemingway: The Short Happy Life of
Francis Macomber" by R. S. Crane. See Crane
above.
pp. 137-141: "Macomber and the Critics" by Robert B. Holland,
from *Studies in Short Fiction*, V (Winter 1967).
pp. 142-144: " 'The Snows of Kilimanjaro': Commentary" by
Caroline Gordon and Allen Tate. Reprinted, E165.
pp. 145-149: "The Leopard and the Hyena: Symbol and Meaning in 'The Snows of Kilimanjaro' " by Marion
Montgomery. Reprinted, H1227[1].
pp. 150-157: " 'The Snows of Kilimanjaro': A Revaluation"
by Oliver Evans. Reprinted, H1358.
pp. 158-161: " 'The Snows of Kilimanjaro': Harry's Second
Chance" by Gloria R. Dussinger, from *Studies in
Short Fiction*, V (Fall 1967).

Jobes, Katharine T., ed. *Twentieth Century Interpretations of The
Old Man and the Sea: A Collection of Critical Essays.* Englewood
Cliffs, N. J.: Prentice-Hall, 1968. [Spectrum Books, S-831.]
vi + 120 pages. Paperback.
pp.   1- 17: Introduction by Katharine T. Jobes.
pp. 18- 26: "*The Old Man and the Sea*: Vision/Revision" by
Philip Young. Reprinted, G460.
pp. 27- 33: "The Boy and the Lions" by Carlos Baker. Reprinted, G26.
pp. 34- 40: "Fakery in *The Old Man and the Sea*" by Robert P.
Weeks. Reprinted, H1430.

pp.   41- 55: "New World, Old Myths" by Claire Rosenfield. Previously unpublished.
pp.   56- 63: "A Ritual of Transfiguration: *The Old Man and the Sea*" by Arvin R. Wells. Reprinted, H1480.
pp.   64- 71: "The Heroic Impulse in *The Old Man and the Sea*" by Leo Gurko. Reprinted, H961.
pp.   72- 80: "*The Old Man and the Sea:* Hemingway's Tragic Vision of Man" by Clinton S. Burhans, Jr. Reprinted, H1173.
pp.   81- 96: "Hemingway's Extended Vision: *The Old Man and the Sea*" by Bickford Sylvester, reprinted from *PMLA*, LXXXI (March 1966).
pp.   97-102: "*The Old Man and the Sea* and the American Dream" by Delmore Schwartz. [Editor's title.] Reprinted, H959.
pp. 103-112: "View Points" by Frederick I. Carpenter, Earl Rovit, Malcolm Cowley, Leslie A. Fiedler, Nemi D'Agostino, Robert Gorham Davis, Philip Rahv, and Philip Toynbee.
pp. 112-113: Hemingway quoted from George Plimpton's interview. See H1066.

Joost, Nicholas. *Ernest Hemingway and the Little Magazines: The Paris Years.* Barre, Mass.: Barre Publishers, 1968. 186 pages. A study of EH's contributions during 1922-1925 in the *Double Dealer, Little Review, Poetry: A Magazine of Verse, Der Querschnitt, This Quarter,* and *Transatlantic Review.*

Josephson, Matthew. *Infidel in the Temple: A Memoir of the Nineteen-Thirties.* New York: Knopf, 1967. pp. 414, 416-435, 477. pp. 416-435: Ch. Twenty: "Hemingway Goes to Spain." Reminiscences of the author's visit to Key West during the winter of 1936-1937.

Kaplan, Harold. *The Passive Voice: An Approach to Modern Fiction.* Athens: Ohio Univ. Press, 1966. pp. 17, 93-110, 120, 133n., 173. pp. 93-110: "Hemingway and the Passive Hero."

Karsh, Yousuf. *Karsh Portfolio.* London: Nelson, 1967. Photograph. pp. 81-83. The story behind the photographs of EH taken by Karsh in 1957.

Kermode, Frank. *Continuities.* London: Routledge & Kegan Paul, 1968. [New York: Random House, 1969.] pp. 161-167:

"Hemingway's Last Novel" (1964). Review of *AMF*, see H1535.

Kristensen, Sven Møller, ed. *Fremmede digtere i det 20. århundrede.* Vol. II. Copenhagen: G. E. C. Gads Forlag, 1968. Photographs. pp. 257-278: "Ernest Hemingway" by Klaus Rifbjerg. List of translations of EH's work into Danish on pp. 624-625.

Landis, Arthur H. *The Abraham Lincoln Brigade.* New York: Citadel Press, 1967. Photograph. pp. xvi, 306, 327-329, 376, 440, 496-497, 500, 574. p. xvi: EH quoted regarding the 11th Brigade.

Levin, Martin, ed. *The Saturday Review Sampler of Wit and Wisdom.* New York: Simon & Schuster, 1966. pp. 288-294: "Havana" by Mary Hemingway, reprinted from *SR*, XLVIII (Jan. 2, 1965).

[Levine, David]. *Pens and Needles.* Literary Caricatures by David Levine. Selected and Introduced by John Updike. Boston: Gambit, 1969. p. 16: Caricature of EH and F. Scott Fitzgerald. p. 17: Caricature of EH standing, with gun, over a second EH. Note: Also published in a limited, signed edition of 300 copies.

[*Life*]. *Ernest Hemingway / William Faulkner. Life* Educational Reprint, 6. New York: Life Education Program, [1968]. 24 pages 13-3/4 x 10-1/2. Photographs. pp. 15-24: "Hemingway." Includes "His Mirror Was Danger" by Archibald MacLeish, on pp. 22-23, see H1274[2] ; "How Hemingway Works" by Malcolm Cowley, on p. 23, see H596; and Editors' Note, "Our Warmest Memories of Hemingway," see H1274.

Lupan, Radu. *Hemingway, Scriitorul.* Bucharest: Editura Pentru Literatura Universala, 1966. 400 pages. Paperback. Selected Bibliography and Chronology on pp. 371-[384].

McAlmon, Robert. *Being Geniuses Together: 1920-1930.* Revised and with supplementary chapters by Kay Boyle. New York: Doubleday, 1968. Photograph. Kay Boyle's reminiscences on pp. 114-115, 201, 204-205, 351-352; McAlmon's autobiography on pp. 175-182, 249, 273-277, 346. See G253.

MacLeish, Archibald. *A Continuing Journey.* Boston: Houghton Mifflin, 1968. pp. 307-312: "Ernest Hemingway" 1961. This essay originally appeared under the title "His Mirror Was Danger," see H1274[2] .

Madden, David, ed. *Tough Guy Writers of the Thirties*. With a Preface by Harry T. Moore. Carbondale: Southern Illinois Univ. Press, 1968. [Crosscurrents Modern Critiques series.] pp. xxi-xxiii, xxxii, 18-50, 89, 90, 102, 129-131, 227, 239n., 240 n. pp. 18-41: "The Tough Hemingway and His Hard-Boiled Children" by Sheldon Norman Grebstein. pp. 42-50: "Focus on *To Have and Have Not*: To Have Not: Tough Luck" by Philip Young.

Meacham, Harry M. *The Caged Panther: Ezra Pound at Saint Elizabeths*. New York: Twayne, 1967. pp. 39, 53, 55-56, 61-62, 65, 94, 96, 113, 117-120, 122-123, 131, 158. pp. 118-119: The Frost-Eliot-Hemingway letter (dated: Jan. 14, 1957), which was drafted by Archibald MacLeish, to the Attorney General of the United States urging Pound's release from Saint Elizabeths Hospital. p. 53: Hemingway letter to Dorothy Pound quoted, regarding his comment on Pound in the *Time* cover story (Dec. 13, 1954).

[Methuen]. *Notes on Hemingway's The Old Man and the Sea*. London: Methuen, 1967. [Study-Aid Series.] iv + 36 pages. Pamphlet. Designed as an aid to students for examination purposes. Includes "Test-yourself" Questions (with answers) on pp. 17-21.

Muste, John M. *Say That We Saw Spain Die: Literary Consequences of the Spanish Civil War*. Seattle: Univ. of Washington Press, 1966. pp. 60-68, 90-119, and *passim*. pp. 60-68: Regarding *The Fifth Column*. pp. 90-119: Regarding *FWBT*.

Poli, Bernard J. *Ford Madox Ford and the Transatlantic Review*. Syracuse, N. Y.: Syracuse Univ. Press, 1967. pp. 12, 14, 15, 17, 58-59, 71, 72, 74-75, 102-111, 112-115, 119-120, 142, 143, 157-158, 161-162. pp. 102-111: Regarding EH's editorship during Ford's absence on a trip to the United States. p. 142: Regarding Ford and Stella Bowen as "Mr. and Mrs. Braddocks" in *SAR*.

Rahv, Philip. *Literature and the Sixth Sense*. Boston: Houghton Mifflin, 1969. pp. 351-357: "Hemingway in the 1950s," reviews of *ARIT* and *OMATS*. See G328.

Randall, David A. *Dukedom Large Enough*. New York: Random House, 1969. pp. 39, 165, 235-241, 243, 256, 257, 259. pp. 235-241: "Hemingway and the Printed Word." See H1403.

Ray, Gordon N., Foreword by. *The American Writer in England: An Exhibition Arranged in Honor of the Sesquicentennial of the University of Virginia.* Introduction by C. Waller Barrett. Charlottesville: Univ. Press of Virginia, 1969. p. 131: Hemingway items in the exhibit. Item 317 contains an excerpt from a "presumably unpublished" letter from EH to Ernest Walsh, from Paris, Feb. 1, 1926.

Richards, Norman. *Ernest Hemingway.* Chicago: Children's Press, 1968. [People of Destiny: A Humanities Series.] 96 pages 11 x 8-3/8. Photographs and drawings. Biography of EH for young people, grade 6-up. Bibliography on pp. 90-91.

Schorer, Mark. *The World We Imagine: Selected Essays.* New York: Farrar, Straus & Giroux, 1968. pp. 299-402: Part Six: "Some Relationships: Gertrude Stein, Sherwood Anderson, F. Scott Fitzgerald, and Ernest Hemingway."

Scott, Nathan A., Jr. *Ernest Hemingway: A Critical Essay.* Grand Rapids, Mich.: Eerdmans, 1966. [Contemporary Writers in Christian Perspective series.] 46 pages. Pamphlet. An examination of the Christian values to be found in EH's novels. Selected Bibliography on pp. 45-46.

Seward, William. *My Friend Ernest Hemingway: An Affectionate Reminiscence.* South Brunswick and New York: A. S. Barnes, 1969. 70 pages. Photographs. Reminiscences by a professor of English of his friendship with EH that began through correspondence in 1940 and continued until Hemingway's death.

Stephens, Robert O. *Hemingway's Nonfiction: The Public Voice.* Chapel Hill: Univ. of North Carolina Press, 1968. xiv + 392 pages. A study of EH's nonfictional writing from his early articles in the *Toronto Star* to the posthumously published *A Moveable Feast.* A Chronological List of Hemingway's Nonfiction on pp. [347]-361.

Stuckey, W. J. [William Joseph]. *The Pulitzer Prize Novels: A Critical Backward Look.* Norman: University of Oklahoma Press, 1966. pp. 70, 82-83, 84, 117, 122-124, 165-170. pp. 122-124: Regarding the Pulitzer prize Advisory Board's recommendation of *FWBT* for the fiction prize in 1941 and Nicholas Murray Butler's "unyielding opposition" to their selection. pp. 165-170: Regarding the Pulitzer prize awarded in 1953 to *OMATS.*

215

Sulzberger, C. L. [Cyrus Leo]. *A Long Row of Candles: Memoirs and Diaries, 1934-1954.* New York: Macmillan, 1969. pp. 4, 611-612, 641, 646, 665, 670. References to correspondence with EH regarding his World War II driver, "Michel Dupont." See Sulzberger's *The Resistentialists* above.

Turnbull, Andrew. *Thomas Wolfe.* New York: Scribners, 1968. pp. 133-134, 192-194, 242-243, 272, 273, 277. pp. 133-134: Regarding Max Perkins and publication of *SAR.* p. 194: Excerpt from an unpublished review of *FTA* by Wolfe.

Tynan, Kenneth. *Tynan Right and Left.* New York: Atheneum, 1967. pp. 285, 287, 330-336, 374, 378-380. pp. 330-336: "Papa and the Playwright." An account of EH meeting Tennessee Williams. See H1509. p. 374: Lawrence Ferlinghetti and Hemingway's *Collected Poems.* pp. 378-380: Regarding EH as guest of the Davises in Málaga in the late 1950s.

Walcutt, Charles Child. *Man's Changing Mask: Modes and Methods of Characterization in Fiction.* Minneapolis: Univ. of Minnesota Press, 1966. pp. 141, 154, 302, 305-314, 316-317, 338. pp. 305-314: "Hemingway's Naked Eyeballs."

Walker, Gerald, ed. *Best Magazine Articles: 1968.* New York: Crown Publishers, 1968. pp. 236-248: "Indian Camp Camp" by Donald St. John. An interview with EH's sister, Sunny (Mrs. E. J. Miller), at the family's old summer home overlooking Walloon Lake in Michigan. Reprinted from the *Carleton Miscellany*, IX (Winter 1968).

Weintraub, Stanley. *The Last Great Cause: The Intellectuals and the Spanish Civil War.* New York: Weybright and Talley, 1968. pp. 179-220, and *passim.* pp. 179-220: Ch. 7: "Things Unsimple: 'Hemingstein' at War."

White, William. *The Merrill Guide to Ernest Hemingway.* Columbus, Ohio: Charles E. Merrill, 1969. iv + 44 pages. Pamphlet. A bio-bibliographical essay, which includes EH's Nobel prize acceptance speech on pp. 28-29.

White, William, compiled by. *The Merrill Studies in The Sun Also Rises.* Columbus, Ohio: Charles E. Merrill, 1969. vi + 106 pages. Paperback. pp. iii-iv: Preface by William White.

Part 1. Contemporary Reviews:

pp. 2- 4: "Expatriates" by Conrad Aiken. See H49.

pp. 5- 8: "Readers and Writers" by Ernest Boyd. See H56.
pp. 9- 11: "Out of Little, Much" by Cleveland B. Chase. See H59.
pp. 12- 14: "Warfare in Man and among Men" by Lawrence S. Morris. See H61.
pp. 15- 16: "Fiction [*Fiesta*]" by Edwin Muir. See H74.
pp. 17- 19: "Hard-Boiled" by Allen Tate. See H60.
pp. 20- 21: "Sad Young Man" from *Time*, see H51.
pp. 22- 23: "Fiesta" from *The Times Literary Supplement*, see H73.

Part 2. Essays:
pp. 26- 36: "The Way It Was" by Carlos Baker. See G26.
pp. 37- 52: "Jake Barnes and Spring Torrents" by Sheridan Baker. Reprinted from Baker's *Ernest Hemingway: An Introduction and Interpretation*, see above.
pp. 53- 57: "*The Sun Also Rises*" by James T. Farrell. See H510.
pp. 58- 72: "*The Sun Also Rises*: An Essay in Applied Principles" by Earl Rovit. See G345.
pp. 73- 85: "The Death of Love in *The Sun Also Rises*" by Mark Spilka. See G363.
pp. 86- 90: "*The Sun Also Rises*: A Commentary" by Philip Young. See G460.
pp. 91-106: "Commencing with the Simplest Things" by Malcolm Cowley. See A29.

White, William, compiled by. *The Merrill Checklist of Ernest Hemingway*. Columbus, Ohio: Charles E. Merrill, 1970. Pamphlet. ii + 46 pages. A checklist of books by EH and books and articles of scholarship and criticism about him.

Wilhelm, Bernard. *Hemingway et Malraux devant la guerre d'Espagne*. Univ. of Berne, 1966. 240 pages.

Wylder, Delbert E. *Hemingway's Heroes*. Albuquerque: Univ. of New Mexico Press, 1969. x + 256 pages. Notes on pp. 227-[244]. Selected Bibliography on pp. 245-[252].

Young, Philip, and Charles W. Mann. *The Hemingway Manuscripts: An Inventory*. University Park and London: Pennsylvania State Univ. Press, 1969. xiv + 138 pages. Facsimiles. An inventory of the 332 manuscripts, fragments, letters, and miscellaneous items in the holdings of Mary Hemingway. Note: Also published in a limited edition of 300 numbered copies specially printed and bound. For additional facsimiles in the limited edition, see above.

Miscellanea

Our Windows. Emmanuel Episcopal Church, Petoskey, Michigan. June 23, 1968. Pamphlet. 28 pages. pp. [16]-[17]: Description and drawing of The Nativity cloister window, which was given to the church: "To the memory of Ernest Miller Hemingway from his sister, Madelaine H. Mainland Miller. 1968." Note: The Emmanuel Episcopal Church program for July 21, 1968, includes in the Sunday service the "Dedication of Ernest Hemingway Memorial Window."

Illustration 1970. A Universe Calendar with 12 original illustrations of *The Sun Also Rises* (cover, Jan. through Aug.) and "The Snows of Kilimanjaro" (Sept. through Dec.) hand-printed by Helmut Ackermann. Signed and numbered edition limited to 100 copies. Universe Books, New York, 1970. 15-1/8 x 12-5/8. $30.00

The "Macomber" Typescript

By

Thomas J. Jackson

Shortly after the appearance of Hemingway's "The Short Happy Life of Francis Macomber" in the September 1936 issue of *Cosmopolitan* magazine, literary scholars began debating whether Margot Macomber intentionally meant to kill her husband. In the past few years "Macomber" has elicited more critical commentary than any other Hemingway short story; yet, none of the articles has ever dealt with what the original typescript had to say, probably because few Hemingway scholars knew its location prior to the publication of the Hanneman bibliography.

The thirty-nine page typescript now permanently resides in the Rare Book Room of Southern Illinois University at Carbondale. Before coming to S.I.U. the typescript belonged to the well-known bibliophile, Mr. Charles Feinberg of Detroit, who had purchased it from a New York rare book dealer in the early 1940's. Unfortunately, the sales records of the book store were destroyed in a fire and the previous provenance of the typescript cannot be determined.

On nearly every page of the typescript which Hemingway submitted to *Cosmopolitan* there are pencil corrections, most of which are in the hand of an unidentified *Cosmopolitan* editor, and virtually all of which are concerned with spelling and punctuation changes. In a few instances the editor inserted short phrases which he felt clarified the time—"many years before," "married eleven years"—and location—"on the side where it had happened," "down to each spot"—in which events took place. These editorial changes were incorporated into the *Cosmopolitan* printing of the story. The editor also questioned Hemingway's use of such inflammatory words as "bitchery," "damned," "virginity" and his mentioning the .505 Gibbs, the Springfield, and the Mannlicher rifles by their brand names. Nonetheless, in spite of these editorial objections, *Cosmopolitan* printed the story with the Hemingway terminology intact.

Nearly all the editorial changes that were made in "Macomber's" *Cosmopolitan* appearance were deleted in 1938 when Scribners reprinted the story in *The Fifth Column And The First Forty-nine Stories*. Subsequent Scribner reprints have adhered to Hemingway's original version. The typescript thus provides few changes, certainly no change that significantly aids or hinders any one interpretation. Consequently, the ambiguity in the story which helped generate the literary controversy remains still.

Southern Illinois University Library

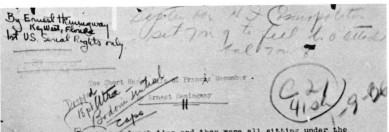

By Ernest Hemingway
Key West, Florida
1st U.S. Serial Rights only

The Short Happy Life of Francis Macomber.

Ernest Hemingway

It was now lunch time, and they were all sitting under the double green fly of the dining tent pretending that nothing had happened.

"Will you have lime juice or lemon squash?" Macomber asked.

"I'll have a gimlet," Robert Wilson told him.

"I'll have a gimlet, too. I need something," Macomber's wife said.

"I suppose it's the thing to do," Macomber agreed. "Tell him to make three gimlets."

The mess boy had started them already, lifting the bottles out of the canvas cooling bags that sweated wet in the wind that blew through the trees that shaded the tents.

"What had I ought to give them?" Macomber asked.

"A quid would be plenty," Wilson told him. "You don't want to spoil them."

"Will the headman distribute it?"

"Absolutely."

Francis Macomber had, half an hour before, been carried to his tent from the edge of the camp in triumph on the arms and shoulders of the cook, the personal boys, the skinner and the porters. The gun bearers had taken no part in the demonstration. When the native boys put him down at the door of his tent, he had shaken all their hands, received their congratulations, and then gone into the tent and sat on the bed until his wife came in. She did not speak to

221

grinning at each other, the gun bearer shouted wildly and they
saw him coming out of the bush sideways, fast as a crab, and the
bull coming, nose out, mouth tight-closed, blood dripping, massive
head straight out, coming in a charge, his little pig eyes blood-
shot as he looked at them. Wilson, who was ahead, was kneeling
shooting, and Macomber, as he fired, not hearing his shot in the
roaring of Wilson's gun, saw fragments like slate burst from the
huge boss of the horns, and the head jerked, He shot again at the
wide nostrils and saw the horns jolt again and fragments fly,
and He did not see Wilson now and aiming carefully, shot again with
the buffalo's huge bulk almost on him and his rifle almost level with
the on coming head, nose out; and he could see the little wicked
eyes and the head started to lower and he felt a sudden white-hot,
blinding flash explode inside his head and that was all he ever felt.

Wilson had ducked to one side to get in a shoulder
shot. Macomber had stood solid and shot for the nose, shooting a
touch high each time and hitting the heavy horns, splintering and
chipping them like hitting a slate roof, and Mrs. Macomber,
in the car, had shot at the buffalo with the 6.5 Mannlicher as it
seemed about to gore Macomber and had hit her husband about two
inches up and a little to one side of the base of his skull.

Francis Macomber lay now, face down, not two yards from
where the buffalo lay on his side, and his wife knelt over him
with Wilson beside her.

" I wouldn't turn him over," Wilson said.

The woman was crying hysterically.

" I'd get back in the car," Wilson said. "Where's
the rifle?"

She shook her head, her face contorted. The gun bearer
picked up the rifle.

Francis Macomber and Francis Fitzgerald

It seems more than possible that the first name of Francis Macomber was a reference to F. Scott Fitzgerald, and that we are supposed to see certain connections between the two Francises. "The Short Happy Life of Francis Macomber" was written right before "The Snows of Kilimanjaro" in 1936 (See Hanneman C 353) at a time when Hemingway was appalled by Fitzgerald's confessional articles in *Esquire*, the articles which prompted the "poor Scott Fitzgerald" remark in "Snows." Moreover, Hemingway saw both Francises as men dominated by their wives.

—M.J.B.

F. Scott Fitzgerald and
The Wedding Night

By

Alan Margolies

A minor yet curious holding in the Fitzgerald Papers at the Princeton University Library is an unsigned ninety-nine page typed carbon titled "Broken Soil," an early treatment of the 1935 Samuel Goldwyn-United Artists motion picture *The Wedding Night*. Film buffs will recall that Gary Cooper and Helen Vinson were cast as Tony and Dora Barrett, a once-successful author and his wife who move to a rural area in Connecticut. Anna Sten portrayed the Polish girl, Manya, who becomes the inspiration for the novelist's latest book. Eventually she dies in an accidental fall on her wedding night after Barrett, who has fallen in love with her, brawls with her new husband, a Polish lout played by Ralph Bellamy. At the end of the film Barrett is reconciled with his wife. The "Broken Soil" version is somewhat different, however, especially in its many veiled references to Zelda and F. Scott Fitzgerald.

In the treatment at Princeton, the hero is a thirty-year-old novelist named Scott Fitzpatrick; his wife, Zelda, is five years younger. In a conversation soon after the beginning of the story, Fitzpatrick and Lee Heywood, his agent, discuss the novelist's many best-sellers over the past ten years, and, among others, mention his first, *This Side of Heaven*, published the year he left college. Heywood soon reveals that Scribners has rejected the novelist's latest volume, and, further, that he is unable to find work in Hollywood for him. Fitzpatrick first considers going to the Riviera, but then, responding to Heywood's suggestions, decides to write about the Polish farmers who reside in the area, and, specifically, about the eighteen-year-old girl who lives on a nearby farm. Much of the rest of the treatment is similar to the film. At the end, however, Manya lives, having fled from her husband on their wedding night. Scott and Zelda are divorced, and Manya is reunited with the novelist at Macy's where he is autographing copies of his newest best-seller, appropriately titled *Broken Soil*.

Both Edwin H. Knopf, who wrote the treatment and eventually received film credit for the original story, and King Vidor, director of *The Wedding Night*, admired Fitzgerald's work and knew the novelist socially. Knopf first met him in Antibes during the summer of 1928 and continued to be friendly with him, especially during the late 1930s when Knopf was story editor at MGM. Vidor, in his autobiography *A Tree Is a Tree*, describes his acquaintanceship with the Fitzgeralds one summer in France during the late 1920s and tells of a conversation with the novelist about plans for a joint film project that, unfortunately, never materialized.[1] Vidor and Fitzgerald, too, remained friends through the 1930s; in addition, Fitzgerald admitted using aspects of the director's life in "Crazy Sunday" and "Two Old-Timers."[2]

Knopf, in correspondence to me, has stated that "Broken Soil" was the result of a summer vacation in 1932 in an area in Maine populated by Poles where he met, on a purely friendly basis, a young Polish girl who became the model for Manya. He says that he based the hero in part upon himself and in part upon Fitzgerald.[3] Vidor, in a letter to me, has corroborated this, suggesting that Fitzgerald was a prototype for the hero.[4] The treatment at Princeton is further evidence for this.

Unfortunately, by the time the film was completed, the more obvious allusions to the Fitzgeralds had been deleted. Yet sufficient similarity remains between "Broken Soil" and *The Wedding Night* to suggest that Zelda and F. Scott Fitzgerald were, at least partially, the original models for Dora and Tony Barrett.

John Jay College, CUNY

---

[1] *A Tree Is a Tree* (New York: Harcourt, Brace and Company, 1953), p. 171. Vidor, in a letter to me (October 1, 1968), suggests the possibility that the film project was to be about Napoleon.

[2] See, e.g., Fitzgerald to Harold Ober, February 8, 1936, *The Letters of F. Scott Fitzgerald*, ed. Andrew Turnbull (New York: Charles Scribner's Sons, 1963), p. 403, and Fitzgerald to Arnold Gingrich, [December 25, 1939], Arnold Gingrich, introd. *The Pat Hobby Stories*, by F. Scott Fitzgerald (New York: Charles Scribner's Sons, 1962), p. xv.

[3] Knopf to the author, October 26, 1968, and January 9, 1970.

[4] Vidor to the author, October 1, 1968.

James Agee's Early Tribute to
Tender is the Night

By

James L. W. West III

In *Permit Me Voyage* (1934)[1] James Agee saluted the artists whose work had informed his own with a long, devotional prose-poem called "Dedication." Two of the tributes were "to Ernest Hemingway; to Scott Fitzgerald." Hemingway's name is no surprise: his reputation was high in 1934. But Fitzgerald's name was a less likely one for Agee to mention. Fitzgerald's writings were not current then in college or artistic circles, and *The Great Gatsby* had appeared when Agee was fifteen years old and in boarding school. It therefore seems likely that the young poet's tribute was in response to his reading of *Tender is the Night* which was published earlier in the same year, 1934, that he composed "Dedication."[2] Agee was one of the people who immediately recognized the achievement of *Tender is the Night*. He though highly enough of the novel to place its author in the company of Joyce, Yeats, Housman, Picasso, and Toscanini in the second section of "Dedication." As Agee put it, Fitzgerald was among the artists "living and soon to die who tell truth or tell of truth, or who honorably seek to tell, or who tell the truths of others."

University of South Carolina

---

[1] New Haven: Yale Younger Poets Series, [October,] 1934; more conveniently available in *The Collected Poems of James Agee*, ed. with an intro. by Robert Fitzgerald, Boston: Houghton Mifflin, 1968.

[2] Editor Robert Fitzgerald, Agee's close friend at the time, says in his introduction (p. x) that "by all reasonable conjecture" the poem was written in

1934 shortly before the October publication date of *Permit Me Voyage*. Agee would have had ample opportunity to read *Tender is the Night*; it had been serialized in *Scribner's Magazine* from January to April of 1934 and was on the market in book form shortly thereafter.

Another Lost Hemingway Review

From *A Moveable Feast* (p. 203): "One Christmas there was a play by Hans Sachs that the school master directed. It was a good play and I wrote a review of it for the provincial paper that the hotel keeper translated." Somebody ought to find it.

Fitzgerald's List of Neglected Books

[From Malcolm Cowley's "Good Books That Almost Nobody Has Read," *New Republic*, LXXVIII (18 April 1934), 283.]

F. Scott Fitzgerald has just finished a book of his own, "Tender is the Night," his first novel since 1925. From Baltimore he sends a list of "the books that seem to me to have cashed in least on their intrinsic worth in recent years":

"Miss Lonelyhearts," by Nathanael West (Liveright, 1933)—though it's really a long short story.

"Sing Before Breakfast," by Vincent McHugh (Simon and Schuster, 1933).

"I Thought of Daisy," by Edmund Wilson (Scribner's, 1927).[1]

"Through the Wheat," by Thomas Boyd (Scribner's, 1927).

He also mentions "a book called 'Spring Flight,' by whom I've forgotten—he never appeared again," and "the detective stories of Raoul Whitfield, who I think is as good as Hammett—in fact I once suspected he was Hammett under another name." We could find no trace of "Spring Flight" or its author—perhaps Fitzgerald remembered the wrong title.[2] As for Raoul Whitfield's detective stories, most of them are published by Knopf, and "Danger Circus," which appeared last year, is the most recent.

"There are probably other neglected books," Fitzgerald continues, "but these occur to me especially. When the most violent emotional hysteria takes place over any rehash of Lenin's 'Imperialism,' any story about a steel mill made out of the dry bones of Upton Sinclair and Jack London, or any version of Hamsun's 'Growth of the Soil,' I think the novels above certainly deserve a good reading. In each case they are the men who did it first and that means a lot to me in my valuation of people's artistic merit. . . Meanwhile I am waiting for the crash down on 'Tender is the Night.' I expect a lot of good pokes from the wise boys for not having written the Odyssey."

—M.J.B.

---

[1] M.J.B. note: *Daisy* was published in 1929.
[2] M.J.B. note: Lee J. Smits, *The Spring Flight* (New York: Knopf, 1925).

The Wrong Duel in *Tender is the Night*

By

James L. W. West III

Shortly before the duel in *Tender is the Night*, Albert McKisco and his second, Abe North, sit talking in a hotel room:

> "There's a wonderful duel in a novel of Pushkin's," recollected Abe. "Each man stood on the edge of a precipice, so if he was hit at all he was done for."
>
> This seemed very remote and academic to McKisco, who stared at him and said, "What?"

The scene is not from a Pushkin novel but from *A Hero of Our Own Times* by Pushkin's contemporary Mikhail Lermontov. Fitzgerald may have deliberately erred to reinforce his portrayal of North as absent-minded and unconcerned, but it is doubtful. So obscure a point would escape nearly every reader. Fitzgerald's mistake was probably unintentional.

University of South Carolina

A Note on Jordan Baker

The name Jordan Baker is contradictory. The Jordan was a sporty car with a romantic image. The well-known ad for it showed a beautiful young woman at the wheel with the caption "Somewhere west of Laramie" that suggested a spirit of adventure and freedom. The Baker was an electric car, a lady's car—in fact, an old lady's car. Therefore the name Jordan Baker combines conflicting connotations. This contradiction is appropriate to her character: although she initially seems to share Nick's conservative standards, he is compelled to reject her because of her carelessness—her Buchanan-like quality.

From a 1923 *Saturday Evening Post* ad:

Somewhere west of Laramie there's a broncho-busting, steer roping girl who knows what I'm talking about.

She can tell what a sassy pony, that's a cross between greased lightning and the place where it hits, can do with eleven hundred pounds of steel and action when he's going high, wide and handsome.

The truth is—the Playboy was built for her.

Built for the lass whose face is brown with the sun when the day is done of revel and romp and race.

She loves the cross of the wild and the tame.

There's a savor of links about that car—of laughter and lift and light—a hint of old loves—and saddle and quirt. It's a brawny thing—yet a graceful thing for the sweep o' the Avenue.

Step into the Playboy when the hour grows dull with things gone dead and stale.

Then start for the land of real living with the spirit of the lass who rides, lean and rangy, into the red horizon of a Wyoming twilight.

                                                                        —M.J.B.

Hemingway's Colonel Appropriately Quotes Jackson

By

David M. McClellan

In Hemingway's *Across the River and Into the Trees,* Colonel Richard Cantwell quotes as he is dying the last words of Stonewall Jackson, ". . . let us cross over the river and rest under the shade of the trees."

Why, in the final moments of his life, does Cantwell quote Jackson?

The professional careers of the renowned Confederate commander and the fictional colonel generally are too dissimilar for Jackson to serve Cantwell as final exemplar. Jackson was usually successful, triumphant over Union forces from the celebrated Valley campaign to the Chancellorsville battle which cost him his life. Cantwell, on the other hand, became a general only to lose his unit in the Hurtgens Forest hostilities of World War II and as a consequence to be reduced in rank.

The answer is indicated in the section of Chapter 42 where the colonel is lamenting to himself his lack of appropriate gifts for his rich and aristocratic young mistress. "I could give her my ring from V. M. I., he thought, but where the hell did I lose that?" This thought of Cantwell's reveals that the colonel was a graduate of the Virginia Military Institute where Jackson taught before the Civil War. As one of the most famous and revered military figures ever to be associated with V. M. I., Jackson would be powerfully present in the memories of its graduates and his dying words might be expected to flash into the fading consciousness of one who also had been a general and was dying.

University of South Carolina

"A Lake Superior Salmon Fisherman"

By

Constance Drake

In a 1926 letter to Fitzgerald, Hemingway wrote a mock-plan of a novel which was, he announced, "to follow the outline and spirit of *The Great Gatsby*." "The hero, like Gatsby," Hemingway continued, "is a Lake Superior Salmon Fisherman. (There are no salmon in Lake Superior)."[1] This latter declaration was apparently intended as a correction of Fitzgerald's depiction in *The Great Gatsby* of the young James Gatz "beating his way along the south shore of Lake Superior as a clam-digger and a salmon-fisher or in any other capacity that brought him food and bed."[2]

But Hemingway's sporting knowledge had failed him. Professor Richard Tubb of the Ohio State University Fishery Unit stated in an interview on May 19, 1969 that about the time of the First World War "salmon fishing" in the Great Lakes was an extremely popular sport (and still is), but that the term was a popular rather than a scientific one. To the local fishermen, Professor Tubb explained, "salmon" were actually steelhead trout. Although trout are members of the salmon family, the term is not, of course, technically accurate, yet we might expect Hemingway, a native Michigan fisherman, to know at least as much about the terminology of Great Lakes fishing as Fitzgerald.

---

[1] Quoted in Matthew J. Bruccoli, *The Composition of Tender is the Night* (Pittsburgh: University of Pittsburgh Press, 1963), p. 19.

[2] *The Great Gatsby* (New York: Scribners, 1925), p. 99.

"Oh, Give Them Irony and Give Them Pity"

Nicholas Joost has shown in his *Ernest Hemingway and the Little Magazines* that Hemingway blamed Gilbert Seldes for *The Dial's* rejection of his work. That this resentment underlies Bill Gorton's "irony and pity" routine in *The Sun Also Rises* has not been noted:—

> As I went downstairs I heard Bill singing, "Irony and Pity. When you're feeling. . . Oh, Give them Irony and Give them Pity. Oh, give them Irony. When they're feeling. . . Just a little irony. Just a little pity. . ." He kept on singing until he came down-stairs. The tune was: "The Bells are Ringing for Me and my Gal." I was reading a week-old Spanish paper.
>
> "What's all this irony and pity?"
>
> "What? Don't you know about Irony and Pity?"
>
> "No. Who got it up?"
>
> "Everybody. They're mad about it in New York. It's just like the Fratellinis used to be."

The source of the "irony and pity" gag had to be Seldes' 1925 *Dial* review of *The Great Gatsby* which commended Fitzgerald for "regarding a tiny section of life and reporting it with irony and pity and a consuming passion." And Hemingway knew this review, for in *A Moveable Feast* he recalls that Scott "showed me a review by Gilbert Seldes that could not have been better. It could only have been better if Gilbert Seldes had been better."

—M.J.B.

Eggs As Huevos in *The Sun Also Rises*

By

J. M. Linebarger

The Spanish word "huevos" is literally translated "eggs" but also carries a vulgar meaning of "cojónes" or their equivalents. The several eggs in *The Sun Also Rises*,[1] although they are never called "huevos," imply such a meaning and add to the patterns of the novel, especially since all the important male characters except Romero are concerned about their masculinity.

The most significant eggs are eaten on the last day of the festival by Jake Barnes, Bill Gorton, and Belmonte the bullfighter:

> Bill and I sat in the down-stairs dining-room and ate some hard-boiled eggs and drank several bottles of beer. Belmonte came down in his street clothes with his manager and two other men. They sat at the next table and ate. Belmonte ate very little. They were leaving on the seven o'clock train for Barcelona. Belmonte wore a blue-striped shirt and a dark suit, and ate soft-boiled eggs. The others ate a big meal. Belmonte did not talk. He only answered questions.
>
> Bill was tired after the bull-fight. So was I. We both took a bull-fight very hard. We sat and ate the eggs and I watched Belmonte and the people at his table.

(pp. 230-231)

All three of these men need to eat eggs, symbolically to replace their own "huevos": Jake lost his during the war; Belmonte, during the afternoon's bullfights, demonstrated his lack of masculinity (pp. 222-223); and Bill Gorton, although not noticeably unmasculine, still is the only major male character (except of course for Jake) who does not manage to end up in bed with Brett Ashley. Since the Circean Lady Brett delights in symbolically castrating her lovers, it may be that she is not attracted to Bill because of an inherent lack of maleness in him that she senses. Some such indication of Bill's lack of symbolic *cojónes* may be inferred from the fishing scene, when Jake and Bill go up into the pure mountains near Burguete and prepare to eat eggs together:

> We unwrapped the little parcels of lunch.
> "Chicken."
> "There's hard-boiled eggs."
> "Find any salt?"
> "First the egg," said Bill. "Then the chicken. Even Bryan could see that."
> "He's dead. I read it in the paper yesterday."
> "No. Not really?"
> "Yes. Bryan's dead."
> Bill laid down the egg he was peeling.
> "Gentlemen," he said, and unwrapped a drumstick from a piece of newspaper. "I reverse the order. For Bryan's sake. As a tribute to the Great Commoner. First the chicken; then the egg. . . ."
> "Eat an egg."

(p. 125)

Eggs in the novel may not always be symbolic. Bill expresses a desire for eggs in one instance and Jake argues for "a regular meal" (p. 75). And Jake at another point mentions eggs as the first course of any Spanish lunch (p. 97); since there is a great deal of gourmandizing in the novel, apparently many characters eat unsymbolic eggs. But the scene with Jake, Belmonte, and Bill clearly is meaningful and relates directly to the concern with masculinity that dominates the discussions about "bulls" and "steers" that occur soon after the clan has gathered (p. 137, pp. 144-147). Lady Brett is particularly fascinated by bulls: "My God, isn't he beautiful?" she remarks of one specimen (p. 144). Mike, in one of these scenes, accuses Robert Cohn of following "Brett around like a steer all the time," since Cohn has been unmanned by her (p. 146). Later, Mike angrily shouts to Romero that "bulls have no horns" (p. 181) and repeats it twice more (p. 182), but the 1953 Scribner's edition happily changes the phrase in all three cases to "bulls have no balls" (pp. 175-76).[2] Mike only wishes that were so, for Brett has openly set her cap for the brave bullfighter. Romero himself never eats eggs during the novel, since he does not lack them; indeed, it is his "huevos" that Brett is attracted to but that she gracefully allows him to retain after their brief fling in Madrid.

North Texas State University

---

[1] Ernest Hemingway, *The Sun Also Rises* (New York: Charles Scribner's Sons, 1926). Hereinafter cited internally.

[2] Audre Hanneman, *Ernest Hemingway: A Comprehensive Bibliography* (Princeton: Princeton University Press, 1967), p. 19. Miss Hanneman points out that "the word 'horns' was changed to the original scatalogical term, on p. 175/line 18, and on p. 176/lines 13, 17. This change has also been made in later printings of other editions." Carlos Baker, in a letter to me, explains the events as he recalls them from his study of the Hemingway materials: "I remember very sharply that in 1926 when EH's typescript was being set up for publication, Maxwell Perkins, his editor, and Charles Scribner, his publisher, were both worried about the reference to the bulls' balls. They were both still somewhat Victorian in their orientation and conservative in the matter of language. EH complied, and said without rancor that the references to the 'bulls' appendages' had all been excised. I cannot remember any correspondence around 1954, but would guess that EH arranged to have the original reading restored. Perkins had died in 1947 and Mr. Scribner in 1952, and anyway the climate had changed toward the use of candid words in print. His editor at that time was Wallace Meyer. I am quite sure that EH himself engineered the change. The original MS in the possession of Mrs. Hemingway shows clearly that the first reading was 'balls,' not 'horns.' " Obviously Hemingway's word is the more appropriate one thematically for *The Sun Also Rises*.

The Last Time I Saw Hemingway

These memories are from a letter Caresse Crosby wrote C. E. F. Clark, Jr. on 7 January 1970. She died 23 January.

...I feel that I've told all I wish to say about Hemingway. The Scott Fitzgerald story began and ended just as I told it. I never saw him again after he waved goodbye from the pier in Baltimore with his chamois gloves. The last time I saw Hemingway was in the Ritz bar in Paris before he became Papa Hemingway. I do not remember the year but only the mustache, no beard. When I said to him 'I have heard that you are one of my authors who didn't fall for my charms' and he replied 'Sue him!' Then we drank to each other with champagne.

Sincerely,

Caresse Crosby

Caresse Crosby

240

The Reception of *Dearly Beloved*

By

Bryant Mangum

F. Scott Fitzgerald's "Dearly Beloved" was published for the first time in the *Fitzgerald/Hemingway Annual 1969*. Six months after its initial appearance, the story had been reprinted eight times; three of the reprintings were made within two days after the *Annual* was issued. Each of the following newspapers and periodicals carried the entire text of the story with a headnote or article about its author and its discovery: *New York Times, Paris International Herald-Tribune, Louisville Courier-Journal, Akron Beacon Journal, San Francisco Examiner, London Daily Telegraph Magazine*, and *National Cash Register World*.[1] The Windhover Press at the University of Iowa published a limited edition in 1970.[2] Although *Time* and *Newsweek* did not reprint the story, it was noted in both magazines within two weeks after its appearance.[3] The rapid reprintings of "Dearly Beloved" raise interesting questions. Was the story received with interest only because it was written by Fitzgerald, the artist; or was it greeted warmly because it was a story about a Negro by a well-known author? An examination of the ways in which the story was presented by the various newspapers and periodicals suggests several reasons for the enthusiastic reception of the story. In most reprintings, the packaging of "Dearly Beloved" reflects a curious blend of nostalgic affection for Fitzgerald as Chronicler of the Jazz Age coupled with an emphasis on the fact that he was writing serious fiction in 1940 about today's favorite serious subject, the Negro.

On 20 August 1969 the *New York Times* reprinted the text of "Dearly Beloved" beneath the headline "Short Story by Fitzgerald is Discovered." In addition to the story, the *Times* included familiar profile pictures of Hemingway and Fitzgerald and a reproduction of the cover of the *Fitzgerald/Hemingway Annual 1969*. The layout also contained an article by Alden Whitman in which he gave a capsule description of the contents of the *Annual*. It is noteworthy that Whitman emphasized the importance of Hemingway's lost review of Sherwood Anderson's *A Story-Teller's Story*, which also appeared in the journal with "Dearly Beloved." But the *Times* reprinted only "Dearly Beloved."

Other publishers appear not to have shared Whitman's enthusiasm for the Hemingway review, because no attempts have been made to reprint it. They keyed, rather, on the first sentence of Whitman's article: "A hitherto unknown short story by F. Scott Fitzgerald, believed to be his only serious fiction about a Negro, has been discovered among his papers at the Princeton University Library." On the day following the *New York Times'* reprinting of "Dearly Beloved," the *Paris International Herald-Tribune* carried the *Times'* copyrighted article by Whitman and placed it beneath the following headline: "Unknown Fitzgerald Story Found; Hero is a Negro." The newspaper also reprinted the complete text of "Dearly Beloved" beneath a picture of Fitzgerald that had been taken in the early 1920's. Also on 21 August 1969, the *Louisville Courier-Journal* reprinted the story and included Whitman's article from the *Times*. The headline, which spread across the top of the page, read: "'Dearly Beloved,' A Long Lost F. Scott Fitzgerald Short Story." Accompanying the text was a picture which showed Fitzgerald working. On the same day, the *London Times* carried Whitman's article with international news.[4] The following day's *Toronto Globe and Mail* reprinted the same article.[5]

The most imaginative treatment of "Dearly Beloved" appeared in the *Akron Beacon Journal* on September 14, 1969. The headline, "Discover New Fitzgerald Story," covered the top of an entire page. This newspaper did not use Whitman's article, but rather printed a headnote which identified Fitzgerald as "the voice of America's Jazz Age" and echoed the comment that "Dearly Beloved" was believed to be Fitzgerald's "only serious fiction work about a Negro." The headnote also stated the newspaper's reason for carrying the story: "Because of its importance in the literary world, the *Beacon Journal's* Lively Arts section is reprinting the Fitzgerald story in its entirety . . . ." Not only was the story published; it was considerably embellished. Editors added six section breaks and placed in capitals all the letters of seventeen key words at the beginnings of the new sections. Midway through the story, the text was broken by the bold-faced words, "Beauty Boy became golf champion of all Heaven." There was, in addition, an illustration that pictured Beauty Boy running from the path of an oncoming train. Accompanying the text was a picture of Fitzgerald captioned "F. Scott Fitzgerald . . . Jazz age writer . . . ."

One week later, the *San Francisco Examiner* reprinted the text of "Dearly Beloved." Whitman's article appeared beneath the headline, "The First Hemingway/Fitzgerald Annual," and a profile sketch of Fitzgerald was included in this full-page treatment. The November-December 1969 *National Cash Register World* also reprinted the text of the story, and in addition, supplied a history of the *Annual*, original sketches of Hemingway and Fitzgerald, and photographic reproductions of the covers of the *Annual* and the *Fitzgerald Newsletter*. Microcard Editions, a part of National Cash Register's Industrial Products Division, publishes the *Fitzgerald/Hemingway Annual*. The latest American reprinting of the story is especially noteworthy— a limited edition by the Windhover Press of the University of Iowa, one of the best little presses.

In England, "Dearly Beloved" appeared in the 28 November 1969 *Daily Telegraph Magazine*. Accompanying this reprinting was an illustration in which Beauty Boy and Lilymary are standing on top of clouds made of golf balls. And on the two pages that follow the text, Alan Coren attempted to put the discovery of the story "into perspective." Coren's discussion includes little except a summary of the events of Fitzgerald's life. A headnote to the story, however, states that the story "has been hailed by many as the Great Lost Manuscript." And while there is no evidence to indicate that this assertion has ever been made in print, it does raise a question about the amount of discussion about Fitzgerald that may have evolved from the discovery of the story.

After its appearance in the *Fitzgerald/Hemingway Annual 1969*, "Dearly Beloved" became news in the United States, England, France, and Canada. No doubt, many editors were prompted to reprint the story because of the current interest in Black literature. But the various packagings of the story indicate that the interest runs deeper than this. Many of the publications that reprinted "Dearly Beloved" reflected the feeling that Fitzgerald remains, even now, in the popular mind the Chronicler of the Jazz Age. The idea that this man could have considered a Negro as suitable material for serious fiction in 1940 has mass appeal.

University of South Carolina

[1] *New York Times*, August 20, 1969, p. 42. *Paris International Herald-Tribune,* August 21, 1969, p. 14. *Louisville Courier-Journal,* August 21, 1969, Sec. A, p. 5. *Akron Beacon Journal*, September 14, 1969, Sec. D, p. 7. *San Francisco Examiner*, September 21, 1969, Literary Supplement, p. 35. *London Daily Telegraph Magazine*, November 28, 1969, p. 65. *National Cash Register World*, II (November-December 1969), 21.

[2] Iowa City, 1969—300 numbered copies. Dated 1969, but published 1970.

[3] "Newsmakers," *Newsweek* (September 1, 1969), 41. "People," *Time* (August 29, 1969), 30.

[4] "New Scott Fitzgerald story," *London Times*, August 21, 1969, p. 4.

[5] "F. Scott Fitzgerald Short story found in author's papers," *Toronto Globe and Mail*, August 22, 1969.

REVIEWS

Ernest Hemingway. *Islands in the Stream.* Scribners, 1970. $10.

By Matthew J. Bruccoli

Remembering Hemingway's comment about how he felt when he used up all his Conrad, I am grateful for 460 good pages after I thought all the Hemingway was gone. Good:—not great, but good pages. As good as *Across the River and Into the Trees. Islands in the Stream* was worth publishing. Scribner and Mrs. Hemingway have done the right thing.

As I have argued elsewhere, Hemingway's stature is based on his great work; nothing that is published now can injure that great work. No matter how good or bad *Islands in the Stream* really is, *The Sun Also Rises* and "Big Two-Hearted River" will not be altered. Publication of these literary remains will give pleasure to many general readers and should help critics and scholars.

Islands consists of three episodes set on the Gulf Stream—"Bimini," "Cuba," and "At Sea"—all dealing with a painter named Thomas Hudson. The first episode, which is the longest and best, covers a visit at Hudson's Bimini home from his three young sons by his two former wives. The central action in this section is the account of one boy's long fight with a big game fish. There are also reminiscences of Paris in the twenties—Mr. Joyce and Mr. Pound—so that the first section resembles a combination of *The Old Man and the Sea* and *A Moveable Feast*. It ends with the news that two of the boys and their mother have been killed in a car crash.

The interlocked second and third sections are based on Hemingway-Hudson's Q-boat activities during the war. In "Cuba," Hudson, now separated from a bitchy third wife, encounters his first wife—a blend of Hadley Richardson and Marlene Dietrich—with whom he is still in love and tells her that their son has been killed flying in the war. "At Sea" covers the pursuit of German sailors off Cuba by Hudson and his crew. It ends with the wounded Thomas Hudson being told: "You never understand anybody that loves you."

There are no surprises in *Islands in the Stream*—no new techniques or themes. The writing, especially in the conversations, is wordy for Hemingway, but then he did not have the chance to revise and cut. There is no strong thematic line, although *Islands* reaffirms the Hemingway code of discipline and integrity—the avoidance of shit, the necessity for balls, and the difficulty of love. Probably the final importance of *Islands in the Stream* lies in its clearly autobiographical basis. It should help Hemingway pros to understand what he was like in the late fifties.

If there is any more this good, it should be published. Nothing can hurt Hemingway's stature now. It is not grave-robbing to publish his unfinished work. It is the duty of good executors and publishers. Unless the work-in-progress of a major author is destroyed by his literary executor, it will be published sometime:—maybe after a long time, but it will be published. It should be published while the people who know what to do with it are around.

George Zuckerman. *The Last Flapper*. Boston: Little, Brown, 1969. $6.95.

By George Frazier

The problem with writing a *roman à clef* is that your key better fit without fuss, slipping in so swiftly and smoothly that there's never any doubt about its being the right one. If it doesn't, then you're in trouble. And bloody well you should be, too. Naturally, if a novel is merely rumored to be *à clef* (with its writer inquiring in umbrage where in the world could anybody have gotten *that* idea), it is exempt from attack on the grounds that it is unfaithful to fact. But when an author practically has a notary witness an avowal that the characters are drawn from life, he better do no disservice to the prototypes, or he's in *terrible* trouble. And if we happen to be not only informed about, but fascinated by a person he made a bad fit for, he better be prepared either not to publish or be damned—or, worse still, to be all but utterly ignored.

Ordinarily, I am diminished when a writer goes down to honorable defeat, his work of months or maybe even years suddenly all for nothing, his high hopes smashed to smithereens by the smart-alecky fascination-with-the-sight-of-his-own-polysyllabic-words exhibitionism of such as the unhyphenated adolescent in *The New York Times*. But there is nothing honorable about *The Last Flapper*, either in its aspiration or execution. It is, in fact, a thoroughly dishonorable enterprise, trading so palpably on the possibility that it might sell if the word went out that it was the story of Zelda Fitzgerald. God, it's disgusting—and its author is obviously a meretricious man who is apparently embarrassed by nothing, not even that James Montgomery Flaggish sketch of him on the jacket, that oh-so-coy concession to the Twenties. But the arrogance of Mr. Zuckerman's ignorance is staggering, the badness of his taste beyond belief. What, for instance, of his sanctioning the copy on the jacket?

But the pity is that the jacket blurb isn't all there is to the novel, for it is infinitely more entertaining than what follows for four hundred and thirty-nine interminable and insensitive pages.

"It was told," runs the jacket copy, "that without Rannah O' Donnell there would have been no Jazz Age. Certainly the vivid, mercurial Southern belle married to the country's handsomest and most talented young writer epitomized the frenetic gaiety and tinsel glitter of the period. Her madcap escapades made wonderful copy; the press and public loved her.

"But it was also said, when the tinsel began to tarnish and the gay North Shore parties were a bad taste in the mouth, that Rannah Gedney O'Donnell was more mad than madcap, and that she was to blame for her handsome young husband's blighted career and his sad, sordid death."

And so on for a little longer—and I'll drink to that, for no harm done so far. But then there is this: "It is not difficult to recognize the real-life counterparts of the characters in THE LAST FLAPPER: the fabulous O'Donnells themselves, beautiful and damned; Harry Ingram, the writer who owed his initial success to Davis O'Donnell and whose reputation eclipsed O'Donnell's during his lifetime."

Somehow I do not think those lines have Tess or Arthur Schlesinger, Sr. in mind—or Robert Hitchens, or that cute couple, the Will Durants, anyone like that. I really don't.

But if that bit of the blurb is not enough to spell out Zelda, there is, in the biographical note on Mr. Zuckerman, a non sequitur that is rather more relevant than not. Mr. Zuckerman, it says—and out of a clear blue sky, without a previous word about Scott or Zelda—"got to know Zelda Fitzgerald during the last few years of her tormented life and conceived the idea then of the present novel." Naturally, it's too late to do anything about it now, but do you suppose it was the thought of his writing a novel about her that tormented Zelda?

The *roman à clef* has been carried off with conviction and grace on any number of occasions, although almost always without any admission that the inspiration was then, or ever had been, flesh. Schulberg succeeded in *The Disenchanted*; Fitzgerald in, among other things, *Tender* and *Tycoon*; Hemingway again and again; and, of course, Maugham in his laceration of Hugh Walpole. Moreover, I have heard that Mrs. Irving Mansfield has been inspired by fact in her fiction, though I won't know for sure until her *oeuvres* are translated into English. The point is that the *roman à clef* can command our admiration, all the more so if we merely suspect that the characters come from life. That is part of the fun. But it's a little late now for that to do Mr. Zuckerman any good.

But what *really* offends and, at times, outrages me is that the author of *The Last Flapper* should be so insensitive to the prodigious chic and style of the Fitzgeralds. They may have been besotted and dissolute and mad, but, by God, they had a sense of style—that they had above all else.

And though their transgressions may have been numerous and egregious, what did they ever do to deserve George Zuckerman? But someone, it seems, is always slandering their shades. Now there is a rumor that Artie Shaw is going to produce a musical of *Gatsby*. Artie *Shaw*!

Stanley Weintraub. *The Last Great Cause*. New York: Weybright & Talley, 1969. $8.50.

Frederick R. Benson. *Writers in Arms*. New York: New York University Press, 1969. $5.95.

By Cecil Eby

Sure, Hugh Thomas was only joking when he estimated that more non-Spaniards have written about the Spanish Civil War than ever fought in it, but his hyperbole is not without point—even barb. For it is certainly true that more intellectuals have rallied round the banner of the Spanish Republic than any other pattern of stripes,

sickles, or stars of our time. That war was holy crusade, conflict between GOOD and evil, wholehearted—but half-headed?—commitment
to every libertarian slogan since the French Revolution. For intellectuals of the Thirties, Spain was where the action was and where
the men were. They journeyed there on dingy day-coaches to fight,
or lightly sped there on wings of thought to poetize. They came;
they saw; they wrote. Everybody who was anybody—right through
the alphabet from Hugh Auden to Leane Zugsmith. For once, or so it
seemed, intellectuals were riding in the locomotive—right up there
with the engineers and power—rather than in the caboose, where
they had always camped out before.

In view of the traditional predilection among intellectuals for
hair-splitting and in-fighting, their monolithic unity of collective
enterprise regarding the Spanish Republic was wondrous to behold.
One senses that these intellectuals surprised even themselves: they
went to war against a common enemy instead of each other. Contemplation moved over for action. Palace-revolution was more po-
tent brew than palace-of-art. The common enemy was, of course,
that obscene nebulosity, "Fascism." Maybe no one exactly knew
what it was, with respect to its Spanish mask, but they hated it just
the same. Thus the holy cause was *against* something, not really *for*
anything in particular. (And at the time no one knew that Franco
himself was engaged in stamping out the Falange, the Spanish Fascist
party.) The essentially negative goal of the war—that commitment to
oppose something—was tremendously appealing to intellectuals who
had thought too long about too much (or too little) to conclude
much of anything. The call to action pushed into the background the
necessity for self-dividing contemplation. Doubts occurred only
much later, after the action was done.

Even today, to write about the Spanish Civil War is to plunge—or
to be plunged—up to the neck in searing debate, to be convicted
without trial (and often without reason) of fascistic or communistic
tendencies, and to function as target for fanatical partisans of one
side or the other—or sometimes for both sides simultaneously. The
corpse of the Republic, though long dead, is still warm enough to
generate books still strangely polemical, books which reflect not
what was or what is but what ought to have been. To account for
this polemical tone in books about Spain written three decades after
the fact, one has to remember that by its expiration the Republic became a lost cause. Like a lost love, a lost cause makes no rigorous demands. No disillusionment is possible because the lovely lady did
not live long enough to become a whore. Intellectuals fondly re-

member Spain; Ethiopia, that other commitment of the Thirties, is better left forgotten.

The books at hand assess the role of writters in the Spanish Civil War. Stanley Weintraub easily outdistances his competitors both in the range of his research and in the conversion of data into smooth narrative. Hemingway, Malraux, Orwell—they are here and within easy reach. In researching his book, he has like Melville "swum through libraries" and his book is an organic whole, battened down and tightly caulked. Then we have Benson, whose subtitle "The Literary Impact of the Spanish Civil War" (lettered as it is across a blood-stained dust jacket) seems unadulterated nonsense. Bullets, Mr. Benson, have *impact*, but as Robert Jordan said, "Paper bleeds little." *Writers in Arms* is a heavy-sided book with the detritus of dissertation (long block quotations and endless summations) all over it. When the writer says of Hemingway's *The Fifth Column* that it was an "attempt to portray conditions in Madrid . . . as they might have appeared in the uncensored dispatches of a very objective war correspondent" and when we think of Philip Rawlings' cloak-and-dagger adventures between the lines, then we have to conclude that Mr. Benson has had access to some version of the play that no one else has ever seen. The writer has done, however, what few others have ever succeeded in doing—in making the Spanish Civil War an abjectly dull affair. Weintraub's book was a labor of love, but for Benson, only a labor.

More pertinent than specific criticism of these books, however, is the mass of assumptions, for the most part never questioned, underlying them. We assume, I suppose, that the way intellectuals respond to a war is of vital importance. But is it, really? Are we not, as intellectuals, guilty of special pleading in concluding, without much evidence, that whatever intellectuals do or say must be important enough to render into a book? If plumbers wrote, they would probably write about plumbers. And imagine the roars of laughter from critics and reviewers on high if a book crossed their desks titled "Plumbers in Arms: Jointers and Fitters in the Spanish Civil War." Such a work would be dismissed as frivolous, immaterial garbage, despite the fact that any of the trade-unions in Spain had considerably more "impact" upon the outcome of the war than did the intellectuals. The difference is that writers write, and writers like to write about writers. From hearing them tell about Spain, one might infer that Orwell, Hemingway, and Malraux lost the war all by themselves, yet in fact, no writer had the power to influence the war at all, for ill or for good.

For all his cherished isolation, the intellectual seems to hunger for action and for recognition. He stands apart from other men, pretending to prefer his fine detachment but secretly envying the noisy party downstairs among the proles. While ordinary men go off to war without fuss or fury, the intellectual insists upon having a forty-piece band to announce his departure and a battalion of intellectuals to record his arrival. Locked within his monumental and nearly onanistical self-esteem, he performs deeds of Everyman as though he were Superman. Yet why should his role, or his death, in war be regarded with more attention than that of any other person? When writers inflate the importance of other writers they betray their alienation from humanity at large, yet perversely they construe this as a virtue. War becomes a guerrilla theatre which they attend to enjoy the virtuosity of their favorite actors. The collective catastrophe of war is converted into a series of personal tragedies, filled with pity and fear but signifying nothing. Even more contemptible is the behavior of that second-generation warrior-intellectual who writes of the Spanish Civil War as though it were an unambiguous morality play.

As a "military game" war is atrocious, but as a "literary game" it is obscene. What Hemingway ate or whom he slept with in Madrid is entertaining gossip, but it has nothing much to do with real people in a real war. That John Cornford was killed near Huesca may be terrible, but certainly no more terrible than the death of Francisco Alonso, a sixteen-year-old baker's apprentice, at the two-kilometer stone on the Toledo road. The only difference is that Cornford's few lines of muggy poetry have transmogrified him from man into literary celebrity. Literary folk find his death poignantly touching. Alonso was a nobody, and he smelled of yeast.

"The Last Great Cause" or "The Last Great Carnival?" Somehow I find it hard to be impressed by those hundreds of writers from the Great Democracies who swarmed across the Iberian landscape in order to record, with passionate detail, the agony of Spain and Spaniards. So many of them turned their notebooks into beautiful books, yet so few of them have ploughed their royalties back into the Spanish earth. We like to think that our intellectuals found a worthy cause, not that they found a worthwhile subject. Hemingway's *For Whom the Bell Tolls* gives us an illusion of the first; Spender's *World Within World* provides us with a glimpse of the other in his account of the megalomania hovering over the Writers' Congress in Madrid. Artists had found, not themselves, but the secret sources of power politics.

We now know all about intellectuals in the Spanish Civil War. The contribution of the plumbers or bakers has not been recorded. This is unfortunate because one suspects that they did a great deal more. Who weeps for Francisco Alonso? Alas, there is none.

University of Michigan

Carl Bode. *Mencken.* Carbondale: Southern Illinois University Press, 1969. $10.

Betty Adler, compiler. *Man of Letters: A Census of the Correspondence of H. L. Mencken.* Baltimore: Enoch Pratt Free Library, 1969. $6.

By William H. Nolte

Judged solely on its literary merits—that is, as a piece of writing, sentence by sentence, paragraph by paragraph—Carl Bode's long-awaited *Mencken* is a botch. It is probably the worst written biography of an important literary figure to appear in years. For the reader who enjoys good prose, who likes to see neatly turned phrases, who is conscious, in short, of all those delicacies that we associate with the craft of writing, wading through this book might be compared to swallowing a bucket of croton oil without even an orange-juice chaser. The thing heaves and labors, grinds and bumps, rumbles and bumbles its zigzag course through nearly 400 pages, charting its course this way and then that, and invariably foundering in a quagmire of triteness and turgidity. It performs the miracle of making Mencken seem dull. An ordeal to the quick, it constitutes a crime against the dead. Alas, that a Prince of American Letters should be thus interred!

One example of the soporific prose should suffice. Here Mr. Bode describes Mencken's close friendship with Hamilton Owens:

> He paid particular attention to the *Evening Sun*. It soon became a far brighter paper than before. He took an immediate liking to Hamilton Owens, who was named its managing editor early in 1922. Eight years younger than Mencken and with somewhat less newspaper experience, Owens valued his help, the more so since it was never heavy-handed. Mencken would drop into his office nearly every afternoon, talking wittily or explosively about newspaper matters of all sizes. His advice was all the better because it came in small doses. Much of it concerned the artful management of trifles; some of it concerned matters of major policy; and some of it concerned man's view of the world. From the first month Owens accepted many of Mencken's minor suggestions; it was not long

before he adopted some of the major ones. And it did not take years before he saw life as a whole in a Menckenian way. During World War I Owens had worked readily enough for the Creel Committee on American propaganda and after the war for an American bank in England. But now he began to see the war and England more nearly as Mencken did. He showed it in both his editing and writing.

For the insomniac such stuff offers a sure-cure, but for the reader who wishes to remain conscious it poses an obstacle of frightening dimensions. If this book were only a little worse than it is, it would tickle the midriff. Were it a great deal better, it would have been a triple-delight.

For we certainly need a good biography of Mencken. The one by Isaac Goldberg, written when Mencken was in mid-career, tells only part of the story. Besides, Goldberg's book is less a biography than a collection of materials, most of it undigested and some of it prefabricated by Mencken himself. The biographies of Edgar Kemler and William Manchester, both appearing in 1950, are useful works but no more than that. Kemler had his own axe to grind, which caused him to leave large areas of the "life" in darkness. He seemed to approach his subject with a few a priori assumptions which he attempted to flesh out; he knew from the beginning what he wanted to find, and he often found what was simply not there. Manchester's book, though a good deal better than Kemler's, strove too much for a racy flavor to complement the "public" personality of its subject. It, too, suffers from being incomplete; the real Mencken, or at least a convincing facsimile thereof, never quite breaks through the surface colors which Mr. Manchester laid on the portrait. We know that Mencken helped Kemler and Manchester with their books, and though he encouraged each to interpret the evidence as he saw fit, there is reason to believe he was selective in just what they should have at their disposal. There can be no doubt that Mencken shied from allowing anyone to look too closely at his private life. Indeed, he tells us very little in his *Days* books about that private world of emotions. The fascination of those volumes depends upon what Mencken tells us about the world around him—about the Baltimore of his early years, his newspaper experiences, the men he encountered along the way, and so forth. My point is that biographers heretofore have been, partially at least, hamstrung in their efforts to visualize the man behind the mask.

Not so with Mr. Bode, who has had access to a wealth of documentary evidence that no one else has been privileged to use. Moreover, he researched the lode far more extensively than any other worker in the field. Not long after Mencken's death in 1956, August Mencken offered him the truly golden opportunity to write the complete biography. Which is to say, he offered to open files that had been closed to previous investigators. At the same time, I understand, Alfred Knopf, Mencken's longtime friend and publisher, agreed to open his files and to underwrite the expense of the research with the option of publishing the book. It is not difficult to guess why he chose not to print the final product. The Enoch Pratt Free Library in Baltimore gave Mr. Bode unrestricted use of its collection of Menckeniana, the size of which is frankly awesome. The letters housed at Princeton were made available. Add to all that the numerous interviews given by Mencken's friends and acquaintances, many of whom had personal files, and you get some idea of the enormity of evidence Mr. Bode had at his disposal. In effect, he was given the chance to write one of the most important biographies of the age. His failure is therefore all the more regrettable.

In his Afterword, Mr. Bode informs us that he wanted "to analyze Mencken's writing in relation to his life" and "to describe the relation between the life and times." Vague as those declared intentions are, I can still say with certitude that he does neither. There's almost no analysis of Mencken's published work; and he relates the "life" and "times" only in so far as he shows that Mencken was interested in a wide variety of subjects—a fact already known to all literate people. Mencken was preeminently The American as Critic, having taken for his text the entire spectrum of American civilization. Or perhaps I should say that Mencken sought to isolate the causes for the absence of civilization in the Republic. We have produced a native *language*, yes. And Mencken's study of that speech must be considered one of his greatest achievements. (Ironically, Mencken encountered more hostility against his belief that our language was uniquely American than he did in his debunkings of other 100-percent-American institutions.) But he would doubtless have agreed with Frank Lloyd Wright's remark that America will be unique in history, unless the wind changes very soon, in that it moved from barbarism to decadence without having created a civilization in between.

As I have said, we learn precious little about Mencken's mind or art from this biography. What, then, about his personality? What sort of man was he? What were his likes and dislikes—aside from those that are clearly underlined in his published work? The sad and simple answer is that we are never told. We don't even learn much about his relations with the literary giants of the period when, as Tom

Wolfe recently put it, American letters commuted from Baltimore. To find out about his stormy friendship with, and defense of, Dreiser one must still go to W. A. Swanberg's biography of the novelist. To learn about his friendship with Sinclair Lewis, one must go to Mark Schorer's book. The same is true of other figures. We don't even learn anything about Mencken's and Fitzgerald's friendship. Did he really like Fitzgerald, as James Farrell (another good friend) wrote me, better than either Lewis or Dreiser? If so, why? Here is all I'm told:

> [Fitzgerald] himself lived, as Mencken saw when their paths crossed in Baltimore, like a character from one of his books. In *This Side of Paradise* the hero, Amory Blaine, goes to Princeton, then to war, and returns to have a pair of love affairs, but he finds no peace in them. Everything is cynical and stylish. In *The Great Gatsby* the main character is a young war veteran, Jay Gatsby, turned bootlegger. On coming back to this country Gatsby meets again the rich girl he has never forgotten, wins her briefly from her rich, hulking husband, and then is shot by a garageman. This hero dies; the other lives. But love proves brittle for them both, as well as for the pretty women they go to bed with. The point here is that in Fitzgerald's fiction the women act as unconventionally as the men.

Don't ask me what on earth this means. I merely sweat and transcribe. I have read Fitzgerald, however, and am thus doubly appalled.

Is *Mencken*, then, without merit altogether? Not quite. A number of dry bones have been exhumed and exhibited to view. That no flesh adheres to the bones must be attributed to the low-grade quality of the writing. Mr. Bode can find "facts"; he just doesn't know how to make them stand up and walk. And he most certainly cannot make them dance with arms and legs.

Most reviews of *Mencken* that I've read have simply acknowledged publication of the book and then moved on to a discussion of HLM— his strengths and weaknesses, as the reviewer understood them, his enormous power as a literary force during the decade following the first World War, his almost incredible energies and diversity of interests, and so on. These reviews usually conclude with a guess concerning just which of the books will endure the erosions of time. One review in particular warrants comment. Written by Tom Wolfe, it appeared in "Book World," the literary supplement of the Washington *Post*, on September 28, 1969. After remarking that he has no doubt concerning the durability of Mencken's reputation, Wolfe predicts that if anyone is interested, in the year 2000, in putting together a collection of the finest English prose of the 20th century, he will probably feature the work of Mencken, George Orwell,

Malcolm Muggeridge, and possibly Shaw. (He refers to non-fiction, of course.) He comments on the extraordinary effects Mencken was capable of in his essays: "Mencken's great gift is also Orwell's and Muggeridge's: namely, he combines the forte of the essayist—the dazzling insight—with the short-story writer's eye for detail and metonymy." That judgment strikes me as not only sound but incapable of improvement.

A final note that may be of interest to some. Not long ago, when Muggeridge was on one of his American speaking tours, I had the opportunity to hear him and then chat with him briefly following his talk. I asked him about Mencken. Where would he place the Baltimore Sage in his pantheon of departed gods? "Very high," he answered. And then, after a pause: "Yes, there's no doubt. Mencken was the greatest of our century."

While working as a newspaperman, first for the Baltimore *Herald* and then the *Sunpapers*, editing magazines (*The Smart Set* and *The American Mercury*) to which he contributed monthly articles, collecting and shaping the language notes that resulted in the great volumes on that subject, writing two dozen books and co-authoring or editing some forty more, traveling widely and still maintaining an active social life, Mencken somehow found time to write an estimated quarter of a million letters. That is to say, over a period of fifty years, he averaged about a dozen letters a day. The mind boggles. The man was a writing machine. And Mencken, probably more than any other of our major figures, was a stickler for *le mot juste*. With the publication of *Man of Letters: A Census of the Correspondence of H. L. Mencken*, compiled by Betty Adler, we now have a neat index to a sizeable hunk of that correspondence. The names of about five thousand individuals are alphabetically arranged and locations of their correspondence given. While most of the letters to and from twentieth-century authors were donated to the New York Public Library and are restricted until 1971, much of the correspondence is presently available in the eighty-three different collections (mostly libraries) listed by Miss Adler. For example, a thousand letters to Dreiser are in libraries other than the New York Public; just how many are in that library is anybody's guess since neither the number of letters nor the inclusive dates covered by the correspondence is known about the restricted material. Since Mencken seldom made carbons of his letters, those written before 1932 that have survived have done so largely through the foresight of his correspondents. After that date, Mrs. Rosalind C. Lohrfinck, Mencken's secretary, typed most of his letters, and though she made no carbons she did preserve the stenographic notebooks from which copies were later made. *Man of Letters* is a valuable contribution to the field of Menckeniana—for which the Enoch Pratt, and Miss Adler in particular, deserve highest praise.

University of South Carolina

Philip Young and Charles W. Mann. *The Hemingway Manuscripts: an Inventory.* University Park: Pennsylvania State University Press, 1969. $5.95 (trade), $20.00 (limited).

By William Cagle

The individual author bibliography came into prominence as a collector's guide and then matured as a scholar's tool. The process has taken half a century during which time experiment and investigation have evolved the standards which today are the guidelines scholarly bibliographers follow. On the other hand, the descriptive catalogue of an author's manuscripts is a relatively new tool and one on which much pioneer work remains to be done. Yet, while the principles for description of manuscripts have not been codified as they have been for books, workers in this new field will find certain basic concepts which apply equally to bibliographies and manuscript catalogues and will do well to benefit from the work which has gone before in the older discipline and to apply these concepts in their work.

An excellent example of how this can be done, and with an all too brief discussion of some of the problems involved, is Kenneth Lohf's *The Literary Manuscripts of Hart Crane*, published in 1967 as the first volume of a proposed series of "Calendars of American Literary Manuscripts." It must be regretted that such a major undertaking as the publication of a catalogue of Hemingway's manuscripts did not more closely follow this excellent model.

The authors of *The Hemingway Manuscripts: an Inventory* state "It should be made clear, first off, that this publication pretends to be no more than what it says: an 'inventory' . . . and not the much more elaborate catalogue . . . that should be made when the papers have reached their permanent repository." The inventory, as they also explain, is limited to those manuscripts in the possession of Mrs. Hemingway. It may be bad form to criticize a book for not being what it does not pretend to be, but one cannot help wondering why, given the opportunity to do this work, the authors did not prepare the "more elaborate catalogue" they admit must follow, and why, having examined what they describe as "the great bulk of the surviving manuscripts of Ernest Hemingway," they did not seek out the other manuscripts and present the more complete picture. Just as a good author bibliography must be based on examination of many books, not merely those in the compiler's own collection as in the case of T. J. Wise or in some other collection as with Harvey's unfortunate bibliography of Ford Madox Ford, so a good author manuscript catalogue must describe all known manuscripts, not merely those in a single location. In effect, *The Hemingway Manuscripts* has gone off half-cocked, and consequently misfired. What is worse, the publication of this inventory is likely to discourage other scholars from undertaking, or another publisher from considering, an adequate descriptive catalogue of the manuscripts of one of our most important writers.

Aside from certain technical inadequacies in the descriptions—most notably lack of any attempt to date the manuscripts—the user of the inventory is most likely to regret the failure of the authors to establish the relationships between the various versions of the several manuscripts described. For example, under item 3, *The Dangerous Summer*, are listed five manuscripts. The first three, lettered A, B, and C, are holograph in ink and, judging only from the pagination, appear to be three parts of a single manuscript, though one cannot be certain from the brief descriptions. The fourth manuscript, lettered D, is as follows: "Typescript, original. Very few corrections in pencil and ink. Pagination 1-688." The fifth manuscript, lettered E, is: "Typescript, carbon, triple-spaced, few corrections in ink and pencil. Pagination 1-688." Is E a carbon of D? If so, why is it specifically designated as triple-spaced? Are the corrections on D and E the same? Are typescripts D and E unrevised copies of manuscript (or manuscripts?) A-C? The reader is not left with a very clear picture of these relationships or, indeed, of exactly what the manuscripts described are.

But perhaps the most frustrating section of the whole book is that for "letters." Take the entry B under item 304, "Letters by EH": "In shopping bag, many originals, photocopies, typed copies, to Harvey Breit, Hadley Hemingway, C. T. Lanham, Bernard Berenson, William Smith, etc." Or if that does not raise your curiosity and leave all your questions unanswered, try item 305, "Letters to EH," A "Seven folders from family and friends." Vague? Yes, rather.

Though *The Hemingway Manuscripts* must be rejected as an adequate descriptive catalogue it serves another and interesting function: it shows us what of Hemingway's manuscripts, published and unpublished, he regarded worth keeping. The arrangement of the book in sections treating different types of work is intelligently done and is helpful when the book is viewed from this last point of view. It is of interest, for example, to see how much poetry Hemingway had written and saved though, in fact, he had published only very little poetry, and that rather early in his career.

Finally, it should be noted that the publishers have produced a handsomely designed, well made book. This is the "trade edition." There is also a "limited edition" (i.e. printing) of 300 copies for the dedicated *aficionado* (at $20.00), bound in quarter leather and adding an illustration not included in the trade printing. The new plate shows pages 2 and 3 of the typescript of "Fifty Grand" on the latter of which is an annotation in Fitzgerald's hand so faintly written, the caption tells us, as to be "illegible in the reproduction."

Lilly Library, Indiana University

B. Poli, A. E. Le Vot, G. et M. Fabre. *Francis Scott Fitzgerald. The Great Gatsby; Tender is the Night.* Paris: Librarie Armand Colin, 1969.

By Pierre Kaufke

This book is published in the excellent "Collection U," the leading series of critical studies of literature aimed especially at the French college student and is therefore written in French. It has by no means the pretention to be written for scholars or Fitzgeraldnicks, but for the person who is interested enough in Fitzgerald's two major works to want to gain a deeper insight into them. This purpose is perfectly accomplished. It makes available to the reader a great amount of material on subjects ranging from the genesis of *The Great Gatsby* and *Tender is the Night* up to the symbolic correspondences of the characters' possessions.

The book itself is divided into two parts, one devoted to *The Great Gatsby* and the other to *Tender is the Night*. Their general plans are very similar, and it is only the detail organization that changes—according to what elements are the most important, the color symbolism of *The Great Gatsby* and the echo-words in *Tender is the Night*.

Both parts begin with the genesis of Fitzgerald's masterpieces—

which works helped shape them, and Fitzgerald's aims. Here also, the myth of the fatal facility of a drunken artist is attacked. Then the structure of the two books is analysed along with those elements which help sustain that structure: language, symbolism, plot, character, time levels, parallelism, correspondences. The styles also receive a careful examination. Another part deals with thematic elements and their networks, while the conclusion of each section is given to a study of the fortunes of the two novels, especially their spread and influence in France.

The analyses in this book are all very pertinent and very deep. The authors cover their subjects with French logic and clarity. At the same time, they hint at many aspects of Fitzgerald's work which, though interesting enough, would not be worth a whole paragraph in the book, and which can easily be amplified by further research.

However, most of the information presented in the book is not original, but consists of all kinds of borrowed critical material that is compiled in such a way that it is easily and readily available. The critical interpretations are almost always well documented and illustrated with examples from Fitzgerald's novels—one time even to an excessive four pages. The sources of the quotations from *The Great Gatsby* and *Tender is the Night* are clearly indicated, but the American student will be puzzled by finding only a few textual references and no footnotes. All the data that he receives about critical sources is included in the bibliography placed at the end of each main chapter, and which is a kind of combination of both footnote and bibliography. But again, the purpose of the book itself is not to be scholarly, but to make the already existing scholarship available to those people who are not Fitzgerald specialists, but who still want to gain a deeper insight into his works without having to plow their way through long research.

University of South Carolina

Nancy Milford. *Zelda.* New York: Harper & Row, 1970

By Sara Mayfield

By the time that Lieut. F. Scott Fitzgerald met Zelda Sayre, in 1918, she was already a legendary southern belle. Her beauty, her prismatic charm, and her scintillating wit had made her famous as the most sought-after prom queen in the Deep South. She was, as Scott proudly noted, "the most popular girl in Alabama *and* Georgia."

As a member of one of Alabama's most aristocratic families and as the daughter of a distinguished justice of the state supreme court, she had a glamorous background of generals, senators, and judges and an unquestioned position in Montgomery. Since Scott was then only an unknown infantry lieutenant, whose hopes for a future rested on an unpublished novel, Zelda's superior status awed him almost as much as her beauty and her fantastic popularity attracted him. However, the competitive spirit was so strong in Scott that he set out to win Zelda despite his lowly rank and scanty funds—and her array of wealthy suitors.

After Scribners published *This Side of Paradise* in March 1920, Scott found that, like Byron, he had become famous overnight. Meanwhile, discouraged by Fitzgerald's inability to make money, Zelda had broken her engagement to him. But reassured by his literary success and the jingle of money in his pocket, Scott persuaded Zelda that he could now offer her a more interesting and a more cosmopolitan life than she had known in Montgomery. Convinced that she could not only contribute to Fitzgerald's success but also make a name for herself as a dancer on the larger stage of a great city, Zelda married Scott on April 3, 1920.

It has been said that, between them, the Fitzgeralds created that fabulous era known as the Jazz Age. However that may be, to say the least, they became its eponymous figures and its laureates. During the twenties they starred in the glittering, syncopated world of café society in New York, Paris, Hollywood, and on the Riviera. Wherever they went they left a trail of stories of their pranks, escapades, and parties, of their overnight success and of their turbulent romance.

With their genius for synchronizing their lives with the *Zeitgeist*, their romantic dreams of eternal youth, an endless honeymoon, and perpetual affluence crashed after the irridescent bubbles of the Jazz Age burst against the harsh realities of the Depression. Faced with hard times, illness, "emotional bankruptcy," and the deterioration of her marriage, Zelda drove herself into a breakdown in an effort to attain some measure of financial security for herself and her child; she wrote and she danced at such a furious pace that she soon wore herself out. While she was hospitalized, she wrote numerous stories as well as an autobiographical novel, *Save Me the Waltz* (1932), which has recently been reprinted in both hardback and paperback.

Zelda's life, from her teen-age triumphs as a belle to her tragic death in a fire that swept through the Highlands Hospital, where she was then being treated, offers fascinating material for a biographical study of a brilliant, capricious, undisciplined charmer. Her relations with her famous husband, and the exciting, if precarious, years that she spent with him add to the interest of her story.

In *Zelda*, Nancy Milford has concentrated on those years and emphasized "how deeply dependent the Fitzgeralds were on each other, and to what an extraordinary degree their dreams were matching ones. Even in the worst years, when the trust was broken, when Zelda was sick and Scott blamed her for his alcoholism, each could still draw on a reservoir of feeling in the other. Their tragedy lay in being too close; at their worst they fought for the same ground."

Mrs. Milford has done a service to Fitzgerald scholars in unearthing the letters that Zelda wrote to Scott during her periods of hospitalization and publishing them. Zelda's letters are poignant, witty, and deeply moving documents, which Mrs. Milford has used effectively in her book. Since she was born too late to have known Scott and Zelda or to have had firsthand knowledge of their lives and times, Mrs. Milford's biography of Mrs. Fitzgerald is necessarily derivative. However, the inclusion of many hitherto-unpublished letters in Mrs. Milford's book give it an immediacy that it might otherwise have lacked. Moreover, her biography of Zelda is well written and carefully researched.

Perhaps the salient defect of the book lies in the fact that its author has done her research *too* well, with the result that she has relied heavily on secondary sources and hearsay, frequently contributed by people who were envious or jealous of Zelda and inclined to slander her. Consequently, Zelda's character as revealed by her letters is very different from Mrs. Milford's interpretation of it in her book. Her accounts of Zelda, many of which are derived from anonymous sources, are not only unconvincing but they also tend to turn the book into a pastiche of quotations, a biographical collage, in which the people who knew Zelda will find little more resemblance to her than they did in George Zuckerman's fictionalized distortion of her career in *The Last Flapper* (1969).

However, if Mrs. Milford's *Zelda* is not a portrait from life, it is nevertheless a most interesting study of a *femme fatale* and her marriage to an *homme manqué*. It is a book that will appeal to the student of life and letters in the Jazz Age as well as to the general reader. For in her biography of Zelda, Mrs. Milford has made a noteworthy contribution to Fitzgeraldana and incorporated it in a readable and engrossing book.

University of Alabama Press

Matthew J. Bruccoli, ed., *Ernest Hemingway, Cub Reporter
Kansas City Star Stories*. Pittsburgh: University of Pittsburgh
Press, 1970. $4.95 (trade), $15 (limited).

By Arnold Gingrich

Matthew Bruccoli has done the study of style a considerable service
by assembling, in book form, the distinguishable writings of Ernest
Hemingway in his brief stint as a cub reporter on the *Kansas City
Star* in the winter and spring of 1917-1918. Note that the operative
word here is "distinguishable" and not "distinguished." There are
only the most fleeting glimpses, or the faintest of hints, of anything
like real literary distinction in these routine reportings. But they
make fascinating reading nevertheless, because the yield of any inti-
mations of immortality in this journeyman prose is so low that the
few that are indubitably there stand out more strikingly than they
would in a setting of more finished work.

Reading these stories I felt the same kind of mixed admiration and
mystification that was provoked by my reading, many years ago, of
some of Hemingway's first printed efforts, in the pages of the *Tabula*,
the Oak Park High School magazine. One story there in particular,
"Sepi Jingan," combined shakiness of syntax and awkwardness of
expression to such a degree that it was hard to understand how it
could nevertheless convey any thrust of power. And yet it did. Bad
as it was, it packed a punch. It was like watching a kid get into the
ring without knowing any of the ropes, and while almost literally
falling all over his own feet, nevertheless manage to deliver a damag-
ing body blow.

Similarly in the *Kansas City Star* stories, it is thrilling to come
across, in the context of reportorial prose that might just as well have
been phoned in as written out, a sentence that seems of a piece with
the later Hemingway style, like this one: "That Christmas season the
workmen in a sugar refinery near Kiev made a cross of ice and set it
up on the frozen river."

Not a word wasted. No pretense at fine writing. But the magic of
the Hemingway prose posture is anticipated there by half a dozen
years. By 1925 and the Boni & Liveright *In Our Time*, that sentence
would not have stood out, against the background of the by-then
fully formed and later famous "stripped style," as it does here where
it gleams like a solitaire in a dustpan.

There are not many times, in the course of reading these pedes-
trian accounts of petty crimes, pickups, raids, mishaps and accidents,

the grist of daily and nightly local news, that you will get the *frisson* of spotting a sentence that might have survived the rigorous self-editing of Hemingway's later writing. Most of the time it's "the prisoner explained" or "narrowly escaped injury" or "elements of a mysterious nature" or "developments leading to the affair," etc. Dull, shoddy stuff like "unable to make a statement," or "said he could not disclose its contents." But just as you're beginning to nod as you plod through paragraphs of things like that, you're suddenly reminded of the presence of hairs on the back of your neck by something like "comes in on the soiled bloody stretcher and the rags are stripped off and his naked broken body lies on the white table in the glare of the surgeon's light." And now and then you're jerked bolt upright from your torpor by such a glimpse as "the big car speeds down the Cherry Street hill, the headlights boring a yellow funnel into the darkness."

A small book, *Ernest Hemingway, Cub Reporter* is none the less seminal, for no serious student of the Hemingway canon will want to miss these relatively few but extremely significant examples of how, in literature too, coming events cast their shadows before.

Editorial

F. Scott Fitzgerald once wrote this note to his secretary: "If you can manage it please get someone to read this with you—it's so important—and a few missing words would destroy so much."

Fitzgerald's *The Great Gatsby: The Novel, The Critics, The Background* (New York: Scribners, 1970), a Scribner Research Anthology edited by Henry Dan Piper nowhere specifies the text of *Gatsby* it prints. It turns out to be set from the Scribner Library edition—which itself silently departs from the 1925 first printing more than 200 times. But this new setting does not even follow its bad copytext accurately:—between the last 1969 printing of the Scribner Library edition and this Scribner Research Anthology there are 25 variants, of which 11 are substantives.

	Scribner Library	Scribner Research Anthology
P-9.69 [C]		A-3.70 [H]
	epigraph	*omits*
	dedication	*omits*
20.22	Daisy	Daily
28.4	startlingly	startling
45.22	staring	starring
67.28	just some nobody	just nobody
79.29	stars to which	stars which
86.23	she said innocently	she innocently
145.20	said.	said ˄
161.19-20	*section break*	*no section break*
175.20-21	*section break*	*no section break*

—and a few missing words would destroy so much.

—M.J.B.

Andrew Turnbull, 1921–1970

By

Burke Wilkinson

Andrew Turnbull's death last January at 48 leaves an unfillable gap in the ranks of those who knew Scott Fitzgerald. Out of their friendship, backed up by brilliant research, came Turnbull's biography, which Scribner published in 1962 and which remains the most understanding and sympathetic portrait of the novelist yet written.

Turnbull was eleven years old when Fitzgerald came to live at La Paix, his family's place near Baltimore. Here is how he recalled how this affected the family:

> Under the impact of this charming, unpredictable man with his gift of intimacy, life on our place began to vibrate on a faster, subtler rhythm than we had ever known.

The purpose of the biography was to try to find the man behind the legends. In this search he drew fully on his own memory of Fitzgerald's tenancy at La Paix. The novelist and young Andy played tennis, boxed, had long discussions on many subjects. Fitzgerald took him to football games and, when the boy went away to school, wrote him letters full of word-play and wonderfully erratic advice.

So, like many first-class biographies, Turnbull's book was a matter of involvement, of caring. In reviewing it for *The New York Times* I gave it the full marks it deserved:

> Beginning with the Baltimore interval, the understanding deepens and the tragic pattern emerges in full. It is as if there were a sudden off-stage click galvanizing the central character into life. Zelda and Scottie, Hemingway, Edmund Wilson, Maxwell Perkins, the editor, Harold Ober, the agent, and

Sheilah Graham, the last love—all these are supporting characters now, and they all supply Turnbull with material that his own sensitivity and affection have well used.

. . . If Fitzgerald was in part the 'spoiled priest' that he himself sought to create in Dick Diver, Turnbull the acolyte has served him well. If he was prodigal moralist, Turnbull the friend sees the prodigal streak and the underlying morality in true proportion, and does not seek to judge.

In its essence, and particularly its final phase, this dramatic memoir and uncritical biography of a man of great talent but an uneven gift for life, stirs the spirit and touches the heart.

Turnbull also edited the letters of Fitzgerald, which Scribners published in 1963. Later, he did a competent biography of Thomas Wolfe. He tried hard to find in Wolfe a talent equal to Fitzgerald's. But some of the spontaneity and conviction of the earlier biography are missing here.

There could have been many more years of creative work, and it is sad that these are not to be. Andy Turnbull's impeccable research, his taste and judgment and lasting gift for friendship, will be greatly missed.

(Mr. Wilkinson wrote "Scott Fitzgerald: Ten Years After" in 1950.)

Serialization of *This Side of Paradise* in the *New York Daily News*, June 1923.

The O'Hara Set

By

George Frazier*

It is strange the things we think about when we hear of the death of a celebrity whom we admired enormously. With the report of the passing of John O'Hara, there was that first icy stab of shock, then curiosity as to the manner of his dying, and, finally, impatience to learn what the *Times* would say in its obit. Would it be long or short, devout or dismissive? Would it be on page one? We felt very protective about what it would say. After all, in a way it would be a reflection on us, the O'Hara set, and to read it would be ourselves to know, at least a little. Would the *New York Times* share our feelings about John O'Hara?

Perhaps now all the wrongs, to us as well as to him, would be redressed; his reputation restored, our judgment confirmed; his genius granted, our hurrahs in order—all of it permitting his soul to rest in peace and authorizing us to tell such patronizing appraisers of his special gifts as Louis Auchincloss and Alfred Kazin and Clifton Fadiman that now they could go straight to hell. We, not they, had been proved correct. The obit in the *Times* would be the imprimatur of his immortality—and better posthumous than premature. It would say, very simply, that John O'Hara was one terrific writer. And then, convinced of that, we thought of all the wonders he had wrought, all the people who had come alive in his pages to touch our lives.

But it wasn't to be that way, for all that the *Times* gave him were a few perfunctory paragraphs that seemed embarassed by beginning

---

*Reprinted from the *Boston Evening Globe* (27 April 1970), 20—with the permission of Mr. Frazier.

on page one. Was the *New York Times* out of its mind or something? What is this thing America has about its best writers? In France a man wins the Goncourt and he's suddenly 10 feet tall and terribly important. What is it with us that we give short shrift to such national treasures as O'Hara while genuflecting to the products of press agents? Is E. B. White as well known as Bill Blass? Nor is it only the press, for just what the hell has Harvard to say for itself, bestowing the kudos of June on a palpable politician one year and the next year on a man whom Freud would have called "an eminent sausage maker," all the while apparently unaware of John O'Hara? We of the O'Hara set become incensed by that sort of thing.

We are so odd, we O'Hara people. We have such a special feeling about him, refusing even to listen to the slightest aspersion on his words at their most wondrous. We are really rather like him, you know—opinionated and always at the ready to curtsy to grace and elegance, and if you do not agree, who invited you anyway? Or has it ever occurred to you that maybe we enjoy being snobbish? Naturally, one reason we have this affinity for O'Hara is that he knows about court tennis and custom tailoring and chic clubs, and if Alfred Kazin doesn't like it, why doesn't he review writers who know about stick ball and where to buy a suit with two pairs of pants and a catcher's mitt?

If Alfred Kazin's your kind of critic, please don't let us disturb you. But you mustn't mind if we of the O'Hara set are out to lunch or tied up with a previous engagement or not to be awakened until the day after tomorrow. Put Alfred Kazin on our bill, and please don't mention it—he comes with the blue plate special.

Temper, temper, temper, we are forever telling ourselves, yet it does no good, for we are very spiteful. We are terrific haters to whom the adversity of an enemy is more fun than a barrel of people. Never, not ever in our lives, were we more delighted than when Pegler called Henry Seidel Canby of *The Saturday Review of Literature* "an antedeluvian crud." After all, we had never forgotten how the antedeluvian crud had sneered at "Appointment in Samarra." Just let anybody question the divinity of our master and we become Hate, Incorporated.

But when with our own kind, we are childlike in our enthusiasm. The kind of people we are, we take off our hats as we pass the Pickwick Arms, for it was there that he wrote "Appointment" on a new portable typewriter with an all-black ribbon. And snobs? Of course we are snobs, nor is there a single member of our set who wouldn't offer his pink bottom to the birching block for the privilege of

wearing an Eton tie. To be in Pop, to wear a boutonniere and a bro-
cade waistcoat.

But don't think O'Hara was the only writer who was snobbish.
Didn't Hemingway talk about Eton in "The Torrents of Spring" and
about Skull & Bones in "To Have and Have Not," and didn't
Faulkner, bowlered and bespoke shape-suited and desirous of returning to earth as a buzzard when reincarnated, didn't he inform a
class of West Pointers what it means to be Bones? And in "Tender,"
when Abe North had been found lying outside the Racquet Club
dead of a beating, didn't Fitzgerald have one of the characters maintain that North had been beaten up elsewhere and had crawled to
the Racquet so that he could die at a good address?

And yet, though the snobbishness is part of the reason why we are
O'Hara people, it isn't the big part. The big part is that he was, above
all else, a fantastically gifted writer who was never not learning. "If
you are an author, and not just a writer," he once said, "you keep
learning all the time." And how he loved to work, having, he said, a
religous feeling about writing.

"The thing I am going to miss most is the strength to work," he
said a few years ago. "The writer who loafs after he has made a
financial success is confessing that the money was all he was after
in the first place . . . Much as I like owning a Rolls-Royce, for instance, I could do without it. What I could not do without is a typewriter, a supply of yellow second sheets, and the time to put them to
good use."

Nobody every put the tools of his trade to better use than John
O'Hara. Perhaps that is why we have a religious feeling when we
read him.

271

Checklist

F. Scott Fitzgerald

Bruccoli, Matthew J. *Checklist of F. Scott Fitzgerald.* Columbus, Ohio: Merrill, 1970.

Bryer, Jackson P. "F. Scott Fitzgerald," *Fifteen Modern American Authors A Survey of Research and Criticism,* ed. Bryer. Durham: Duke University Press, 1969, pp. 211-238.

Cassill, R. V. *La Vie Passionnée of Rodney Buckthorne.* New York: Geis, 1968. A character named Amory Blaine.

Coren, Alan. "Scott Fitzgerald—refractions of a strange Peter Pan," *Daily Telegraph Magazine* #268 (28 Nov 1969), 65-67. Includes "Dearly Beloved."

Durham, Philip. "Jay Gatsby and Hopalong Cassidy." *Themes and Directions* in American Literature, ed. Ray B. Browne & Donald Pizer. Lafayette: Purdue University Studies, 1969, pp. 163-170.

Fitzgerald, F. Scott. *Dearly Beloved.* Iowa City. Windhover Press, 1969. Illustrated by Byron Burford. 300 numbered copies, of which 30 are signed by the artist. Published 1970.

———. *This Side of Paradise 26 March 1920 26 March 1970.* Columbia, S. C.: Fitzgerald/Hemingway Annual, 1970. 50 numbered copies of keepsake that reprints "The Author's Apology."

Fitzgerald, F. Scott. "Dearly Beloved," *NCR World,* II (Nov - Dec 1969), 21. See Mangum note in this issue of *F/H.*

Gessner, Robert. *The Moving Image*. New York: Dutton, 1968. Analysis of *Cosmopolitan* ["Babylon Revisited"] script.

Graham, Sheilah. *College of One*. Harmondsworth: Penguin, 1969.

La Hood, Marvin J., ed. *Tender is the Night Essays in Criticism*. Bloomington: Indiana University Press, 1969.

Littlejohn, David. *Interruptions*. New York, Grossman, 1970. Includes articles on Fitzgerald.

Litz, A. Walton. "Maxwell Perkins: The Editor as Critic," *Editor Author and Publisher*, ed. Wm. J. Howard. Toronto: University of Toronto Press, 1969, pp. 96-112.

Mayfield, Sara. "Scott and Zelda: Exiles from Paradise," *Atlanta*, IX (Jan. 1970), 49-50, 86, 88-90, 92, 94.

Milford, Nancy. *Zelda*. New York: Harper & Row, 1969.

Minter, David L. *The Interpreted Design as a Structural Principle in American Prose*. New Haven & London: Yale University Press, 1969. Includes chapter on *GG*.

Nason, Thelma. "Afternoon (and Evening) of an Author," *Johns Hopkins Magazine*, XXI (February 1970), 2-15.

Piper, Henry Dan. *Fitzgerald's The Great Gatsby*. New York: Scribners, 1970. Scribner Research Anthology.

Poli, B.; Le Vot, A.; Fabre, G. & M. *Francis Scott Fitzgerald. The Great Gatsby; Tender is the Night*. Paris: Librairie Armand Colin, 1969. French study guide.

Randall, David. "Wolfe and Fitzgerald," *Dukedom Large Enough*. New York: Random, 1969, pp. 242-259. But Fitzgerald was never in *American First Editions*.

Wickes, George. *Americans in Paris*. New York: Paris Review—Doubleday, 1969.

Zuckerman, George. *The Last Flapper*. Boston: Little, Brown, 1969. Appalling—see review.

Checklist

General

Adler, Betty, compiler. *Man of Letters A Census of the Correspondence of H. L. Mencken.* Baltimore: Enoch Pratt Free Library, 1969.

Atkinson, Hugh C. *Checklist of Theodore Dreiser.* Columbus, Ohio: Merrill, 1969.

Bode, Carl. *Mencken.* Carbondale: Southern Illinois University Press, 1969.

Bruness, Tad. *Cars of the Early Twenties.* Philadelphia: Chilton, 1968.

Cunard, Nancy. *These Were the Hours*, ed. Hugh Ford. Carbondale: Southern Illinois University Press, 1969.

Engels, John. *Guide to William Carlos Williams.* Columbus, Ohio: Merrill, 1969.

Glassco, John. *Memoirs of Montparnasse.* Toronto & New York: Oxford University Press, 1970.

Gunter, Bradley. *Guide to T. S. Eliot.* Columbus, Ohio: Merrill, 1970.
Checklist of T. S. Eliot. Columbus, Ohio: Merrill, 1970.

Hellman, Lillian. *An Unfinished Woman.* Boston: Little, Brown, 1969.

Hénault, Marie. *Checklist of Ezra Pound*. Columbus, Ohio: Merrill, 1970.

Herrick, William. *Hermanos!* New York: Simon & Schuster, 1969. Spanish Civil War novel with character named Richard Jordan Prettyman.

Huguelet, Theodore L. *Checklist of Wallace Stevens*. Columbus, Ohio: Merrill, 1970.

Kennedy, Richard S. and Paschal Reeves, eds. *The Notebooks of Thomas Wolfe*. Chapel Hill: University of North Carolina Press, 1970.

Lundquist, James. *Guide to Sinclair Lewis*. Columbus, Ohio: Merrill, 1970.

Nolte, William H. *H. L. Mencken's Smart Set Criticism*. Ithaca: Cornell University Press, 1968.

———. *Guide to H. L. Mencken*. Columbus, Ohio: Merrill, 1969.

North, Joseph, ed. *New Masses An Anthology of the Rebel Thirties*. New York: International, 1969.

Reeves, Paschal. *Checklist of Thomas Wolfe*. Columbus, Ohio: Merrill, 1969.

Ross, Ishbel. *The Expatriates*. New York: Crowell, 1970.

Rosenstone, Robert A. *Crusade of the Left*. New York: Pegasus, 1969.

Shapiro, Charles. *Guide to Theodore Dreiser*. Columbus, Ohio: Merrill, 1969.

White, Ray Lewis. *Checklist of Sherwood Anderson*. Columbus, Ohio: Merrill, 1970.

Briefs

The Cabellian—Julius Rothman, Editor (75 Noble St., Lynbrook, N.Y. 11563), $7 per year. . . . The 1970 meeting of The Rocky Mountain Modern Language Association will be held at Sun Valley in October and will focus on Hemingway. . . . A bust of Ernest Hemingway is the first in a series of literary sculptures being commissioned by Frederick Ruffner of Gale Research in Detroit. The Hemingway head was done by James Gardner and shows a pensive, bearded Hemingway. A limited number of castings of the Gardner bust have been made and are available through Gale Research, Book Tower, Detroit, Michigan 48226.